ICNS 2016

The Twelfth International Conference on Networking and Services

June 26 - 30, 2016

Lisbon, Portugal

ICNS 2016 Editors

Carlos Becker Westphall, Federal University of Santa Catarina, Brazil

Eugen Borcoci, University 'Politehnica' Bucharest, Romania

Kevin Daimi, University of Detroit Mercy, USA

Printed from e-media with permission by:

Curran Associates, Inc.
57 Morehouse Lane
Red Hook, NY 12571

Some format issues inherent in the e-media version may also appear in this print version.

Printed by Curran Associates, Inc. (2016)

International Academy, Research, and Industry Association (IARIA)
412 Derby Way
Wilmington, DE 19810

Phone: (408) 893-6407
Fax: (408) 527-6351

petre@iaria.org

Additional copies of this publication are available from:

Curran Associates, Inc.
57 Morehouse Lane
Red Hook, NY 12571 USA
Phone: 845-758-0400
Fax: 845-758-2633
Email: curran@proceedings.com
Web: www.proceedings.com

Table of Contents

Increasing Information Capacity in Ultra-High-Speed Optical Networks 1
Milorad Cvijetic

5GMobile Communication Systems: Innovation, Convergence and Ubiquitous 5
Abdulrahman Yarali, Masoud Fateh, and Nasrin Razmi

Client Driven Rate Adaptation Algorithm for Streaming over HTTP 12
Waqas ur Rahman and Kwagsue Chung

Basic System Implementation of the Cloud Type Virtual Policy Based Network Management Scheme for the Common Use Between Plural Organizations 17
Kazuya Odagiri, Shogo Shimizu, and Naohiro Ishii

Power Consumption of Packet Processing Engines and Interfaces of Edge Router: Measurements and Modeling 23
Akram Galal Mahmoud Ibrahim, Mohamed Essam Khedr, and Mohamed Shaheen

Securing Vehicle's Electronic Control Units 29
Kevin Daimi, Mustafa Saed, Scott Bone, and John Robb

Wireless Ticket Exchange Boosts Telecommunication Sector 35
Wieslawa Wajda

An Automated Approach for Selecting Web Services 41
Alysson Alves and Gledson Elias

Simulation of Real Time Multi Radar Data With a Non-Real Time Simulator 47
Atakan Simsek, Ahmet Murat Ozdemiray, and Alper Yildirim

Open Source Tool for Networks Management Communication 53
Nuno Simoes and Carlos Rabadao

Island-Based Sensor Relocation in Wireless Sensor Network to Improve Connectivity 60
Sahla Masmoudi and Leila Saidane

Layer-2 Failure Recovery Methods in Critical Communication Networks 66
Ferdinand von Tullenburg and Thomas Pfeiffenberger

ICNS 2016

Foreword

The Twelfth International Conference on Networking and Services (ICNS 2016), held between June 26 - 30, 2016 - Lisbon, Portugal, continued a series of events targeting general networking and services aspects in multi-technologies environments. The conference covered fundamentals on networking and services, and highlighted new challenging industrial and research topics. Network control and management, multi-technology service deployment and assurance, next generation networks and ubiquitous services, emergency services and disaster recovery and emerging network communications and technologies were considered.

IPv6, the Next Generation of the Internet Protocol, has seen over the past three years tremendous activity related to its development, implementation and deployment. Its importance is unequivocally recognized by research organizations, businesses and governments worldwide. To maintain global competitiveness, governments are mandating, encouraging or actively supporting the adoption of IPv6 to prepare their respective economies for the future communication infrastructures. In the United States, government's plans to migrate to IPv6 has stimulated significant interest in the technology and accelerated the adoption process. Business organizations are also increasingly mindful of the IPv4 address space depletion and see within IPv6 a way to solve pressing technical problems. At the same time IPv6 technology continues to evolve beyond IPv4 capabilities. Communications equipment manufacturers and applications developers are actively integrating IPv6 in their products based on market demands.

IPv6 creates opportunities for new and more scalable IP based services while representing a fertile and growing area of research and technology innovation. The efforts of successful research projects, progressive service providers deploying IPv6 services and enterprises led to a significant body of knowledge and expertise. It is the goal of this workshop to facilitate the dissemination and exchange of technology and deployment related information, to provide a forum where academia and industry can share ideas and experiences in this field that could accelerate the adoption of IPv6. The workshop brings together IPv6 research and deployment experts that will share their work. The audience will hear the latest technological updates and will be provided with examples of successful IPv6 deployments; it will be offered an opportunity to learn what to expect from IPv6 and how to prepare for it.

Packet Dynamics refers broadly to measurements, theory and/or models that describe the time evolution and the associated attributes of packets, flows or streams of packets in a network. Factors impacting packet dynamics include cross traffic, architectures of intermediate nodes (e.g., routers, gateways, and firewalls), complex interaction of hardware resources and protocols at various levels, as well as implementations that often involve competing and conflicting requirements.

Parameters such as packet reordering, delay, jitter and loss that characterize the delivery of packet streams are at times highly correlated. Load-balancing at an intermediate node may, for example, result in out-of-order arrivals and excessive jitter, and network congestion may manifest as packet losses or large jitter. Out-of-order arrivals, losses, and jitter in turn may lead to unnecessary retransmissions in TCP or loss of voice quality in VoIP.

With the growth of the Internet in size, speed and traffic volume, understanding the impact of underlying network resources and protocols on packet delivery and application performance has assumed a critical importance. Measurements and models explaining the variation and interdependence of delivery characteristics are crucial not only for efficient operation of networks and network diagnosis, but also for developing solutions for future networks.

Local and global scheduling and heavy resource sharing are main features carried by Grid networks. Grids offer a uniform interface to a distributed collection of heterogeneous computational, storage and network resources. Most current operational Grids are dedicated to a limited set of computationally and/or data intensive scientific problems.

Optical burst switching enables these features while offering the necessary network flexibility demanded by future Grid applications. Currently ongoing research and achievements refers to high performance and computability in Grid networks. However, the communication and computation mechanisms for Grid applications require further development, deployment and validation.

We take here the opportunity to warmly thank all the members of the ICNS 2016 Technical Program Committee, as well as the numerous reviewers. The creation of such a high quality conference program would not have been possible without their involvement. We also kindly thank all the authors who dedicated much of their time and efforts to contribute to ICNS 2016. We truly believe that, thanks to all these efforts, the final conference program consisted of top quality contributions.

Also, this event could not have been a reality without the support of many individuals, organizations, and sponsors. We are grateful to the members of the ICNS 2016 organizing committee for their help in handling the logistics and for their work to make this professional meeting a success.

We hope that ICNS 2016 was a successful international forum for the exchange of ideas and results between academia and industry and for the promotion of progress in the fields of networking and services.

We are convinced that the participants found the event useful and communications very open. We also hope that Lisbon provided a pleasant environment during the conference and everyone saved some time for exploring this beautiful city.

ICNS 2016 Chairs:

ICNS Advisory Chairs
Pedro Andrés Aranda Gutiérrez, Telefónica I+D - Madrid, Spain
Carlos Becker Westphall, Federal University of Santa Catarina, Brazil
Eugen Borcoci, University 'Politehnica' Bucharest, Romania
Jaime Lloret Mauri, Polytechnic University of Valencia, Spain
Sathiamoorthy Manoharan, University of Auckland, New Zealand
Simone Silvestri, Missouri University of Science and Technology, USA
Yoshiaki Taniguchi, Kindai University, Japan
Go Hasegawa, Osaka University, Japan
Abdulrahman Yarali, Murray State University, USA
Emmanuel Bertin, Orange Labs, France
Steffen Fries, Siemens, Germany
Rui L.A. Aguiar, University of Aveiro, Portugal
Iain Murray, Curtin University of Technology, Australia
Khondkar Islam, George Mason University - Fairfax, USA

ICNS Industry/Research Relation Chairs
Eunsoo Shim, Samsung Electronics, Korea
Tao Zheng, Orange Labs Beijing, China
Bruno Chatras, Orange Labs, France
Jun Kyun Choi, KAIST, Korea
Michael Galetzka, Fraunhofer Institute for Integrated Circuits - Dresden, Germany
Mikael Gidlund, ABB, Sweden

Juraj Giertl, T-Systems, Slovakia
Sinan Hanay, NICT, Japan

ICNS 2016

Committee

ICNS Advisory Committee

Pedro Andrés Aranda Gutiérrez, Telefónica I+D - Madrid, Spain
Carlos Becker Westphall, Federal University of Santa Catarina, Brazil
Eugen Borcoci, University 'Politehnica' Bucharest, Romania
Jaime Lloret Mauri, Polytechnic University of Valencia, Spain
Sathiamoorthy Manoharan, University of Auckland, New Zealand
Simone Silvestri, Missouri University of Science and Technology, USA
Yoshiaki Taniguchi, Kindai University, Japan
Go Hasegawa, Osaka University, Japan
Abdulrahman Yarali, Murray State University, USA
Emmanuel Bertin, Orange Labs, France
Steffen Fries, Siemens, Germany
Rui L.A. Aguiar, University of Aveiro, Portugal
Iain Murray, Curtin University of Technology, Australia
Khondkar Islam, George Mason University - Fairfax, USA

ICNS Industry/Research Relation Chairs

Eunsoo Shim, Samsung Electronics, Korea
Tao Zheng, Orange Labs Beijing, China
Bruno Chatras, Orange Labs, France
Jun Kyun Choi, KAIST, Korea
Michael Galetzka, Fraunhofer Institute for Integrated Circuits - Dresden, Germany
Juraj Giertl, T-Systems, Slovakia
Sinan Hanay, NICT, Japan

ICNS 2016 Technical Program Committee

Johan Åkerberg, ABB AB - Corporate Research - Västerås, Sweden
Ryma Abassi, Higher School of Communication of Tunis /Sup'Com, Tunisia
Nalin Abeysekera, University of Colombo, Sri Lanka
Ferran Adelantado i Freixer, Universitat Oberta de Catalunya, Spain
Hossam Afifi, Télécom SudParis | Institut Mines Télécom, France
Prathima Agrawal, Auburn University, USA
Javier M. Aguiar Pérez, Universidad de Valladolid, Spain
Rui L.A. Aguiar, University of Aveiro, Portugal
Mehmet Akşit, University of Twente, Netherlands
Basheer Al-Duwairi, Jordan University of Science and Technology, Jordan
Ali H. Al-Bayatti, De Montfort University - Leicester, UK
Markus Aleksy, ABB AG, Germany
Maria Andrade, University of Porto / INESC Porto, Portugal
Annamalai Annamalai, Prairie View A&M University, USA

Pedro Felipe Prado, University of São Paulo, Brazil
Juan Flores, University of Michoacan, Mexico
Steffen Fries, Siemens, Germany
Sebastian Fudickar, University of Oldenburg, Germany
Martin Gaedke, Technische Universität Chemnitz, Germany
Michael Galetzka, Fraunhofer Institute for Integrated Circuits - Dresden, Germany
Alex Galis, University College London, UK
Ivan Ganchev, University of Limerick, Ireland
Abdennour El Rhalibi, Liverpool John Moores University, UK
Stenio Fernandez, Federal University of Pernambuco, Brazil
Gianluigi Ferrari, University of Parma, Italy
Kiev Gama, UFPE, Brazil
Miguel Garcia, University of Valencia, Spain
Rosario Garroppo, Università di Pisa, Italy
Amjad Gawanmeh, Khalifa University, United Arab Emirates
Sorin Georgescu, Ericsson Research, Canada
Juraj Giertl, T-Systems, Slovakia
Veronica Gil-Costa, Universidad Nacional de San Luis (UNSL), Argentina
Marc Gilg, University of Haute Alsace, France
Ivan Glesk, University of Strathclyde - Glasgow, UK
Ann Gordon-Ross, University of Florida, USA
Victor Govindaswamy, Concordia University - Chicago, USA
Dominic Greenwood, Whitestein, Switzerland
Jean-Charles Grégoire, INRS - Université du Québec - Montreal, Canada
Vic Grout, Glyndwr University - Wrexham, UK
Ibrahim Habib, City University of New York, USA
Sinan Hanay, NICT, Japan
Go Hasegawa, Osaka University, Japan
Jing (Selena) He, Kennesaw State University, USA
Maryline Hélard, INSA-IETR, France
Hermann Hellwagner, Klagenfurt University, Austria
Enrique Hernandez Orallo, Universidad Politécnica de Valencia, Spain
Shahram S. Heydari, University of Ontario Institute of Technology, Canada
Zhihong Hong, Communications Research Centre, Canada
Per Hurtig, Karlstad University, Sweden
Naohiro Ishii, Aichi Institute of Technology, Japan
Khondkar Islam, George Mason University - Fairfax, USA
Saïd Jabbour, CRIL - CNRS, University of Artois, France
Arunita Jaekel, University of Windsor, Canada
Tauseef Jamal, SITILab Lisbon, Portugal
Peter Janacik, University of Paderborn, Germany
Imad Jawhar, United Arab Emirates University, UAE
Sudharman K. Jayaweera, University of New Mexico - Albuquerque, USA
Wei Jiang, Missouri University of Science and Technology, USA
Eunjin (EJ) Jung, University of San Francisco, USA
Janusz Kacprzyk, Systems Research Institute - Polish Academy of Sciences, Poland
Maxim Kalinin, Peter The Great St. Petersburg Polytechnic University, Russia
Enio Kaljic, University of Sarajevo, Bosnia and Herzegovina

Georgios Kambourakis, University of the Aegean - Karlovassi, Greece
Hisao Kameda, University of Tsukuba, Japan
Kyungtae Kang, Hanyang University, Korea
Nirav Kapadia, Public Company Accounting Oversight Board (PCAOB), USA
Georgios Karagiannis, University of Twente, The Netherlands
Masoumeh Karimi, Technological University of America, USA
Hiroyuki Kasai, University of Electro-Communications, Japan
Aggelos K. Katsaggelos, Northwestern University - Evanston, USA
Sokratis K. Katsikas, University of Piraeus, Greece
Thomas Kemmerich, University College Gjøvik, Norway
Wolfgang Kiess, DOCOMO Euro-Labs, Germany
Ki Hong Kim, The Attached Institute of ETRI, Korea
Younghan Kim, Soongsil University - Seoul, Republic of Korea
Mario Kolberg, University of Stirling - Scotland, UK
Lisimachos Kondi, University of Ioannina, Greece
Jerzy Konorski, Gdansk University of Technology, Poland
Elisavet Konstantinou, University of the Aegean, Greece
Kimon Kontovasilis, NCSR "Demokritos", Greece
Andrej Kos, University of Ljubljana, Slovenia
Diego Kreutz, University of Luxembourg, Luxembourg
Francine Krief, University of Bordeaux, France
Mikel Larrea, University of the Basque Country UPV/EHU, Spain
Anju Lata Yadav, Shri G. S. Institute of Technology and Science, India
Suk Kyu Lee, Korea University at Seoul, Republic of Korea
DongJin Lee, Auckland University, New Zealand
Mark Leeson, University of Warwick, UK
Leo Lehmann, OFCOM, Switzerland
Ricardo Lent, Imperial College London, UK
Alessandro Leonardi, AGT Group (R&D) GmbH - Darmstadt, Germany
Yiu-Wing Leung, Hong Kong Baptist University, Hong Kong
Tonglin Li, Illinois Institute of Technology, USA
Yanhua Li, Huawei Noah's Ark Lab, Hong Kong
Qilian Liang, University of Texas at Arlington, USA
Wen-Hwa Liao, Tatung University - Taipei, Taiwan
Fidel Liberal Malaina, University of Basque Country, Spain
Marco Listanti, Sapienza University of Rome, Italy
Giovanni Livraga, Università degli Studi di Milano - Crema, Italy
Jaime Lloret Mauri, Polytechnic University of Valencia, Spain
Albert Lysko, Meraka Institute/CSIR- Pretoria, South Africa
Zoubir Mammeri, ITIT - Toulouse, France
Sathiamoorthy Manoharan, University of Auckland, New Zealand
Moshe Masonta, Tshwane University of Technology - Pretoria, South Africa
George Mastorakis, Technological Educational Institute of Crete, Greece
Constandinos X. Mavromoustakis, University of Cyprus, Cyprus
Ivan Mezei, University of Novi Sad, Serbia
Klaus Moessner, University of Surrey- Guildford, UK
Mohssen Mohammed, Cape Town University, South Africa
Mario Montagud Climent, Polytechnic University of Valencia, Spain

Fangyang Shen, New York City College of Technology (CUNY), USA
Jian Shen, Chosun University, Gwangju, Republic of Korea
Tsang-Ling Sheu, National Sun Yat-Sen University - Kaohsiung, Taiwan
Eunsoo Shim, Samsung Electronics, Korea
Simone Silvestri, Missouri University of Science and Technology, USA
Alex Sim, Lawrence Berkeley National Laboratory, USA
Thierry Simonnet, ESIEE-Paris, France
Navjot Singh, Avaya Labs Research, USA
Georgios Ch. Sirakoulis, Democritus University of Thrace, Greece
Renaud Sirdey, CEA LIST, France
Charalabos Skianis, University of Aegean - Karlovasi, Greece
Dimitrios Skoutas, University of the Aegean, Greece
Vasco N. G. J. Soares, Instituto de Telecomunicações / Polytechnic Institute of Castelo Branco, Portugal
José Soler, Technical University of Denmark, Denmark
Gritzalis Stefanos, University of the Aegean, Greece
Ronggong Song, DRDC, Canada
Mujdat Soyturk, Marmara University, Turkey
Marc St-Hilaire, Carleton University, Canada
Young-Joo Suh, Pohang University of Science & Technology (POSTECH), South Korea
Akira Takura, Jumonji University, Japan
Yoshiaki Taniguchi, Kindai University, Japan
Olivier Terzo, Istituto Superiore Mario Boella - Torino, Italy
Christian Timmerer, Alpen-Adria-Universität Klagenfurt, Austria
Federico Tonelli, University of Pisa, Italy
Ilaria Torre, University of Genoa, Italy
Stephan Trahasch, Hochschule Offenburg, Germany
Joseph G. Tront, Virginia Tech, USA
Binod Vaidya, University of Ottawa, Canada
Geoffroy R. Vallee, Oak Ridge National Laboratory (ORNL), USA
Fabrice Valois, INSA Lyon, France
Hans van den Berg, TNO / University of Twente, The Netherlands
Ioannis O. Vardiambasis, Technological Educational Institute (TEI) of Crete - Branch of Chania, Greece
Vladimir Vesely, Brno University of Technology, Czech Republic
Dario Vieira, EFREI, France
Bjørn Villa, Norwegian Institute of Science and Technology, Norway
José Miguel Villalón Millan, Universidad de Castilla - La Mancha, Spain
Demosthenes Vouyioukas, University of the Aegean - Karlovassi, Greece
Arno Wacker, University of Kassel, Germany
Bin Wang, Wright State University - Dayton, USA
Junwei Wang, University of Hong Kong, Hong Kong
Mea Wang, University of Calgary, Canada
Tingkai Wang, London Metropolitan University, UK
Zhe Wang, Edinburgh Napier University, UK / University of Technology, Sydney, Australia
Michelle Wetterwald, HeNetBot, France
Alexander Wijesinha, Towson University, USA
Ouri Wolfson, University of Illinois - Chicago, USA
Serhan Yarkan, Istanbul Commerce University, Turkey
Homayoun Yousefi'zadeh, University of California - Irvine, USA

Vladimir S. Zaborovsky, Polytechnic University/Robotics Institute - St.Petersburg, Russia
Sherali Zeadally, University of the District of Columbia, USA
Jie Zeng, Tsinghua University, China
Zhi-Li Zhang, University of Minnesota, USA
Tao Zheng, Orange Labs Beijing, China
Yifeng Zhou, Communications Research Centre, Canada
Ye Zhu, Cleveland State University, USA
Yingwu Zhu, Seattle University, USA
Piotr Zuraniewski, University of Amsterdam (NL), The Netherlands /AGH University of Science and Technology, Poland

Copyright Information

Increasing Information Capacity in Ultra-High-Speed Optical Networks

Milorad Cvijetic
University of Arizona, College of Optical Sciences
Tucson, Arizona, USA
Email: milorad@optics.arizona.edu

Abstract— High spectral efficiency of optical transmission links is essential for the overall throughput increase in optical networks. In this paper, we discuss multidimensional structure and parallel signal processing applied on advanced modulation, coding, and detection schemes and introduce an optimized design scenario for future 4 Tb/s and 10Tb/s Ethernet channels.

Keywords-optical networks; information capacity; modulation.

I. Introduction

It is well known that he Internet traffic has been growing exponentially and it is projected that the zettabyte level in data exchange will be exceeded in year 2017. It is also projected that the traffic from video services and peer-to-peer file sharing will comprise the majority of the Internet traffic. The wireless connectivity through (4/5G+) mobile networks and widespread use of mobile traffic for social networking has also become an integral part of the overall networking picture since it provides a large contribution to the never ending bandwidth demand in optical networks.

All applications mentioned above will demand an extremely large throughput in different optical networking segments (i. e., in access, metro and core), which means that high aggregate information capacity of optical links will be required. It is envisioned that current 100 Gb/s Ethernet (100 GbE) in converged optical packet networks will be eventually overlaid with 400 Gb/s Ethernet (400 GbE) and 1 Tb/s Ethernet (TbE). Down the road, 1+TbE (specifically 4 TbE) and even 10+ TbE) will become a relevant topic when talking about Terabit optical networking [2]. We should also mention that the total data traffic in aggregation (metro and regional) networking segment just recently exceeded the data traffic carried over by core optical networks.

Demand for higher information capacity is closely related to request that the information bandwidth in next generation networks is more flexible and highly dynamic and elastic in nature. The elastic and dynamic behavior requires that the data bit rate and signal spectral efficiency can be changed dynamically based on the traffic conditions and/or signal quality along specified lightpath (which is commonly related to the optical signal to noise ratio (OSNR). The point is that an automated action should be taken to adjust the bit rate/spectral efficiency, which is done by change in modulation/multiplexing scheme or in coding strength. This adjustment becomes necessity for aggregation networks, since their dominance in terms of the overall data traffic [1]. Accordingly, we can say that a higher attention should be given to the metro networking in order to satisfy both high information capacity and dynamic connectivity requests. However, the logic about capacity and connectivity applies also to other networking segments (optical access networks and data center networks, and core networks), which are all connected to the metro networks [3] [4].

In this paper, we will discuss the advanced schemes enabling high information capacity of optical channels and develop scenario for design of future superchannels by using parallelism and multidimensional structure. The paper is organized as follows. In next section, we will analyze spectral efficiency of optical channels through employed basis functions and identify multidimensional modulation and multiplexing schemes that contribute to information capacity increase. In Section III, we will apply optimized channel design to scenarios related to aggregate and core optical networks. Finally, in Section IV, we will make the relevant conclusions.

II. Spectral Efficiency Increase in Next-Gen Networks

It is interesting to observe that the IP traffic growth has the same dynamics as the speed of processors (Moore's law), which we illustrated in Figure 1. Having in mind the past connection between data rates of IP routers ports and speed of processors related to that, we can envision connection between projected dynamics of the speed (or bit rates) of serial optical interfaces carrying IP traffic and speed of processors, which is also illustrated in Figure 1. The key point is that both the driving forces and key enabling components are subjects of an exponential dynamics, which means that the speed of optical line interfaces (channels) should advance with the same pace as speed of processors. Since we will be dealing with ultra-high processor speeds and line bit rates, we can expect that both objectives will be achieved only if parallel approach is applied. The parallelism in design means that multidimensional approach in signal processing is underlining factor for information capacity increase. The parallelism/multidimensionality in optical networks can be imposed through modulation and multiplexing schemes, which is not a trivial task since there are a number of parameters that can be incorporated in an optimum high-speed optical channel design.

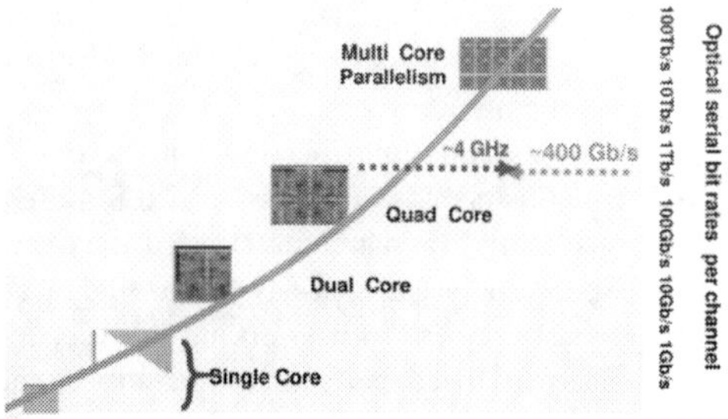

Figure 1. Envisioned parallelization of processors and speed of high-speed in optical channels

The increase in spectral efficiency of optical channels is precondition for overall throughput in high-speed optical networks. Optical channel construction can be done by fully utilizing all available basis function (amplitude, phase, time, frequency, space, and polarization) through parallelization and arrangement that would maximize information capacity of fiber links. Generally, any set of real-valued energy signals $\{s_i(t)\}$ can be expressed as a linear combination of D orthonormal basis functions $\{\Phi_j\}$, as [5]

$$s_i(t)=\sum_{j=1}^{D}s_{ij}\Phi_j(t),\begin{cases}0\le t\le T_s\\ i=1,2,...,M\end{cases} \tag{1a}$$

$$s_{ij}=\int_0^{T_s}s_i(t)\Phi_j dt,\begin{cases}i=1,2,...,M\\ j=1,2,...,D\end{cases} \tag{1b}$$

where M relates to well-known amplitude-phase constellation diagrams containing M states where symbols can reside, while T_s specifies symbol interval. The parallelism in signal representation in (1a,b), should be translated to modulation format design. The illustration of basis functions commonly considered for channel construction is presented in Figure 2.

When talking about increased spectral efficiency of amplitude-phase modulation formats with the constellation diagram of size M, it is possible to design some other structure different than conventional M-QAM formats. The design of these formats, also known as two-dimensional ones, can be done with respect to established constraints and optimization criteria (such as minimum mean square error (MMSE), minimum bit error rate (BER), minimum energy consumption, minimum latency, etc., as presented in [5] [6] [7]. We should outline that construction of advanced modulation formats based on specified criteria is still widely open research process.

Two-dimensional modulation formats with amplitude and phase as basis functions is commonly extended to more complex four-dimensional form if polarization state is used as additional basis. New format is different than polarization division multiplexing scheme since in four-dimensional signaling scheme only one mapper is used with four coordinates (amplitude, phase, x-polarization and y-polarization), which serve as inputs to corresponding I/Q modulators. With this approach, we can increase the Euclidean distance among neighboring points in constellation diagram and thus improve the OSNR, which can be essential in scenario with expected high impact of nonlinearities [5] [8].

The further parallelization in optical channel construction can be achieved by including the frequency as the signaling basis function, while keeping the Nyquist orthogonality criterion represented by raised cosine function spectral shape. In this format, known as the orthogonal frequency division multiplexing (OFDM) [5] [8] [9], the total spectrum is arranged with multiple overlapping optical (sub)-carriers that form a single channel, commonly recognized as superchannel. It has been proven that, with an arbitrary number of optical subcarriers per superchannel, a multiterabit capacity per channel can be realized [10] [11]. The OFDM subcarriers in superchannel are spaced apart by Δf_{SC} , which is equal to the symbol rate R_{SC} of the signal applied to them leading to an aggregate bit rate of an OFDM based channel equal to $R_S = R_{SC} N_{SC}$, where N_{SC} is number of subcarriers (assuming the same rate for each subcarrier). The Nyquist based overlapping can be also achieved in time domain by applying Nyquist WDM scheme, which produces the most efficient way of the signal multiplexing in time domain [10].

The orthogonal polynomials or orthogonal prolate spheroidal wave (OPSW) functions can be considered instead of orthogonal subcarrier [9], which is a promising way of introduction of the time basis function. If OPSW functions are used as orthonormal basis $\{\Phi_j\}$ in Eqn. (1), the pulse duration and the bandwidth of the OPSW functions will stay almost unchanged regardless of the associated order value. The OPSW functions are simultaneously time-limited to symbol duration T_s and bandwidth-limited to bandwidth Ω, which is essential property while considering spectral efficiency increase. They can be obtained as solutions of the following integral equation [9]

$$\int_{-T_s/2}^{T_s/2}\Phi_j(u)\frac{\sin[\Omega(t-u)]}{\pi(t-u)}du=\xi_j\Phi_j(t) \tag{2}$$

where the coefficient ξ_j *is* related to the energy concentration in the interval [$-T_s/2$, $T_s/2$]. The use of orthogonal polynomials/OPSW means that two basis functions (in-phase and quadrature components associated with amplitude/phase arrangement) are replaced with the set of $2M$ basis, thus producing arbitrary multidimensional schemes that can be eventually combined with polarization as a basis function.

The next dimension in parallel multidimensional approach aimed to increase the spectral efficiency is the space basis function employed through spatial multiplexing technique applied within the same optical fiber [13] [14]. By using a novel class of optical fibers known as few-mode fibers (FMF) and few-core fibers (FCF), a number of orthogonal spatial modes can be supported. Since each spatial mode can be independently modulated with signals already employing other basis function mentioned above while essentially occupying the same spectral bands, the total spectral efficiency will be increased in proportion with the number N_{mode} of spatial modes. As an example, the MCF fiber with 7 cores is shown in Fig 2c, in which the central core is FMF supporting 4 modes.

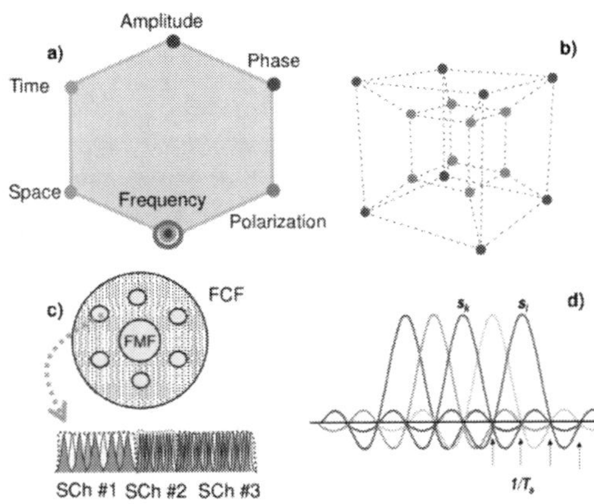

Figure 2. (a) Basis function of an optical channel; (b) coded modulation with amplitude-phase and polarization basis functions; (c) spatial modes with superchannel structure per mode; (d) OFDM spectral arrangement for superchannels

The sophisticated forward error correction (FEC) coding applied on advanced multidimensional modulation and multiplexing schemes is an essential component that contributes to the information capacity increase. The FEC process means that some number of redundant symbols (which is inversely proportional to the code rate R<1; R is the ratio between input information bits/symbols and output coded bits/symbols) have been introduced [5]. They are inserted into data stream in accordance with the specific mathematical algorithms in order to verify the signal health and to make a correction of wrongly detected symbols. With FEC in place, the OSNR requirements for a specific information bit rate and modulation format are relaxed, which means that the channel capacity over specified distance is brought to be closer to the Shannon's limit [15].

Although coding, modulation, and multiplexing are commonly considered as separate serial functions, they can also be performed in parallel manner through coded modulation approach. In such a way, the main functions that involve intense digital signal processing are effectively performed at much lower symbol rates [16]. Also, the coded modulation schemes are inherently adaptive in nature, which is highly desirable for applications in elastic network scenarios when dealing with changing network conditions (dynamic traffic flow and variable impact of impairments). In an adaptive coded modulation scheme, the appropriate code rate (error correction strength) can be selected based on information about the destination and link conditions to match to the required OSNR. Design of advanced coding schemes is still widely open research area, and there is expectation that the coding gain for more advanced FEC schemes will exceed 12 dB with coding rate $R \geq 0.8$, [17] [18]. It appears that a nonbinary low density parity coding LDPC-coded modulation is an approach for achieving a high coding gain. In an adaptive scheme, both the appropriate code rate (error correction strength) and modulation/multiplexing scheme are subject to adjustment based on information about the required data flow and transmission link conditions to match to the required OSNR [19].

III. MULTIDIMENSIONAL ASPECTS IN AGGREGATION AND CORE OPTICAL NETWORKS

Currently, the standardized dual polarization (DP-QPSK) modulation in predominant format used for creation of 100 GbE lightpaths in metro and core optical network segments. However, the need for 400 GbE and 1TbE line transport has become highly evident, thus requiring the most appropriate solutions in design of optical superchannels with an intention to reduce the number of subcarriers by increasing the size of constellation diagram. By using optimized multidimensional structure, we have developed implementation scenarios for future high-speed optical superchannels, with several options presented in Table 1. It quite realistic that practical solution will be based on 400Gb/s rate per carrier in superchannel structure, while the number of amplitude-phase constellation points can vary depending on network conditions and transmission length, with possible interchange between formats. We envision that 32 constellation points are quite realistic in near future, which means that achieved spectral efficiency will be ~6.9 b/s/Hz, while required OSNR will be ~23 dB. As for 1 TbE channels, if faster electronics is used for sampling and only a single carrier modulated with DP-32-QAM is employed, achieved spectral efficiency will be ~6.8 b/s/Hz with the required OSNR of ~27 dB. Some other options for bit rates of various Ethernet interfaces (including futuristic version of 4 TbE and 10 TbE) are also shown in Table 1.

If DP-32-QAM format is applied with the coding rate of 0.8, the required sampling rate would be ~295 GSamples/s, while required OSNR value will be ~27 dB. In such a case, achieved spectral efficiency will be ~6.8 b/s/Hz. If multicarrier superchannel is constructed for 4 TbE and 10 TbE rates bit rates, the required sampling rate can be reduced to be approximately (295 GSamples)/N_{mode}, where N_{mode} is the number of spatial modes that is used. This will also relax the OSNR requirements for at least 3 dB, if two spatial modes are used.

TABLE I: POSSIBLE DESIGN OF HIGH-SPEED SUPERCHANNELS

M (Number of constalation points DP-QAM format)	16	32	64	32	32	32
Bit rate [Gb/s]	400	400	400	1000	4000	10000
FEC Coding Rate; R	0.8	0.8	0.8	0.8	0.8	0.8
Spectral Bandwidth without FEC, Single Carrier; [GHz]	56	47	37	118	N/A	N/A
Spectral Bandwidth with FEC, Single Carrier; [GHz]	70	58.1	46.3	147.5	N/A	N/A
Sampling Rate per Carrier; Gsamples/s	140	116	93	295	116	116
Spatial Modes	1	1	1	1	2	3
Spectral Efficiency, Single Carrierr; [b/s/Hz]	5.7	6.9	8.6	6.8	N/A	N/A
Spectral Eff. (w. spacial mux), Multicarrier; [b/s/Hz]				6.0	11.9	15.1
OSNR per Single Carrier [dB]	~21	~23	~25	~27	~20*	~23**

*400 Gb/s per carrier

IV. CONCLUSION

Design of future high-speed optical networks is a challenging task. Optical channel design is essential and there is a number of possible options to maximize network performance while satisfying both the need for higher information capacity of optical links and the need for dynamic adjustment of data flows along the selected optical lightpaths. In this paper we presented methodology for a multidimensional channel design, which includes and intense signal processing in both time and frequency domains, and applied it to metro/core networking scenarios. We presented multidimensional design of future ultra-high speed 4TbE and 10 TbE interfaces and identified key parameters that would enable not only the highest information capacity, but a dynamic adjustment of date flows as well.

ACKNOWLEDGMENT

This work is partially supported by the NSF CIAN ERC under grant EEC-0812072.

REFERENCES

[1] Cisco Global Cloud Index: www.cisco.com/c/en/us/.../global-cloud-index-gci/ (2014)

[2] M. Cvijetic, "Adaptive multidimensional modulation and multiplexing for next generation optical networks", Proc. SPIE 9388, Optical Metro Networks and Short-Haul Systems VII, 938803 (February 7, 2015)

[3] N. Cvijetic et al, "Terabit optical access networks based on WDM-OFDMA-PON", OSA/IEEE Journal of Lightwave Technology, Vol. 30, Issue 4, 2012, pp. 493-503

[4] X. Zhou, et al, "32 Tb/s (320x114 Gb/s) PDM-RZ-QAM transmission over 580 km of SMF Ultra Low Loss Fiber", OSA/IEEE Optical Fiber Conference OFC'2009, San Diego, CA, 2009, paper PDPB.4.

[5] M. Cvijetic and I. B. Djordjevic: "Advanced Optical Communication System and Networks", Artech House, Boston-London, 2012.

[6] Djordjevic, et al., "Optimum signal constellation design for high-speed optical transmission," Proc. OFC/NFOEC 2012.

[7] M. Cvijetic and I. B. Djordjevic, "Multidimensional aspects of ultra high speed optical networking," Transparent Optical Networks (ICTON), 2015 17th International Conference on, Budapest, 2015, pp. 1-4.

[8] T. J. Xia, et al., "Field experiment with mixed line-rate transmission (112-Gb/s, 450-Gb/s, and 1.15-Tb/s) over 3,560 km of installed fiber using filterless coherent receiver and EDFAs only," in *Proc. OFC/NFOEC*, 2011, paper PDPA3.

[9] I. B. Djordjevic and M. Cvijetic, "Beyond 10 Tb/s Optical Transport based on Adaptive Software-Defined LDPC-Coded Multidimensional Spatial-MIMO-All-Optical-OFDM and Orthogonal Prolate Spheroidal Wave Functions," IEEE 15th International Conference on Transparent Optical Networks, ICTON 2013.

[10] Y. K. Huang, et al., "Terabits Optical Superchannel with Flexible Modulation Format for Dynamic Distance/Route Transmission," in Proc. OFC 2011, Los Angeles, USA.

[11] H. Zhang, et al., "16QAM transmission with 5.2 bits/s/Hz spectral efficiency over transoceanic distance," Optics Express, vol. 20, No. 11, May 2012, pp. 11688-11693.

[12] R. Schmogrow, et al., "Real-time Nyquist pulse generation beyond 100 Gbit/s and its relation to OFDM," Opt. Express 20, 2012, pp. 317-337.

[13] D. Qian et al., 1.05Pb/s Transmission with 109b/s/Hz Spectral Efficiency using Hybrid Single- and Few-Mode Cores", in Proc. of 2012 Frontiers in Optics/Laser Science XXVIII (FiO/LS), Rochester, NY, October 2012.

[14] T. Morioka, et al, "Enhancing optical communications with brand new fibers," IEEE Commun. Mag. 50, 2012, pp. 40-50.

[15] R. J. Essiambre, et al., "Capacity limits of information transport in fiber-optic networks," *Phys. Rev. Lett.*, vol. 101, 17 October 2008, pp. 163901-1 - 163901-4.

[16] I. B. Djordjevic, M. Cvijetic, and C. Lin, "Multidimensional Signaling and Coding Enabling Multi-Tbs Optical Transport and Networking: Multidimensional aspects of coded modulation", IEEE Signal Processing Magazine 31 (2014), pp. 104-117

[17] C. Lin, et al, "Mode-Multiplexed Multi-Tb/s Superchannel Transmission with Advanced Multidimensional Signaling in the Presence of Fiber Nonlinearities," IEEE Transactions on Communications, vol. 62, no. 7, July 2014, pp. 2507-2514.

[18] G. Tzimpragos, et al, "A Survey on FEC Codes for 100G and Beyond Optical Networks", in IEEE Communications Surveys and Tutorials, 10/2014.

[19] M. Cvijetic, I. B. Djordjevic, and N. Cvijetic, "Dynamic multidimensional optical networking based on spatial and spectral processing," OSA Opt. Express 20(1), 2012, pp. 317–337.

5G Mobile Communication Systems: Innovation, Convergence and Ubiquitous Connectivity

Abdulrahman Yarali
Institute of Engineering
Murray State University
Murray, USA
e-mail: ayarali@murraystate.edu

Masoud Fateh, Nasrin Razmi
CITNA, Department of Electrical Engineering,
Isfahan University of Technology
Isfahan, Iran
e-mail: masoudfateh@gmail.com,
Nasrin.razmi@yahoo.com

Abstract— **Wireless technology is one industry which has seen exponential growth in data and capacity in the past decade and it still continues to grow in demand. One big challenge the mobile phones and wireless networks will face in the future is that of supporting mobile traffic efficiently for different phones requirements from diverse applications. More advanced phones will be manufactured and will be expected to properly function. Already we are seeing 4GLTE implementation and some developments of the 5G network that is presumed to be faster and more efficient than their predecessors, but the process of standard and technology ratification is still in its infancy stage. This survey paper focuses on the requirements of 5G network infrastructure and the user experiences and economic benefits that will come along with this new generation of mobile communication network. The core discussion of this paper will be centered on the main features and technological and economic characteristic of 5G mobile systems.**

Keywords-Mobility; Connectivity; Quality; energy efficiency; IoT; small innovations.

I. INTRODUCTION

Just as other global organization, the recent advancement in technology has posed a great advantage and opportunity for the mobile and telecommunication company. One of the greatest revolution and response from the telecommunication industry is the implementation of network sharing strategies that have evolved from the first to the fourth generation. Even though the fourth generation (4G) telecommunication system is undergoing deployment worldwide, individuals are eyeing the development of the 5G telecommunication system, which will lead to greater opportunities from the increased efficiency and effectiveness in network access perspective. From a clear comparison of the changes in evolution between the 1G technology and the recent 4G technology, it is clear that the changes have highly improved in speed, and reliability. The 1G technology provided access at 100 Kilobytes per second (Kbps), the 2G technology improved the speed to 270 Kbps, and the 3G came into play with an access speed of 389 Kbps, whereas the recently most used 4G network increased access to 250 Mbps [1][2]. With this trend, the 5G network technology is expected to provide a great revolution in the telecommunication network access with an access speed of approximately 10 Gbps (Gigabytes per second). This increased speed is based on the recent advancement in telecommunication technology and the urge for businesses to improve their services through enhances communication and telecommunication services [3].

Explosive growth of technology influences consumer behavior. It is estimated that by 2020, almost 80% of the global population will be utilizing mobile technology and over 60% will be using smartphones or tablets. Predictions are that there will be over 50 billion devices on the global network, out of which, mobile devices being the primarily access point for internet connection. With arrival of new 5G system, internet access will be fast and readily accessible; customers will have connections always available to them. Currently, there are over 2.7 million smart phones on the various networks, and this number will increase greatly by the time 5G will go live [4].

Businesses will have to be able to transition from existing offered products and available distribution models to a better way in order to deliver goods and services that customers want. Simpler products are always preferred – it lets consumers make informed choices. It is vital for businesses to recognize the importance of the customer relations, starting with the initial sale and continuing over the lifetime of the contract. It is vital to get customer insights and tailor the services to the individual customer rather than a group of customers.

Even with the recent efficiency status of the 4G technology, businesses have continued to look for alternatives in regards to reliable and efficient telecommunication networks. Latest developments in technology have increased the amount of consumers that are globally connected with networks; they are acutely aware of latest technological trends and attuned to changes. Brands that will respond best to what these customers require now are most will be most likely to succeed; these demands will have to be met in the real time. When businesses will have an understanding of customer needs and wants, it will help with profit margin growth across the organizations.

If current systems make tracking of individual customers difficult, 5G systems will make it much easier. By creating custom tailored services and products based on the individual customer, it will allow businesses increase customer satisfaction and it will lead to customer loyalty. Businesses will be able to pinpoint their customers uniquely and will reward their loyalty. One of the ways to provide loyal customers with a unique option is a personalized pricing. Offered price and the discount will be based on the past history. By utilizing social media (such as Twitter, Facebook, etc.,), businesses will be able to understand what kind of persons their customers are. 5G will be able to analyze customers in real time and businesses will be able to anticipate their customers' future buying plan. Keeping existing customer base is one of the main goals for any service provider; a 2% customer retention increase is equivalent to reducing the cost by 10% [5][6]. By retaining an existing customer instead of acquiring new one businesses can have a larger profit growth – by making an existing customer spend just 10% more on goods and services will produce more profit than to get a 10% growth in new customers. Businesses will be able to deliver solutions that will fulfill the needs of the customer better and offer personalized customer service. Instead of sending bulk/spam messages and emails with general information, more customized messages will be sent to the customers and that will allow better conversion rates and sales increase. Businesses should be able to respond promptly and efficiently to changing market, new customer requests and new regulations.

5G will allow a fully connected network society with unlimited access to information and data sharing anytime to anywhere to anyone. With various environments available, communication will increase exponentially. Businesses should create new services and new experiences based on all the different ways of interaction and connectivity available on the systems. 5G technology will allow brands to hop across customers' different environments using device-to-device discovery. World will become a connected place, the boundaries between developed and developing nations will dissipate.

II. Motivations and Key Drivers of 5G

The 5G network targets various uses including real time gaming, manufacturing or medicine and even extend to wearable technologies. For instance, in the field of medicine operations could be performed by robots which are monitored from a remote access area by a surgeon that he or she is specialized in carrying out similar type of operations

A. When will the next higher generation (5G) of wireless network be deployed?

Considering the statistics presented by the telecommunication network regarding the time period between the deployment of one generation to the other, it is clear that the period presents a sequential matrix whereby a period of five to six years lies between a given network generation deployment and the other. However, the 5G wireless network is expected to break the sequence and take a longer period due to the increased requirements for efficiency. Although the deployment of the 4G network is still on its final stages, operators, leading research teams, and handset developers have launched R&D initiative to develop the 5G network and to ensure that it is fully functional for commercialization by the year 2020.

The ongoing status of the 5G network for the mobile systems are on the very early stages as they underlie the changes and user response in regards to the efficiency and effectiveness of the 4G network. Most of the technological changes to be considered in the formation of the 5G network will be derived from the utilization of the 4G network, which will then be transformed to the 5G network in order to formulate a more concrete system that will be defined by increased efficiency and a positive impact to the operators and mobile industry [8]. The only issue that will lead to delayed deployment is its demanding requirements and intense check over to ensure that it meets all the user demands and transforms the globe to a technological standpoint. With this, the 5G network will not only transform the world by 2020 to a high efficient network connected globe, but also to a community that communicates and shares ideas in an efficient and effective manner.

B. Proposed solutions to key technologies to be considered

As indicated earlier, the development of the 5G technology will mainly lie on the changes and alterations considered after the development of the 4G network. Solutions will mainly rely on end user response and their perception of the efficiency and reliability of the 4G network. Additionally, the changes in technological advancement and consumer demands will highly influence the formation of the 5G network. A clear analysis of the recent development statistics produced by the United Nations indicate that the world will have transformed completely to a technological globe by the year 2020 whereby all nations will be united through a suitable communication network. With this, one of the main proposed solutions would be to enhance reliability and efficiency in order to foster the development of a suitable communication network. Most organization perceives communication as the greatest managerial communication tool towards enhanced performance and productivity. The greatest urge for businesspersons is to have access to a reliable network that fosters appropriate management from appropriate communication.

Additionally, unlike the recent prototype of the 4G network, which does not enhance coverage, increased connectivity, and call frequency thus leading to underperformance, the 5G network will be expected to provide a permanent solution to these problems [9]. The deployment of the 5G network should coincide with the organizational system and become a part of the productivity enhancement strategies for any given organization. With this, the high-speed 5G technology will be expected to present a paradigm movement in the overall design of the mobile industry in order to revolutionize the entire system to encourage enhanced latency, flow, and the scalability requirements, which will be suitable to meet the overarching demands such as the trillion device connection and the augmented reality. With appropriate provision and permanent solution to these problems, the 5G technology will have taken over the business world and transformed it fully to a community defined by enhance performance and productivity.

C. *Is 5G wireless mobile network an evolution or a revolution?*

Through the considerations put forth as well as the expectation by the year 2020 when the 5G network will be deployed, it is clear that the invention will completely change the world to a single entity characterized by increased efficiency and reliability. With this, the worldwide transformation will define the 5G network as a revolution rather than a mere evolution. The development of the 5G network technology is expected to provide appropriate benefits that will surpass the expectation of the previous generation of network technology. Telecommunication industries are already doing away with the term World Wide Web (WWW) and coining into the term World Wide Wireless Web (WWWW), which will define the increased utilization as well as reliability in the efficiency of the 5G wireless network [1].

From an earlier analysis, it is clear that the 5G wireless network will transform the functioning of the entire globe to include the increased use of wireless network. The 5G network will easily carry over 1000 times of mobile data compared to the recent 4G prototype. This therefore indicates an increased reliance and a massive capability for increased communication, which will cater for all individual's need to access and transfer data in a quasi-instantaneous, and sensationalize in their own choice. Then 5G network will also have a direct impact on security deployment, formation of electric transportation systems, ambient policing, and worldwide access to information. With this, the 5G network will change the entire world to a community of both similarity and togetherness, which will give the invention a revolutionary status.

D. *Business opportunities from the deployment of the 5G network*

The deployment of the 5G network will present great business opportunities for both the service providers and the virtual mobile network operators. With the increased agility and reliance on high-speed network, the world will have fully transformed to a technological world with great need for internet connection and network availability. Most organizations will require the installation of network for office use and downloading of business materials. Additionally, online businesses such as transaction and selling of video games and movies will present a great opportunity to the service providers and virtual mobile network operators. Additionally, security systems, tracking devices, ambient policing, internet cars, healthcare monitors, and appliances will need to transform from manual operationalization to a digital platform, which will be highly dependent on high speed network for increased efficiency and accuracy. With this, the service providers will have an increased business opportunity, as they will need to install mobile networks to the respective field. Additionally, most individuals will require high-speed network on their mobile phones in order have access to emails, games, and online transactions. This will provide an opportunity for the virtual mobile network operator to install 5G network to the respective individuals [10]. With the increased access to communication and online interactions, consumers will have a direct access to the service providers and virtual mobile network operators. As communication is a great managerial tool, the consumers will easily voice their concern for further actions, which will increase performance and productivity of the respective network provider. With this, the deployment of the 5G network will pose a great opportunity for increased business functionality and operation efficiency.

The recent technological advancements call for major consideration in the telecommunication industry in order to enhance efficiency and reliability in the general network and communication provision. Deployment of the 5G network will be considered after the complete deployment of the 4G network, as it will be a result of enhancement based on changes required and consumer reaction to the development of the 4G network. From an analysis of the changes that will be presented by the 5G network, it is clear that the invention will be a complete revolution, as it will totally transform the world to a network dependent globe. Additionally, deployment of the 5G network will unionize the world to a single entity defined by similarity and togetherness. With the increased dependence, the 5G network will also present great business opportunities, as it will lead to increased utilization in major fields such as office management, ambient policing, security, formation of technological transport systems, and healthcare monitoring. With a clear consideration of communication efficiency and reliability, it is clear that the 5G network will provide a great platform for increased performance and productivity for the service providers and the virtual mobile network providers.

III. 5G Requirements Framework and Research Direction

The development of 5G technology will be helpful for executing long projects within no time and it will increase the reliability of the global networks because everyone will be connected with high speed internet. Following are the main key points which can be concluded from the research work:

1) It will be helpful in browsing, downloading and uploading data files from any place to anywhere.
2) Network energy usage will be reduced which will in turn increase the battery life of the device.
3) It will increase the users' density over the unit area many times which will help the users to use high bandwidth for a longer period of time.
4) 5G Technology will also be helpful and beneficial for the Internet to things, Machine to Machine Communication and Device to Device Communication. It will increase the object oriented works and data management.
5) Through the deployment of 5G technology, the users will develop frameworks to utilize machine-machine system of communication..
6) RF-EHN is a promising way for future 5G wireless networks.

In a nutshell, 5G technology should be developed as early as possible because of increasing technological usage of the servers and machines.

A. Vision

Any innovation is a product of a vision. The innovation of the 5G Technology is driven by three different visions [11]:

- High efficiency: The efficiency of the 5G Technology is taken as a main parameter and the innovation and design are taken forward with focus on areas like demand based networks, data rate management, etc.
- High Speed: The innovation with focus on speeds concentrates on areas like coverage, clustering of data cells, wide area mobility, dynamic spectrum, etc.
- Converged networks: The use of a joint wireless and fiber operated networks enables the new 5G Technology to be able to employ millimeter wave bands. This would facilitate the support of very high bandwidths. This path of vision makes the emerging 5G Technology to be characterized as more of a Wi-Fi service than a mobile service

B. Goals

The main goals of the innovation of 5G technology can be broadly classified in to Flexibility and Reliability[12].

- Flexibility: 5G technology should be employable in diverse applications and services. All the needs and services required should be embedded into a single operation point. 5G service owned by a person should facilitate all the services and needs required. 5G should not be entitled as "*Services*" but as a "*Service*" which is an embodiment of all the services in one entity of service.
- Reliability: 5G is, hopefully, going to be providing the most reliable set of services the world has ever seen. Security has been taken as a prominent factor in the design of 5G services. Increase of reliability will eventually be a factor in the increase of efficiency, but an unlikely increase in prices too. The specific goals that are indicated in the deployment of the 5G technology services are:
    - High data rates owing to faster modulation and some new innovation technologies
    - Fast response times by node reduction and more intelligent components
    - Whole new and diverse services using automation, cloud and tactile internet

C. Inference to the customers

With reference to the customers, the meaning of 5G in layman's words can be indicated as the ability to download a full length HD movie to a phone in just a few seconds or the services that facilitate video chats in such a way that it may feel like the person on the other side can be touched. This is not an exaggeration, but the factual vision of the network sector. The simple goals that need to be attained by the 5G technology, according to the customers are [13]:

- Faster speeds for data
- Ultra-low latency which refers to the time it takes to send a packet of data between two devices
- Connected devices (cars, home appliances, accessories, etc.) making everything flexible
- Backward compatibility with the devices that are already owned
- Reasonable costs for the 5G services

D. Services

One of the main aspects that is needed a great deal of look up is the requirements for the 5G network, which can affect many other parameters like cost, compatibility, feasibility, standardization, etc. These requirements are subject to the forecasted services that are expected to be fulfilled by the 5G network. Some of the services that 5G technology is needed to provide are[11]:

- Pervasive Video and high quality content
- Tactile Internet and Broad cast Services
- E – Health Services and 50 + MBPS data rate everywhere
- Internet of things and Real time data analytics
- Mobile Broad band and Smart Societies
- Smart Grids and Freight tracking
- Public safety

E. Characteristics forecast

The 5G network will be characterized by its increased power, strength, efficient, and speed, which are promising features that will take the mobile industry to the next level. With the presence of the 5G network, the mobile industry will be considered as the main key to the Internet of Things. This name is given to the act whereby every activity will be tied to the internet and mobile network. The mobile industry will lead to development of billions of sensors, door locks, smartwatches, and health monitors. Additionally, the mobile industry will be characterized with an increased scalability, flow, and latency in order to meet all its overarching demands. A consideration of these factors gives a clear look at the opportunity and efficiency that will be presented to the mobile industry by the development of the 5G network in the year 2020 and beyond. From a look at the recent occurrence after the deployment of the 3G and 4G network, It is clear that by the year 2020, the 5G network will present the with new realities, increased speed, gratification, efficiency, and lightning-fast response. The following s is some of the expected characteristics of 5G networks.

- Ultra-high capacity and Massive MIMO
- Multi hop transmission and New spectrum
- Wide area coverage and Full duplex
- Ultra-dense networks and NFV SDN
- Security and New Waveforms
- Energy Efficient
- Real time inter Machine communication
- Application Awareness and Zero Latency
- Strategy based traffic management

The following graphical representations depict the implementation of a single 5G wireless antenna to facilitate diverse applications and services.

F. Need

Demand on 5G is far more complicated and comprehensive than the previous generations of mobile communication. There is a conflict and tension between factors such as high performance requirement and availability, cost, and efficiency when it comes to only one technology for 5g systems deployment. In order to provide services with variety of requirements there need to be more than one technology implementation for 5G to meet user experiences in terms of availability, speed, reliability and cost. Some of the predominant needs for a new generation technology in spite of already existing 4G and LTE are;

- Growing data demand – It is estimated that the data needs are intended to increase to 12 times per month compared to the data used now.
- Development of Device technologies – The upgrades and developments in technologies of the devices (Android, IOS) lead to an increased need of *coverage, data rates, low latency, etc.*
- Increased use of networks – Unlike the olden days, the use of the network services has been increasing exponentially from more than a decade. This was the main reason that leads to such a heavy innovation in the devices and network industry, which is a main point of motivation for the 5G technology.
- With respect to the 4G technology, the backlogs that provided a motivation for 5G innovation are
  - I. Limited connectivity to specific carriers and geographic regions
  - II. Limited backward compatibility
  - III. Limited network coverage
  - IV. Use of multiple transmitters and antenna leading to poor battery life

G. Technology

The radio access for the 5G Technology will be energized from the already existing technologies like the LTE, HSPA, Wi-Fi and GSM as well as the new radio access technologies which are called as RAT. A successful 5g deployment requires a comprehensive designing, simulating, emulating, calibrating and validating for a new solution.

The employment of millimeter waves (Carrier, BW, MU-MIMO) is going to be the prime supporting aspect for increased speeds, wide area coverage, and reliability. Millimeter waves also support very flexible long distant communication. This will also result in use of very less radio base stations. Millimeter waves are expected to revolutionize the latency times. It is needed that the 5G Technology provide less than 1ms latency from one end to the other. The power requirements, bandwidth standardizations and the commercialization of the millimeter waves are expected to be before the year 2020[14].

Use of bandwidths that are very unlikely to be used by other broadcast technologies (3 MHz – 300 MHZ) resulting in higher speeds and capacity

The multiplexing used for the 5G transmission is under speculation. The evaluation of the 5G networks using CDMA, OFDM with respect to data rate and latency is being studied.

OFDM has always been the most preferred modulation technique right from the time of its acceptance in 4G enhanced mobile broadband accesses. In 5G as we know we need low latency, high data rates and wide channel bandwidth along with low complexity per bit. This modulation technique is very much suitable to these specifications. OFDM has a scalable symbol duration and subcarrier spacing with low complexity receiver for wider bandwidth. This also runs efficiently with special multiplexing and multi user data SDMA. OFDM implementations make way for more number of transmissions and reception filtering based on link and adjacent channel requirements. Also RSMA waveforms have better uplink for short data bursts needed for low power internet of things devices. This supports asynchronous and synchronous contention based access [15].

Advanced technologies that could recognize the surrounding objects and more number of sensors are to be used. Also, real time rendering and hologram technologies that can revive a real image in real time in an all angle (360 degree) view are to be employed. MMT which is an acronym for MPEG Media Transport is a processing technology used to decrease the latency. With the help of MVC which is an acronym for Multi View Video Encoding high efficiency in 3D transmission can be achieved. For agility of network and cost reduction efficient control of the networks based on software and virtualization are done through an orchestration that is integrated. Finally, big data is used for the 5G technologies to compare the required existing data to the whole unstructured data in real time for Traffic analysis to equip the network with intelligence for feedback and decision making. Also, self-organized networks are also the intelligent networks that detect anomalies and take the help of big data to organize a solution.

H. Deployment

It is common expectation that the deployment of the 5G services will be prevalent in 2020. This particular year was foretold taking many surveys into consideration. The factors that led to the forecast of the year 2020 for the deployment of 5G Technology are [16]:

1. Higher number of connected devices:

It is expected that the number of connected devices using the 5G Technology should be 50 to 500 billion and depending on the present surveys it would take at least 4 to 5 years to reach the expected number from the present number (2 billion). The 5G Technology should be deployed into the practical commercial network gradually with respect to the geographical areas and then completely marketed to connect all the 5G enabled devices.

2. Energy efficiency:

The energy drain is likely to be very high with the 5G services with reference to the heavy data rates and connectivity. The use of lithium ion battery devices made a heavy impact on the battery life for the high end devices, but is analyzed to be less efficient in 5G enabled devices. This factor becomes more unsolvable for low power devices. Hence, the research for new, high battery capacity components is also expected to come to a result by 2020.

The Increase in the use of applications on mobile computing and also user needs like portable cell phones and devices will increase the need for the mobile wireless networks in the upcoming years. Cell Phone users will assume more bandwidth and fewer amounts of delays in the cell phone network. All these expectations and assumptions will increase in the infrastructures of mobile industries which will eventually lead to the discharge or emission of carbon dioxide. We can say that by 2020, 181 Megatons of carbon dioxide are emitted by mobile networks, which is almost equal to triple [17].

High energy performance and minimizing the energy usage is the basic requirement of 5G. It reduces the ownership cost and extends the network connectivity to almost everywhere and also the network access is very bearable and very resource efficient way. The main technology to finish the ultra-lean model and separation of user's data on the radio interference, 5G is very costly when compared to other data plans. Its functioning model is different from 3G and 4G. It really plays an important role in the energy saving while the data is transmitted. The device does not transmit the data unless and until a user data transfer is going on. The main two design principles of this technology are; a) being active only when the transmission is required and b) being active only where the transmission is required.

IV. Conclusion

While telecommunication developers have created four generations of mobile technology, a variety of mobile technologies will be included in the 5G technology. Therefore, the 5G will be released in a couple of years, and it will comprise various features such as an increase in efficiency. Establishing the 5G of mobile technology will inevitably provide higher and higher data rate. Even more, it will meet the customers' demands since it is reliable for communication, and the capability of 5G will resist the future challenges in mobile communication.

References

[1] Bhalla, Mudit Ratana, and Anand Vardhan Bhalla. "Generations of mobile wireless technology: A survey." *International Journal of Computer Applications* 5.4 (2010).

[2] Yarali, A., "The Future Connectivity and Technological Advancement in Higher Generation of Telecommunication Systems", 4G and Beyond: The Convergence of Networks, Devices and Services, Nova Inc. Publisher, 2015.

[3] Wang, Li-Chun, and Suresh Rangapillai. "A survey on green 5G cellular networks." *Signal Processing and Communications (SPCOM), 2012 International Conference on*. IEEE, 2012.

[4] Yarali, A., Barrow, K., "The Road Towards Densified and HetNet Gigabit Wireless Networks", 4G and Beyond: The Convergence of Networks, Devices and Services, Nova Inc. Publisher, 2015.

[5] https://5g-ppp.eu/ The 5G Infrastructure Public Private Partnership, 2015

[6] White paper, Ericsson, "5G Energy Performance", Uen 284 23-3265, April2015

[7] Bangerter, B., Talwar, S., Arefi, R., & Stewart, K. (2014). Networks and devices for the 5G era. *Communications Magazine, IEEE, 52*(2), 90-96.

[8] Sharma, Pankaj. "Evolution of mobile wireless communication networks-1G to 5G as well as future prospective of next generation communication network." *International Journal of Computer Science and Mobile Computing* 2.8 (2013): 47-53.

[9] Li, Xichun, et al. "The future of mobile wireless communication networks." *Communication Software and Networks, 2009. ICCSN'09. International Conference on*. IEEE, 2009.

[10] Osseiran, Afif, et al. "Scenarios for 5G mobile and wireless communications: the vision of the METIS project." *Communications Magazine, IEEE* 52.5 (2014): 26-35.

[11] *"What is 5g, 5g visions," GSM History: History of GSM, Mobile Networks, Vintage Mobiles. 20 November 2015.*

[12] Toni Janevski (10–13 January 2009). "5G Mobile Phone Concept". Consumer Communications and Networking Conference, 2009 6th IEEE [1-4244-2308-2]. Facility of Electrical Engineering & Information Technology, University Sv. Kiril i Metodij. Retrieved 20 November 2015.

[13] Xichun Li; Abudulla Gani; Rosli Salleh; Omar Zakaria (February 2009). "The Future of Mobile Wireless Communication Networks" International Conference on Communication Software and Networks. Retrieved 20 November 2015.

[14] Hoydis; S. Ten Brink; M. Debbah (February 2013)."Massive MIMO in the UL/DL of Cellular Networks: How Many Antennas Do We Need?" IEEE Journal on Selected Areas in Communications. vol. 31, no. 2. Bell Labs, Alcatel-Lucent. pp. 160–171. Retrieved 20 November 2015.

[15] Akhtar, Shakil (August 2008). Pagani, Margherita, ed.2G-5G Networks: Evolution of Technologies, Standards, and Deployment (Second ed.). Hershey, Pennsylvania, United States: IGI Global. pp. 522–532. Retrieved 20 November 2015.

[16] Zeadally, Sherali, Samee Ullah Khan, and Naveen Chilamkurti. "Energy-efficient Networking: Past, Present, and Future." (n.d.): n. pag. *Sameekhan.org*. Springer Science+Business Media, LLC 2011, 31 May 2011. Web. 20 Nov. 2015. <http://sameekhan.org/pub/Z_K_2011_SUPE.pdf>.

[17] Moon, Sangwoo, and Yung Yi. "Energy-Efficient User Association in Cellular Networks: A Population Game Approach." *YouTube*. Sogang University, 25 Aug. 2015. Web. 21 Nov. 2015. <https://www.youtube.com/watch?v=Jc2HXP5qwsY>.

Client Driven Rate Adaptation Algorithm for Streaming over HTTP

Waqas ur Rahman and Kwangsue Chung
Department of Electronics and Communications Engineering
Kwangwoon University
Seoul, Korea
Email: waqas@cclab.kw.ac.kr, kchung@kw.ac.kr

Abstract— **Video streaming services make up a large proportion of Internet traffic throughout the world. Adaptive streaming allows for dynamical adaptation of the video bitrate with varying network conditions, to guarantee the best user experience. We propose an adaptive bitrate scheme that intelligently selects the video bitrates based on the estimated throughput and buffer occupancy. We show that the proposed algorithm selects a high playback video rate and avoids unnecessary rebuffering while keeping a low frequency of video rate changes.**

Keywords- Rate adaptation; Quality adaptation; Quality of Experience; HTTP Streaming; Multimedia

I. INTRODUCTION

High speed broadband networks and improvements in display technology of various devices have enabled video streaming to become one of the most popular applications. Video traffic dominates Internet traffic on both fixed and mobile access networks all over the world.

Initially, the video clients completely downloaded the video before the streaming could start. This was followed by the progressive download with which the clients begin the playback at a defined video rate before the download is complete. Recently, video streaming services are based on Hypertext Transport Protocol (HTTP) over TCP for streaming multimedia over computer networks. Network conditions and video clients' capabilities vary with time and place; therefore, adaptive streaming over HTTP allows the adaption of video quality based on the available resources on the path between the server and client. Multiple versions of the multimedia content are stored at the server. The server shares the information about the characteristics of the stored multimedia content with the client. The adaptive bitrate (ABR) algorithm at the video client is responsible for selecting a suitable bitrate depending on the system conditions such as throughput and the occupancy of the playback buffer.

ABR algorithms strive to maximize the user experience by meeting conflicting video quality objectives in different environments. Some of the potential objectives include selecting a set of video bitrates that are the highest feasible, avoiding needless video bitrate switches and preserving the buffer level to avoid interruption of playback [1][2]. Maximizing the video rate increases the risk of playback interruption whereas mitigating the frequency of video rate switches results in lower average video rate.

One way to pick video bitrates is to make an estimate of the future throughput from past observations. An inaccurate estimation may lead to selecting the video bitrate that results in extensive rebuffering. If the selected video rate is higher than the available throughput, the client's playback buffer drains which may result in interrupted playback. To avoid interrupting playback, ABR algorithms add playback buffer occupancy as an adjustment parameter on top of throughput estimation to select video bitrates.

In this paper, we show that the proposed algorithm selects the video rates based on the buffer occupancy by exploiting the variation of the sizes of the upcoming segments. The results show that our approach provides better viewing experience by delivering higher average video rate without unnecessary rebuffering while maintaining a low frequency of video rate changes. The rest of the paper is organized as follows. The related works are presented in Section II. The proposed scheme is presented in Section III. The experimental results are provided in Section IV, and finally the concluding remarks are given in Section V.

II. RELATED WORK

The main objective of all adaptive video rate algorithms is to improve the user's viewing experience. Adaptation algorithms mainly select video rates based on the estimated throughput and the state of the playback buffer. Segment throughput is calculated as the ratio of the segment size to the time that it takes to download the segment [3]. In many commercial clients, the moving average of the throughput of previous segments is used to estimate the throughput [4]. Once the throughput has been estimated, clients pick the video rate of the next segment based on the throughput [5-7].

Many ABR algorithms consider playback buffer along with the throughput to select the video rate of the next segment. The buffer is divided into predefined ranges and different decisions are taken to select the video rates when the buffer level stays in different ranges [8][9]. The method in [9] is more stable as compared to the method in [8] but it is late to react to the changes in the throughput as it waits for the playback buffer to reach a threshold before selecting a higher video rate. We propose an adaptive bitrate scheme [10] that intelligently selects the video bitrates based on the estimated throughput and buffer occupancy. The scheme improves viewing experience by achieving a high video rate without taking unnecessary risks and by minimizing the frequency of changes in the video quality. Huang *et al* [11] propose a video rate adaption algorithm that selects the video rate by observing only the client's playback buffer. The video rate is increased and decreased as the playback buffer builds up and drains respectively. Furthermore, the algorithm selects the video rates considering the sizes of the upcoming segments. In this paper, we propose a scheme that is similar to the schemes proposed in [8][9][13] as it selects the video rates based on both the estimated throughput and the buffer occupancy. The current schemes in the literature pick the video rates based on the predefined buffer ranges whereas the proposed scheme dynamically selects the buffer ranges to optimally pick the video rates based on the upcoming segment sizes to optimize the QoE.

III. Proposed Scheme

A. System Model

The HTTP client downloads a video stream divided into multiple segments. The video stream is stored at the server and the adaptive bitrate algorithm at the client decides which segment to download next. All the segments have an equal duration of τ seconds. The set of representations available for the video stream is denoted by R where $R = \{R_{min}, R_2, R_3, \ldots, R_{max}\}$. The client dynamically selects a video rate from the set R for the next segment. R_{min} and R_{max} are the representations with the highest and lowest video rates in the set R. Any video rate higher and lower than currently selected video rate is denoted by $R\uparrow$ and $R\downarrow$ respectively.

B. Adaptive Bitrate Algorithm

Available bandwidth estimation plays an important part in the selection of the video rate. The clients estimate the throughput of the next segment based on the throughput observed over the download of the previous segments. Segment throughput is calculated as the ratio of segment size divided by the time it takes to download the segment. The selection of the video rate for the next segment based on the throughput $T(i\text{-}1)$ of the last downloaded segment keeps the playback buffer stable but results in a fluctuating video rate curve. In this paper, we use the McGinely dynamic indicator for the throughput estimation measure $T^E(i)$ to overcome the fluctuating video curve which is given by [12]:

$$T^E(i+1) = T^E(i) + \frac{T(i) - T^E(i)}{N \times (\frac{T(i)}{T^E(i)})^4} \quad (1)$$

The numerator of the second term gives a sign, up or down and the power of 4 gives the calculation an adjustment factor which increases more sharply as the difference between the observed throughput of ith segment and estimated throughput of segment i increases. N is the tracking factor which we set equal to 1.

The buffer dynamics are considered when the segment is completely downloaded. Let $B(i\text{-}1)$ be the buffer level at the end of the download of segment i-1, then $B(i)$ is given by:

$$B(i) = B(i-1) + \tau - [\tau \times \frac{R_k(i)}{T(i)}] \quad (2)$$

where $R_k(i)$ is the kth video rate from the set R and $T(i)$ is the throughput observed during the download of segment i. (2) shows that if the selected video rate is greater than the available throughput, the playback buffer drains. As each segment contains duration of τ seconds, $C_k(i)$, the size of the ith segment is $\tau\times R_k$ bits. Given the available throughput $T(i)$ and video rate $R_k(i)$, the change in buffer level during the download of ith segment is equal to B^*:

$$B^* = B(i) - B(i-1) = \frac{C_k(i)}{R_k(i)} - \frac{C_k(i)}{T(i)} \quad (3)$$

where the playback buffer fills with $C_k(i) / R_k(i)$ seconds of data and the buffer drains with $C_k(i) / T(i)$ seconds of data. (2) can now be written as:

$$B(i) = B(i-1) + B^* \quad (4)$$

If $R_k(i) > T(i)$, B^* becomes negative, which means that the buffer is drained at a rate faster than the rate at which it fills, therefore, $B(i)$ will be less than $B(i\text{-}1)$. We assume that the available throughput cannot be less than $R_{min}= R_1$. We denote the change in the buffer level when $T(i) = R_{k-1}$ and the client overestimates the throughput and selects the next higher video rate R_k for the ith segment as B_k^*. We denote $B_k(i)$ as the minimum buffer level occupancy to select the kth video rate for the ith segment.

$$B_k(i) = \tau + \left|\sum_{m=2}^{k} B_m^*\right| = \tau + \left|\sum_{m=2}^{k} \frac{C_m(i)}{R_m} - \frac{C_m(i)}{R_{m-1}}\right| = \tau + \left|\sum_{m=2}^{k} \frac{C_m(i)\times R_m - C_m(i)\times R_{m-1}}{R_m \times R_{m-1}}\right| \quad (5)$$

(5) ensures that if the client selects the kth video rate when at least $B_k(i)$ amount of buffer is available and the throughput drops to R_{min}, there will be one segment (τ seconds) available in the buffer at the end of the segment download. Most of the streaming services encode videos in variable bitrate (VBR) where static scenes are encoded with fewer bits and active streams with more bits. In VBR, video is encoded at an average video rate and the instantaneous video rate of each segment varies around the average rate. This allows flexible and efficient use of bits. As the size of each segment is different and $B_k(i)$ depends on the segment size, the value of $B_k(i)$ will change every time a segment is downloaded. This makes the video rate change frequently. Furthermore, for a given throughput a segment of a larger size will take more time to get downloaded; hence will consume more video in the buffer than a smaller segment. To

this end, we take the average of the next 10 segment sizes and calculate $B_k(i)$ after every 10 segments based on their average sizes.

$$B_k(i) = \tau + \sum_{m=2}^{k} \frac{\bar{C}_m \times R_m - \bar{C}_m \times R_{m-1}}{R_m \times R_{m-1}} \quad (6)$$

where $\bar{C}_m$ is the average of every 10 segment sizes. (6) makes sure that $B_k(i)$ gets its value recalculated after every 10 segments to reduce the video rate switches. If the upcoming segments are larger, the buffer thresholds to select a given video rate will be greater than when segments are smaller to minimize the risk of buffer underflow. If we select the average segment size based on more than 10 upcoming segments, it might not correctly depict the segment size trend whereas calculating $B_k(i)$ based on fewer segments will result in a higher frequency of video rate switches.

The algorithm's pseudo-code is provided in Algorithm 1. We consider that Algorithm 1 is invoked to select the video rate of ith segment. The streaming session is divided into two phases of operation: the startup phase and the steady phase. The startup phase starts when the buffer is building up from being empty, to be followed by the steady phase.

Algorithm 1: Adaptation Algorithm

```
if Startup phase conditions hold true
    if B(i-1) < B_LOW then
        if R↑ < α1 ×T(i-1) then
            Rk(i) = R↑
    else
        if R↑< α2 ×T(i-1) then
            Rk(i) = R↑
else
    if B(i-1) < Bmin then
        R(i) = Rmin
    else if R(i-1)==Rk && Bk-1(i) < B(i-1) then
            R(i) = R(i-1)
    else if R(i-1)≠Rmin && B(i-1)<Bk-1(i) then
            R(i) = R↓
    else if R(i-1)≠Rmax&&B(i-1)>Bk↑&&T^E(i) >T^E(i-1) then
            R(i) = R↑
    else
            R(i) = R(i-1)
```

During the startup phase, the buffer builds up from being empty. A conservative approach is considered at the start and as the buffer gradually fills up and climbs above the buffer threshold B_{LOW}, we take more risk in selecting the video rate. Minimum available video rate R_{min} is selected to download the first segment. This approach reduces the delay after the client requests the video and before the client streams the video. For $B(i\text{-}1) < B_{LOW}$, the client switches to a higher video rate if $R\uparrow < \alpha_1 \times T(i\text{-}1)$. For $B(i\text{-}1) > B_{LOW}$, a higher video rate is selected if $R\uparrow < \alpha_2 \times T(i\text{-}1)$ where α_1 and α_2 are the safety margins and $\alpha_1 < \alpha_2$. When the buffer size is small, the client will increase the video rate faster in the startup phase. When the buffer size is large, it may take time for the client to accumulate buffer up to B_{LOW} which may result in underutilization of the resource when the available throughput is high. To avoid this scenario, we set the condition that if $R_{startupphase} < R_{steadyphase}$ the algorithm switches to steady phase. $R_{startupphase}$ and $R_{steadyphase}$ are the video rates suggested by the client during the startup and steady phase respectively. The proposed scheme stays at the startup phase until any of the following conditions are not satisfied: (i) $B(i\text{-}2) < B(i\text{-}1)$; or (ii), $R_{startupphase} > R_{steadyphase}$. The motivation behind the startup phase is to quickly fill up the buffer without risking playback interruption. Afterwards, we use steady phase to select the video rate of the upcoming segments.

In the steady phase, to select the kth video rate, two conditions should be satisfied:

1) The buffer level should be higher than $B_k(i)$
2) $R_k(i) < \alpha_3 \times T^E(i)$

The client will select $R_k(i)$ if the buffer level is greater than $B_k(i)$. This condition helps in avoiding the buffer underflow in case the client overestimates the throughput or there is a sudden drop in the throughput. The condition of $R_k(i) < \alpha_3 \times T^E(i)$ uses a safety margin α_3 to compute the bitrate to avoid throughput overestimation.

First we consider the scenario where buffer level falls below $B_{min} = B_2(i)$. In this case, R_{min} is always selected. $B_2(i)$ is the minimum buffer occupancy to select the video rate $R_2(i)$. The reason is that it is of the primary importance to avoid interruption of the playback.

Now, we consider the scenario when the throughput and the buffer level drops. We do not immediately react to this drop in the throughput; we stay at the current video rate until the buffer level drops below $B_{k-1}(i)$. This is because we can minimize the number of video rate switches if we don't react to short-term fluctuations. Once the buffer level falls below $B_{k-1}(i)$, we continue to reduce the video rate until the condition $R_k(i) < \alpha_3 \times T^E(i)$ is satisfied.

Next, we consider the scenario of an increase in throughput and the buffer level. To increase the video rate in response to the increase in throughput and buffer level, the following conditions should be satisfied:

1) $T^E(i) > T^E(i\text{-}1)$
2) The buffer level should be greater than $B_k\uparrow$

The first condition makes sure that there isn't a recent drop in throughput while the client decides to increase the video rate. $B_k\uparrow$ is the buffer threshold to select the higher video rate $R\uparrow$. As the video rate cannot be adapted until the download of the next segment, in case of a sudden drop in throughput the second condition reduces the risk of buffer underflow. When the conditions of switching up and switching down the video rate are not satisfied, we maintain the current video rate.

IV. PERFORMANCE EVALUATION

We implement the proposed scheme in ns-3 to evaluate its performance. We compare the proposed method with the schemes proposed in [8] and [9]. We refer to the algorithms proposed in [8] and [9] as AAAS and QAAD respectively. The topology implemented in this paper is shown in Figure 1.

The topology consists of an HTTP server, HTTP client and a pair of network elements. The link between the network elements is our bottleneck link. We add the UDP traffic between the network elements to vary the throughput across the bottleneck. To achieve adaptive streaming, the HTTP server offers the client four different video rates which include 450, 850, 1500 and 2500kbps. The length of each segment and playback buffer size is 4 and 60 seconds, respectively. B_{LOW} is set to 30% of the buffer size. The safety margins are set to (α_1, α_2, α_3)=(0.5, 0.75, 0.9).

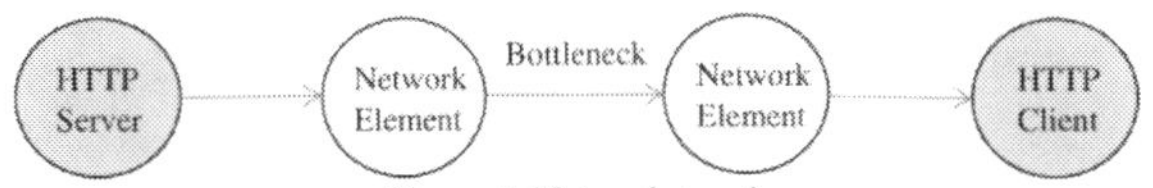

Figure 1. Network topology

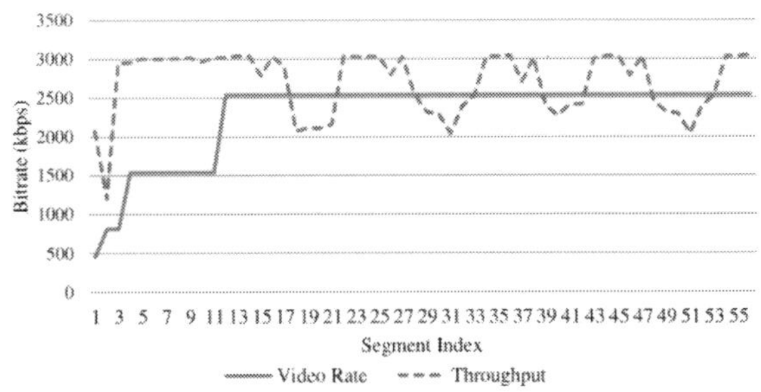

Figure 2. Response of the proposed scheme to small drop in throughput

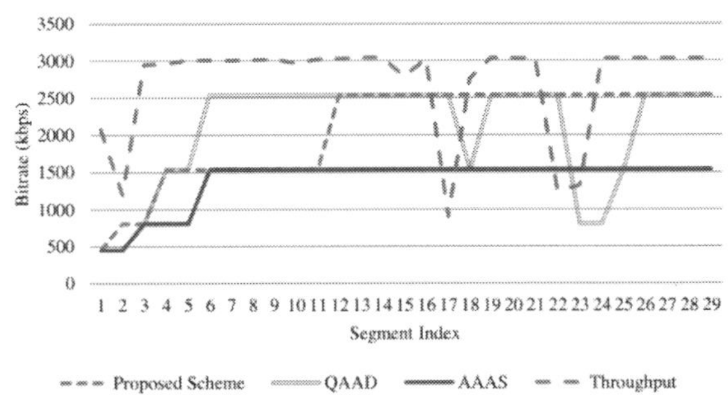

Figure 3. Comparison of the schemes in response to large throughput fluctuation

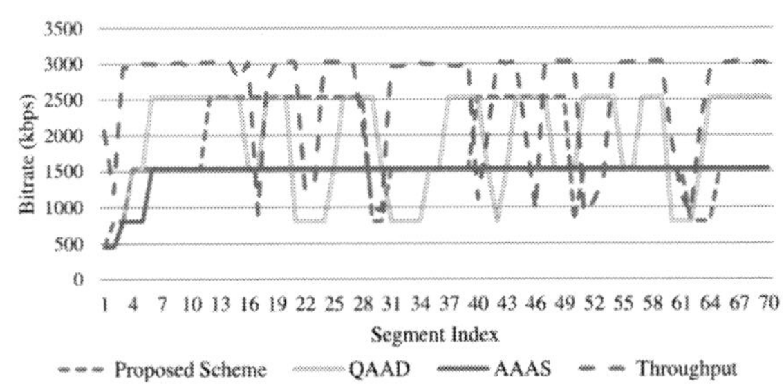

Figure 4. Comparison of the schemes in response to highly variable available bandwidth

Figure 2 shows the response of the proposed scheme to short term throughput fluctuations. It shows that the proposed scheme is stable in the face of short term throughput fluctuations while maintaining a high video rate.

Figure 3 shows that the proposed scheme does not vary the video rate quickly as it maintains video rate at the expense of drop in buffer level below $B_k(i\text{-}1)$. The motivation behind maintaining the video rate at the expense of drop in buffer level is that the objective of ABR algorithm is not to keep the buffer full but to provide better user experience. AAAS scheme shows a stable response to the throughput fluctuations but stays at a lower video rate. QAAD scheme varies the video rate as the throughput fluctuates in order to avoid buffer underflow.

Figure 4 shows that the proposed scheme tries to maintain the higher video rate but reacts swiftly to large drop in throughput to avoid any playback interruption. The AAAS scheme is the most conservative of all the schemes. The reason is that it waits for the playback buffer to cross a predefined threshold before stepping up or down the video rate. The proposed scheme achieves an average of video rate of 350kbps higher than AAAS. QAAD has slightly higher video rate than the proposed scheme but at the expense of twice the number video rate switches which greatly degrades the user experience.

V. Conclusion and Future Work

Video rate adaptation techniques are used to adapt the quality of the video to the varying network resources of the computer network. In this paper, we proposed an adaptive bitrate streaming algorithm to improve the viewing experience of the multimedia streaming applications. The proposed algorithm achieves high video rate and minimizes the frequency of changes in video quality while preventing interruption in playback to guarantee QoE. In this paper, we consider a single client scenario. For the future work, we plan to extend our algorithm to a multi-user scenario where multiple clients share the bottleneck.

Acknowledgment

This work was supported by ICT R&D program of MSIP/IITP. [R0101-16-293, Development of Object-based Knowledge Convergence Service Platform using Image Recognition in Broadcasting Contents]

References

[1] F. Dobrian, V. Sekar, A. Awan, I. Stoica, D. Joseph, A. Ganjam, J. Zhan, and H. Zhang, "Understanding the impact of video quality on user engagement," ACM SIGCOMM Computer Communication Review, vol. 41, no. 4, Sep. 2011, pp. 362-373.

[2] P. Ni, R. Eg, A. Eichhorn, C. Griwodz, and P. Halvorsen, "Flicker effects in adaptive video streaming to handheld devices," Proc. of ACM International Conference on Multimedia, Feb. 2011, pp. 463-472.

[3] T. C. Thang, Q. D. Ho, J. W. Kang, and A. T. Pham, "Adaptive streaming of audiovisual content using MPEG DASH," IEEE Transactions on Consumer Electronics, vol. 58, no. 1, Feb. 2012, pp. 78-85.

[4] T. Y. Huang, N. Handigol, B. Heller, N. McKeown, and R. Johari, "Confused, timid, and unstable: picking a video

streaming rate is hard," Proc. of ACM Conference on Internet Measurement, Nov. 2012, pp. 225-238.

[5] S. Akhshabi, A. C. Begen, and C. Dovrolis, "An experimental evaluation of rate-adaptation algorithms in adaptive streaming over HTTP," Proc. of ACM Conference on Multimedia Systems, Feb. 2011, pp. 157-168.

[6] T. C. Thang, Q. D. Ho, J. W. Kang, and A. T. Pham, "Adaptive streaming of audiovisual content using MPEG DASH," IEEE Transactions on Consumer Electronics, vol. 58, no. 1, Feb. 2012, pp. 78-85.

[7] C. Liu, I. Bouazizi, and M. Gabbouj, "Rate adaptation for adaptive HTTP streaming," Proc. of the ACM Conference on Multimedia Systems, Feb. 2011, pp. 169-174.

[8] K. Miller, E. Quacchio, G. Gennari, and A. Wolisz, "Adaptation algorithm for adaptive streaming over HTTP," Proc. of the IEEE Packet Video Workshop, May. 2012, pp. 173-178.

[9] D. Suh, I. Jang, and S. Pack, "QoE-enhanced adaptation algorithm over DASH for multimedia streaming," Proc. of IEEE Conference on Information Networking, Feb. 2014, pp. 497-501.

[10] W. Rahman and K. Chung, " Buffer-based adaptive bitrate algorithm for streaming over HTTP," KSII Transactions on Internet and Information Systems, vol. 9, no. 11, Nov. 2015, pp. 4585-4622.

[11] T. Huang, R. Johari, and N. McKeown, "Downtown abbey without the hiccups: Buffer-based rate adaptation for http video streaming," Proc. of ACM SIGCOMM workshop on Future Human-centric Multimedia Networking, Aug. 2013 , pp. 9-14.

[12] J. R. McGinley, "McGinley Dynamics," Market Technicians Association Journal, issue 48, 1997, pp. 15-18.

[13] P. Juluri, V. Tamarapalli, and D. Medhi, "SARA: Segment aware rate adaptation algorithm for dynamic adaptive streaming over HTTP," Proc. of IEEE International Conference on Communication Workshop, June. 2015, pp. 1765-1770.

Basic System Implementation of the Cloud Type Virtual Policy Based Network Management Scheme for the Common Use between Plural Organizations

Kazuya Odagiri
Sugiyama Jogakuen University
Aichi, Japan
kodagiri@sugiyama-u.ac.jp,
kazuodagiri@yahoo.co.jp

Shogo Shimizu
Gakushuin Women's College
Tokyo, Japan
shogo.shimizu@gakushuin.ac.jp

Naohiro Ishii
Aichi Institute of Technology
Aichi, Japan
ishii@aitech.ac.jp

***Abstract*— In the current Internet system, there are many problems using anonymity of the network communication such as personal information leaks and crimes using the Internet system. This is why TCP/IP protocol used in Internet system does not have the user identification information on the communication data, and it is difficult to supervise the user performing the above acts immediately. As a study for solving the above problem, there is the study of Policy Based Network Management (PBNM). This is the scheme for managing a whole Local Area Network (LAN) through communication control for every user. In this PBNM, two types of schemes exist. The first is the scheme for managing the whole LAN by locating the communication control mechanisms on the path between network servers and clients. The second is the scheme of managing the whole LAN by locating the communication control mechanisms on clients. As the second scheme, we have studied theoretically about the Destination Addressing Control System (DACS) Scheme. By applying this DACS Scheme to Internet system management, we will realize the policy-based Internet system management. In this paper, as the progression phase of the second phase for the last goal, we implemented the basic prototype system of the cloud type virtual PBNM, which can be used by plural organizations.**

Keywords- policy-based netwok management; DACS Scheme; NAPT

I. INTRODUCTION

In the current Internet system, there are many problems using anonymity of the network communication such as personal information leaks and crimes using the Internet system. The news of the information leak in the big company is sometimes reported through the mass media. Because TCP/IP protocol used in Internet system does not have the user identification information on the communication data, it is difficult to supervise the user performing the above acts immediately. As studies and technologies for managing Internet system realized on TCP/IP protocol, those such as Domain Name System (DNS), Routing protocol, Fire Wall (F/W) and Network address port translation (NAPT)/network address translation (NAT) are listed. Except these studies, various studies are performed elsewhere. However, they are the studies for managing the specific part of the Internet system, and have no purpose of solving the above problems.

As a study for solving the problems, Policy Based Network Management (PBNM) [2] exists. The PBNM is a scheme for managing a whole Local Area Network (LAN) through communication control every user, and cannot be applied to the Internet system. This PBNM is often used in a scene of campus network management. In a campus network, network management is quite complicated. Because a computer management section manages only a small portion of the wide needs of the campus network, there are some user support problems. For example, when mail boxes on one server are divided and relocated to some different server machines, it is necessary for some users to update a client machine's setups. Most of computer network users in a campus are students. Because students do not check frequently their e-mail, it is hard work to make them aware of the settings update. This administrative operation is executed by means of web pages and/or posters. For the system administrator, individual technical support is a stiff part of the network management. Because the PBNM manages a whole LAN, it is easy to solve this kind of problem. In addition, for the problem such as personal information leak, the PBNM can manage a whole LAN by making anonymous communication non-anonymous. As the result, it becomes possible to identify the user who steals personal information and commits a crime swiftly and easily. Therefore, by applying the PBNM, we will study about the policy-based Internet system management.

In the existing PBNM, there are two types of schemes. The first is the scheme of managing the whole LAN by locating the communication control mechanisms on the path between network servers and clients. The second is the scheme of managing the whole LAN by locating the communication control mechanisms on clients. It is difficult to apply the first scheme to Internet system management practically, because the communication control mechanism needs to be located on the path between network servers and clients without exception. Because the second scheme locates the communication control mechanisms as the software on each client, it becomes possible to apply the second scheme to Internet system management by devising the installing mechanism so that users can install the software to the client easily.

As the second scheme, we have studied theoretically about the Destination Addressing Control System (DACS) Scheme. As the works on the DACS Scheme, we showed the basic principle of the DACS Scheme, and security function [14]. After that, we implemented a DACS System to realize a concept of the DACS Scheme. By applying this DACS Scheme to Internet system, we will realize the policy-based Internet system management. Then, the Wide Area DACS system (wDACS system) [15] to use it in one organization was showed as the second phase for the last goal. As the first step of the second phase, we showed the concept of the cloud type virtual PBNM, which could be used by plural organizations [16]. In this paper, as the progression phase of the second phase for the last goal, we describes the basic prototype system to confirm the possibility of the cloud type virtual PBNM for the use in plural organizations. In Section Ⅱ, motivation and related research for this study are described. In Section Ⅲ, the existing DACS Scheme and wDACS Scheme is described. In section Ⅳ, the proposed scheme is described.

II. Motivation and Related Reserach

In the current Internet system, problems using anonymity of the network communication such as personal information leak and crimes using the Internet system occur. Because TCP/IP protocol used in Internet system does not have the user identification information on the communication data, it is difficult to supervise the user performing the above acts immediately.

As studies and technologies for Internet system management to be comprises of TCP/IP [1], many technologies are studied. For examples, Domain name system (DNS), Routing protocol such as Interior gateway protocol (IGP) such as Routing information protocol (RIP) and Open shortest path first (OSPF) , Fire Wall (F/W), Network address translation (NAT) / Network address port translation (NAPT) , Load balancing, Virtual private network (VPN), Public key infrastructure (PKI), Server virtualization. Except these studies, various studies are performed elsewhere. However, they are for managing the specific part of the Internet system, and have no purpose of solving the above problems.

As a study for solving the above problem, the study area about PBNM exists. This is a scheme of managing a whole LAN through communication control every user. Because this PBNM manages a whole LAN by making anonymous communication non-anonymous, it becomes possible to identify the user who steals personal information and commits a crime swiftly and easily. Therefore, by applying this policy- based thinking, we study about the policy-based Internet system management.

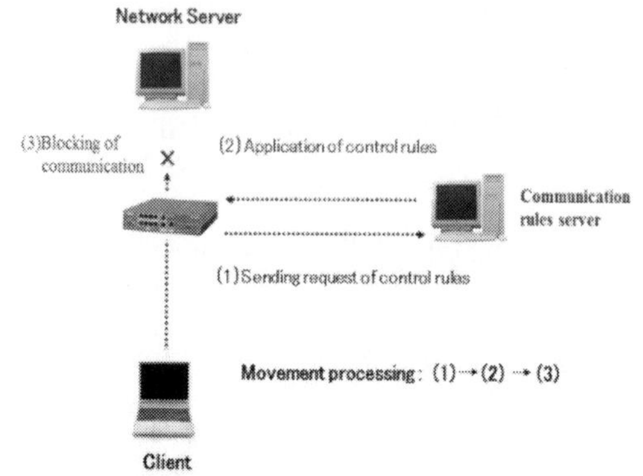

Figure 1. Principle in First Scheme

In policy-based network management, there are two types of schemes. The first scheme is the scheme described in Figure 1. The standardization of this scheme is performed in various organizations. In IETF, a framework of PBNM [2] was established. Standards about each element constituting this framework are as follows. As a model of control information stored in the server called Policy Repository, Policy Core Information model (PCIM) [3] was established. After it, PCMIe [4] was established by extending the PCIM. To describe them in the form of Lightweight Directory Access Protocol (LDAP), Policy Core LDAP Schema (PCLS) [5] was established. As a protocol to distribute the control information stored in Policy Repository or decision result from the PDP to the PEP, Common Open Policy Service (COPS) [6] was established. Based on the difference in distribution method, COPS usage for RSVP (COPS-RSVP) [7] and COPS usage for Provisioning (COPS-PR) [8] were established. RSVP is an abbreviation for Resource Reservation Protocol. The COPS-RSVP is the method as follows. After the PEP having detected the communication from a user or a client application, the PDP makes a judgmental decision for it. The decision is sent and applied to the PEP, and the PEP adds the control to it. The COPS-PR is the method of distributing the control information or decision result to the PEP before accepting the communication.

Next, in DMTF, a framework of PBNM called Directory-enabled Network (DEN) was established. Like the IETF framework, control information is stored in the server storing control information called Policy Server, which is built by using the directory service such as LDAP [9], and is distributed to network servers and networking equipment such as switch and router. As the result, the whole LAN is managed. The model of control information used in DEN is called Common Information Model (CIM), the schema of the CIM (CIM Schema Version 2.30.0) [11] was opened. The CIM was extended to support the DEN [10], and was incorporated in the framework of DEN. In addition, Resource and Admission Control Subsystem (RACS) [12] was established in Telecoms and Internet converged Services and protocols for Advanced Network (TISPAN) of European Telecommunications Standards Institute (ETSI), and Resource and Admission Control Functions (RACF) was established in International Telecommunication Union Telecommunication Standardization Sector (ITU-T) [13].

However, all the frameworks explained above are based on the principle shown in Figure 1. As problems of these frameworks, two points are presented as follows. Essential principle is described in Figure 2. To be concrete, in the point called PDP (Policy Decision Point), judgment such as permission and non-permission for communication pass is performed based on policy information. The judgment is notified and transmitted to the point called the PEP, which is the mechanism such as VPN mechanism, router and Fire Wall located on the network path among hosts such as servers and clients. Based on that judgment, the control is added for the communication that is going to pass by.

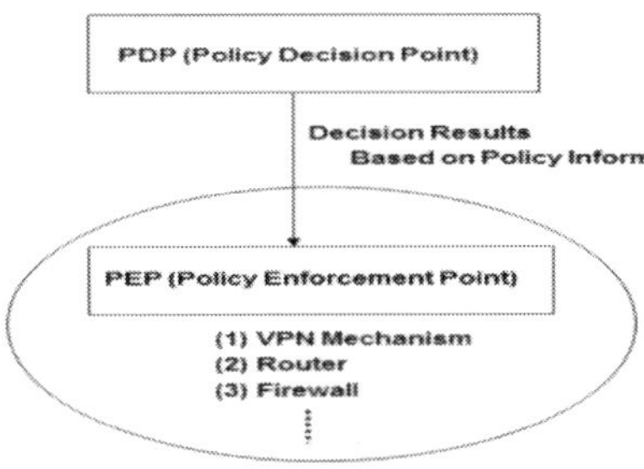

Figure 2. Essential Principle

The principle of the second scheme is described in Figure 3.By locating the communication control mechanisms on the clients, the whole LAN is managed. Because this scheme controls the network communications on each client, the processing load is low. However, because the communication control mechanisms need to be located on each client, the work load becomes heavy.

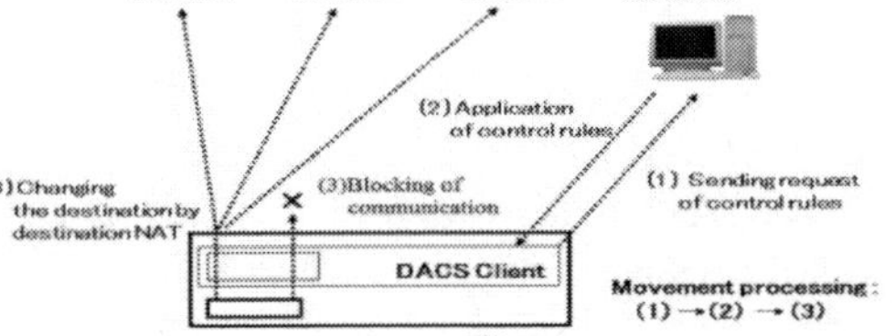

Figure 3. Principle in Second Scheme

When it is thought that Internet system is managed by using these two schemes, it is difficult to apply the first scheme to Internet system management practically. This is why the communication control mechanism needs to be located on the path between network servers and clients without exception. On the other hand, the second scheme locates the communication controls mechanisms on each client. That is, the software for communication control is installed on each client. So, by devising the installing mechanism letting users install software to the client easily, it becomes possible to apply the second scheme to Internet system management. As a first step for the last goal, we showed the Wide Area DACS system (wDACS) system [15]. This system manages a wide area network, which one organization manages. Therefore, it is impossible for plural organizations to use this system. Then, as the first step of the second phase, we showed the concept of the cloud type virtual PBNM, which could be used by plural organizations in this paper.

III. EXISTING DACS SCHEME AND WDACS SYSTEM

In this section, the content of the DACS Scheme which is the study of the phase 1 is described.

A Basic Principle of the DACS Scheme

Figure 4 shows the basic principle of the network services by the DACS Scheme. At the timing of the (a) or (b) as shown in the following, the DACS rules (rules defined by the user unit) are distributed from the DACS Server to the DACS Client.

(a) At the time of a user logging in the client.

(b) At the time of a delivery indication from the system administrator.

According to the distributed DACS rules, the DACS Client performs (1) or (2) operation as shown in the following. Then, communication control of the client is performed for every login user.

(1) Destination information on IP Packet, which is sent from application program, is changed.

(2) IP Packet from the client, which is sent from the application program to the outside of the client, is blocked.

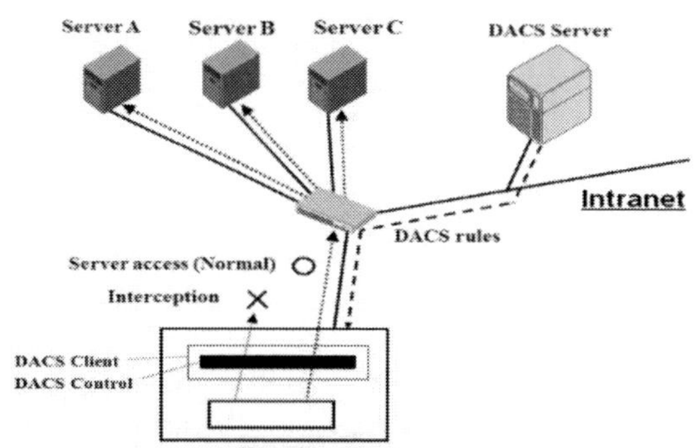

Figure 4. Basic Principle of the DACS Scheme

An example of the case (1) is shown in Figure 4. In Figure 4, the system administrator can distribute a communication of the login user to the specified server among servers A, B or C. Moreover, the case (2) is described. For example, when the system administrator wants to forbid a user to use MUA (Mail User Agent), it will be performed by blocking IP Packet with the specific destination information.

In order to realize the DACS Scheme, the operation is done by a DACS Protocol as shown in Figure 5. As shown by (1) in Figure 5, the distribution of the DACS rules is performed on communication between the DACS Server and the DACS Client, which is arranged at the application layer. The application of the DACS rules to the DACS Control is shown by (2) in Figure 5.

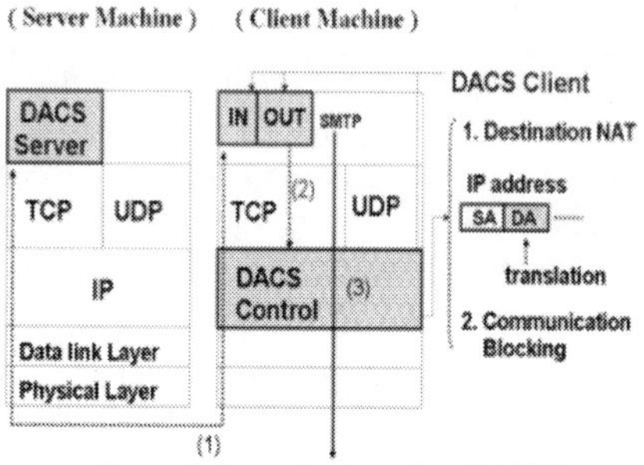

Figure 5. Layer Setting of the DACS Scheme

The steady communication control, such as a modification of the destination information or the communication blocking is performed at the network layer as shown by (3) in Figure 5.

B Communication Control on Client

The communication control on every user was given. However, it may be better to perform communication control on every client instead of every user. For example, it is the case where many and unspecified users use a computer room, which is controlled. In this section, the method of communication control on every client is described, and the coexistence method with the communication control on every user is considered.

When a user logs in to a client, the IP address of the client is transmitted to the DACS Server from the DACS Client. Then, if the DACS rules corresponding to IP address, is registered into the DACS Server side, it is transmitted to the DACS Client. Then, communication control for every client can be realized by applying to the DACS Control. In this case, it is a premise that a client uses a fixed IP address. However, when using DHCP service, it is possible to carry out the same control to all the clients linked to the whole network or its subnetwork for example.

When using communication control on every user and every client, communication control may conflict. In that case, a priority needs to be given. The judgment is performed in the DACS Server side as shown in Figure 6. Although not necessarily stipulated, the network policy or security policy exists in the organization such as a university (1). The priority is decided according to the policy (2). In (a), priority is given for the user's rule to control communication by the user unit. In (b), priority is given for the client's rule to control communication by the client unit. In (c), the user's rule is the same as the client's rule. As the result of comparing the conflict rules, one rule is determined respectively. Those rules and other rules not overlapping are gathered, and the DACS rules are created (3). The DACS rules are transmitted to the DACS Client. In the DACS Client side, the DACS rules are applied to the DACS Control. The difference between the user's rule and the client's rule is not distinguished.

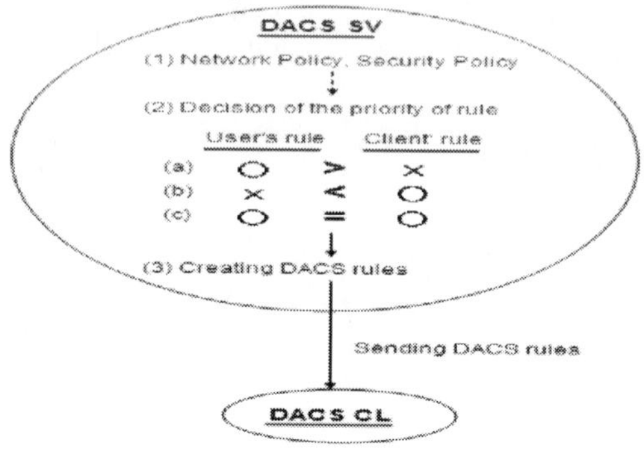

Figure 6. Creating the DACS rules on the DACS Server

C Security Mechanism of the DACS Scheme

In this section, the security function of the DACS Scheme is described. The communication is tunneled and encrypted by use of SSH. By using the function of port forwarding of SSH, it is realized to tunnel and encrypt the communication between the network server and the, which DACS Client is installed in. Normally, to communicate from a client application to a network server by using the function of port forwarding of SSH, local host (127.0.0.1) needs to be indicated on that client application as a communicating server. The transparent use of a client, which is a characteristic of the DACS Scheme, is failed. The transparent use of a client means that a client can be used continuously without changing setups when the network system is updated. The function that doesn't fail the transparent use of a client is needed. The mechanism of that function is shown in Figure 7.

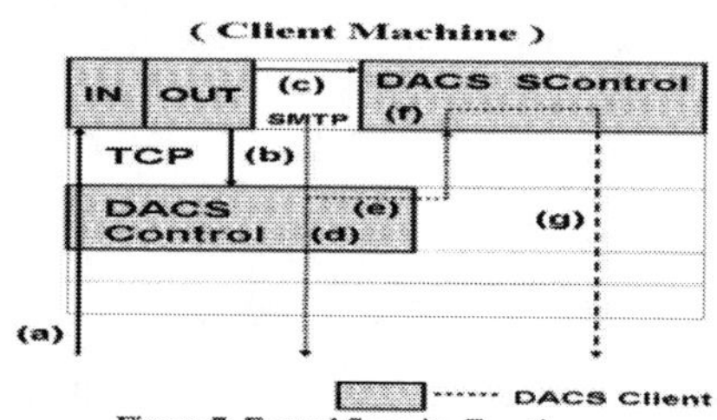

Figure 7. Extend Security Function

D Application to cloud environment

In this section, the contents of wDACS system are explained in Figure 8. First, as preconditions, because private IP addresses are assigned to all servers and clients existing in from LAN1 to LAN n, mechanisms of NAT/NAPT are necessary for the communication from each LAN to the outside. In this case, NAT/NAPT is located on the entrance of the LAN such as (1), and the private IP address is converted to the global IP address towards the direction of the arrow. Next, because the private IP addresses are set on the servers and clients in the LAN, other communications except those converted by Destination NAT cannot enter into the LAN. But, responses for the communications sent form the inside of the LAN can enter into the inside of the LAN because of the reverse conversion process by the NAT/NAPT. In addition, communications from the outside of the LAN1 to the inside are performed through the conversion of the destination IP address by Destination NAT. To be concrete, the global IP address at the same of the outside interface of the router is changed to the private IP address of each server. From here, system configuration of each LAN is described. First, the DACS Server and the authentication server are located on the DMZ on the LAN1 such as (4). On the entrance of the LAN1, NAT/NAPT and destination NAT exists such as (1) and (2). Because only the DACS Server and network servers are set as the target destination, the authentication server cannot be accessed from the outside of the LAN1. In the LANs form LAN 2 to LAN n, clients managed by the wDACS system exist, and NAT/NAPT is located on the entrance of each LAN such as (1). Then, F/W such as (3) or (5) exists behind or with NAT/NAPT in all LANs.

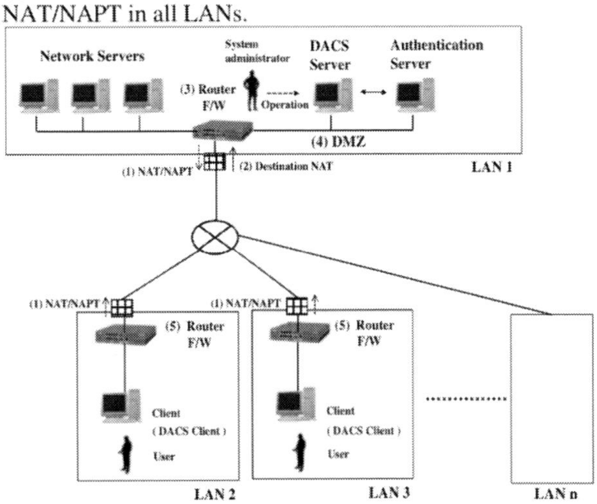

Figure 8. Basic System Configuration of wDACS system

IV. THE CLOUD TYPE VIRTUAL PBNM FOR THE COMMON USE BETWEEN PLURAL ORGANIZATIONS

In this section, the concept and implementation of the proposed scheme are described.

A Concept of the Cloud Type Virtual PBNM for the Common Use Between Plural Organizations

In Figure 9 which is described in [16], the proposed concept is shown. Because the existing wDACS Scheme realized the PBNM control with the software called the DACS Server and the DACS client, other mechanism was not needed. By this point, application to the cloud environment was easy.

The proposed scheme in this paper realizes the common usage by plural organizations by adding the following elements to realize the common usage by plural organizations: user identification of the plural organizations, management of the policy information of the plural organizations, application of the PKI for code communication in the Internet, Redundant configuration of the DACS Server (policy information server), load balancing configuration of the DACS Server, installation function of DACS Client by way of the Internet

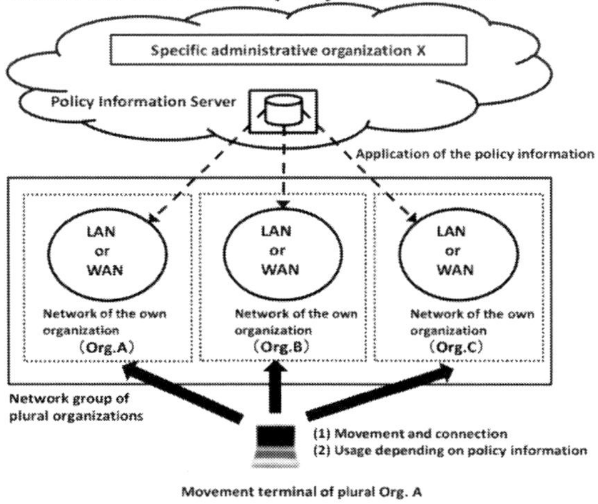

Figure 9. Concept of the proposed scheme

B Implementation of the basic function in the Cloud Type Virtual PBNM for the Common Usage Between Plural Organizations

In the past study [14], the DACS Client was operated on the windows operation system (Windows OS). It was because there were many cases that the Windows OS was used for as the OS of the client. However, the Linux operating system (Linux OS) had enough functions to be used as the client recently, too. In addition, it was thought that the case used in the clients in the future came out recently. Therefore, to prove the possibility of the DACS Scheme on the Linux OS, the basic function of the DACS Client was implemented in this study. The basic functions of the DACS Server and DACS Client were implemented by JAVA language. From here, it is described about the order of the process in the DACS Client and DACS Server as follows.

(Processes in the DACS Client)

(p1) The information acquisition from Cent OS

From the Linux OS (Cent OS), which the user logs in, the login user name and Internet domain name, the IP address, which is setting on the Cent OS are acquired through the system environment variable.

(p2)Transmission from the DACS Client to the DACS Server

This part was implemented by use of the Socket class. The IP address and port number is set to the Socket, and the DACS Client is connected to the DACS Server on the server machine.

(p3) The information transmission from the DACS Client to the DACS Server

By use of getInputStream() in Socket class, this part was implemented. The information, which is acquired from the Cent OS as described in (p1) is sent to the DACS Server.

(p4) The reception of the DACS rules from the DACS Server

This part was implemented by using getInputStream() in the Socket class. This process is performed after the server side process.

(p5) Application of the DACS rules of the DACS Control

This function was implemented by the Runtime class. Because this function uses the function of "firewalld", which is equipped normally, the command of "firewall-cmd" to execute packet filtering and destination nat. After the DACS rules are received from the DACS Server, the DACS rules are applied to the DACS Control in the DACS Client by this process.

(Processes in the DACS Server)

(p1) The information reception from the DACS Client

In this process, the DACS Server receives the information, which is sent from the DACS Client. This process was implemented by the ServerSocket().

(p2) Connection to the database

In this process, the connection from the DACS Server to the PostgreSQL database is performed. This process was realized by the function of JDBC driver. To be concrete, it is implemented by the DriverManager class of JAVA.

(p3) Inquiry of the Database

Based on the information, which receives at the process (1), the inquiry is performed in the form of using SQL language.

(p4) Transmission of the DACS rules to the DACS Client

The DACS Server sends the DACS rules, which are created based on the information to the DACS Client. This Process was implemented by the createStatement method defined by the Connection Interface in JAVA. About the basic system, which is realized by these processes, the prototype system was implemented.

V. Conclusion

In this paper, we implemented the basic function of the cloud type virtual PBNM, which could be used by plural organizations. This study is the second step of the second phase for the final goal of Internet management by the PBNM. In this study, the DACS Client was implemented and operated on the Cent OS. As the processing processes of the DACS Client, five processes were implemented. By these processes, it becomes possible to pass the DACS rules as the communication control rules to the DACS Control which was a communication control mechanism. As a future work, we are going to perform a function experiment and the performance experiment of this system.

Acknowledgment

This work was supported by JSPS KAKENHI Grant Number 26730037. We express our gratitude.

References

[1] V. CERF and E. KAHN, "A Protocol for Packet Network Interconnection," IEEE Trans. on Commn, vol.COM-22, May 1974, pp.637-648.

[2] R. Yavatkar, D. Pendarakis and R. Guerin, "A Framework for Policy-based Admission Control," IETF RFC 2753, 2000.

[3] B. Moore at el., "Policy Core Information Model -- Version 1 Specification", IETF RFC 3060, 2001.

[4] B. Moore.,"Policy Core Information Model (PCIM) Extensions", IETF 3460, 2003.

[5] J. Strassner, B. Moore, R. Moats, E. Ellesson, " Policy Core Lightweight Directory Access Protocol (LDAP) Schema", IETF RFC 3703, 2004.

[6] D. Durham at el.,"The COPS (Common Open Policy Service) Protocol", IETF RFC 2748, 2000.

[7] S. Herzog at el.,"COPS usage for RSVP", IETF RFC 2749, 2000.

[8] K. Chan et al.,"COPS Usage for Policy Provisioning (COPS-PR)", IETF RFC 3084, 2001.

[9] CIM Core Model V2.5 LDAP Mapping Specification, 2002.

[10] M. Wahl, T. Howes, S.Kille, "Lightweight Directory Access Protocol (v3)", IETF RFC 2251, 1997.

[11] CIM Schema: Version 2.30.0, 2011.

[12] ETSI ES 282 003: Telecoms and Internet converged Services and protocols for Advanced Network (TISPAN); Resource and Admission Control Subsystem (RACS); Functional Architecture, June 2006.

[13] ETSI ETSI ES 283 026: Telecommunications and Internet Converged Services and Protocols for Advanced Networking (TISPAN); Resource and Admission Control; Protocol for QoS reservation information exchange between the Service Policy Decision Function (SPDF) and the Access-Resource and Admission Control Function (A-RACF) in the Resource and Protocol specifica-tion", April 2006.

[14] K. Odagiri, R. Yaegashi, M. Tadauchi, and N. Ishii, " Secure DACS Scheme, " Journal of Network and Computer Applications," Elsevier, Vol.31, Issue 4, 2008, pp.851-861, November.

[15] K. Odagiri, S. Shimizu,M. Takizawa and N. Ishii,"Theoretical Suggestion of Policy-Based Wide Area Network Management System (wDACS system part-I)," International Journal of Networked and Distributed Computing (IJNDC), Vol.1, No.4, November 2013, pp.260-269.

[16] K. Odagiri,S. Shimizu, N. Ishii, M. Takizawa, "Suggestion of the Cloud Type Virtual Policy Based Network Management Scheme for the Common Use between Plural Organizations," Proc of Int. Conf. on International Conference on Network-Based Information Systems (NBiS-2015),pp.180-186,Septmber, 2015

Power Consumption of Packet Processing Engines and Interfaces of Edge Router: Measurements and Modeling

Akram Galal Mahmoud Ibrahim, Mohamed Essam Khedr, Mohamed Shaheen
Electronics and Communications Engineering department
Arab Academy for Science, Technology and Maritime Transport
Alexandria, Egypt

email: akram_galal@yahoo.com, email: khedr@vt.edu, email: mohamed.shaheen@aast.edu

Abstract—**Power management is a key feature in today's Internet Protocol/ Multi-Protocol Label Switching (IP/MPLS) network across all market segments. With the aim of controlling the power consumption in core networks, we consider energy aware devices that are able to reduce their energy requirements by adapting their performance. We focus on packet processing engines, and router interfaces, which generally represent the most energy consumption components of network devices data plane. Our goal is to control both the power configuration of pipelines, as well as to study the effect of the packet size onto the power consumption of an edge router. The results show that the packet size is closely related to the power consumption of the edge router. It is also shown that there is a tradeoff between power consumption and packet latency times. Based on these results, we model the formal power consumption equation of the edge router.**

Keywords-power consumption; green networking; packet processing engine; packet size; edge router; interface power; packet processing power.

I. Introduction

By the continuous growth of customers, broadband access, and number of services being offered by telecom operators and Internet Service Providers (ISPs), the energy efficiency issue has become a high priority objective, and a significant concern for network infrastructure and next-generation network devices. The rapid growth of traffic has resulted in a related increase in energy consumption. ISPs, and telecom operators reported alarming statistics of network energy requirements and of the related carbon footprint [1]. The Global e-Sustainability Initiative (GeSI) estimated the overall carbon footprint of European network devices and infrastructure to be about 349 MtCO2e (Million Metric Tons of Carbon) in 2020, with a 131% increase with respect to 2007 if no green network technologies (GNTs) would be adopted [2]. In order to support this rapid increase in energy consumption, ISPs need a larger number of devices with architectures able to perform more complex operations in a scalable way. The majority of current network devices operate at their maximum capacity and have a constant power consumption independent of the actual traffic load, and thus the most of the energy consumed in networks is wasted. It is well known that network links and devices are generally provisioned for busy or rush-hour load, which typically exceeds their average utilization by a wide margin [3]. Although this margin is seldom reached, network devices are designed on its basis so their power consumption remains more or less constant even in the presence of fluctuating traffic load.

The data plane certainly represents the most energy consuming and critical element in the largest part of network device architectures since it is generally composed by special purpose hardware (HW) elements (packet processing engines, network interfaces, etc.) that have to perform per-packet forwarding operations at very high speeds. Certain studies estimated that the power required at the data plane weighs for 54% on the overall device architectures, versus 11% for the control plane and 35% for power and heat management. Internal packet processing engines require about 60% of the power consumption at the data plane of a high end router, network interfaces weigh for 13%, switching fabric for 18.5%, and buffer management for 8.5 [4][5]. Starting from these data, we decided to focus on the power consumption of packet processing engines and the power consumption of the router interface trying to study the effect of the packet size variation onto the power consumption of an edge router. After that, we analyze the measurement results from numerous cases and show that the packet size is closely related to the power consumption of the edge router. Through the analysis, it is possible to draw a power consumption function of the edge router against the packet size.

In this paper, our main objective is to consolidate two factors of power consumption (packet processing engines and router interfaces) and find a closed relation between them, and provide an analytical model able to capture the trade-off between energy consumption and network performance (delay) by controlling the power state configurations according to the actual traffic load to minimize the power consumption while meeting the performance constraints.

The paper is organized as follows. Section II introduces literature review and related work. Then we describe the power consumption of the packet processing engines in section III, and the power consumption of the router interface in section IV. Section V shows the analytical model, while measurements and analysis are shown in section VI. Finally, the conclusions are in section VII.

II. LITERATURE REVIEW AND RELATED WORK

Most of the approaches that study the power consumption of data plane of the edge router are directed to study the effect of one separate factor from the previous discussed aspects in section I, and show the effect of it on the total power consumption of the data plane, assuming no variation for the other factors. Bolla et al. [6] provide an up-to-date survey on the current state-of-the-art in energy efficiency for fixed telecommunication networks, and improvements that can be introduced in today's networking equipment. Bolla et al. [7] aimed at studying the power consumption of packet processing engines by proposing an analytical model able to capture the impact of power management of the packet processing engines, and tried to optimize it by dynamic adaptation of network device resources. Ahn et al. [8] provide measurement of the power consumption of a router interface and draw an analytical model against the packet sizes. Nedevschi et al. [3] present the design of two forms of power management schemes, that reduce the energy consumption of network. The first form is based on putting network components to sleep during idle times, reducing energy consumed in the absence of packets. The second form is based on adapting the rate of network operation to the offered workload, reducing the energy consumed when actively processing packets. Zouaoui et al. [9] achieve to adapt the router queue-length by dynamic buffer management in such a way, that reduced the energy. In this paper, our objective is to consolidate two merged factors of power consumption (packet processing engines and router interfaces) and find a closed relation between them to study the best suitable power configuration of pipelines in both high traffic volume (rush hours) and low traffic volume, and achieve the best way to optimize the tradeoff between energy consumption and network performance indexes (delay) using different packet sizes. By merging both contributions [7][8], we proposed an analytical model able to capture the impact of packet size on the link utilization factor and the packet processing capacity, which will affect the power consumption of packet processing inside the data plane. The obtained results show that for low traffic volumes, it is recommended to use a power state corresponds to the minimization of energy consumption constrained to low packet latency with high packet size. For high traffic volumes, it is recommended to use power state corresponds to the maximization of energy consumption constrained to low packet latency with high packet size.

III. POWER CONSUMPTION OF PACKET PROCESSING ENGINES

In order to reduce the energy requirements of the packet processing engine, there are two basic techniques. Firstly, Adaptive rate (AR) that allows dynamically modulating the capacity of a processing engine (or single pipeline) in order to meet traffic loads and service requirements. Secondly, Low power idle (LPI) that forces processing engines to enter low-power states when not sending/processing packets. As previously evaluated and sketched in preliminary studies [6][7], LPI and AR have different impacts on packet forwarding performance. Figure 1 illustrates the effect of AR and LPI on packet forwarding performance. We can tune AR and LPI mechanisms for each parallel pipeline (interaction between AR and LPI). Figure 1(c) shows how AR causes a stretching of packet service times, while the sole adoption of LPI Figure 1(b) introduces an additional delay in packet service, due to the wake-up times.

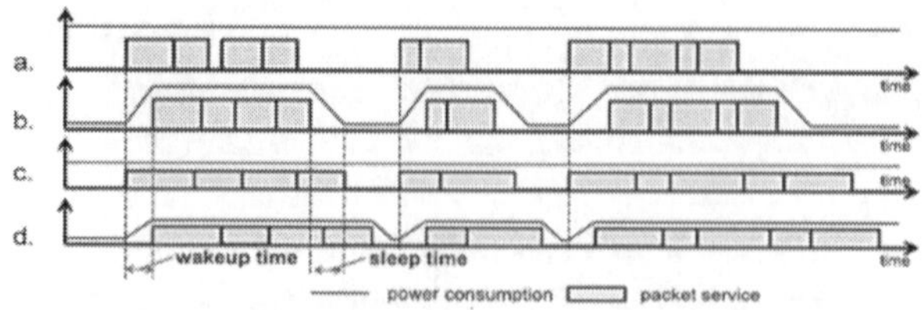

Figure 1. Packet service times and power consumptions in the cases with (a) no power- ware optimizations, (b) only LPI, (c) only AR, and (d) AR and LPI [6][7].

As sketched LPI and AR have different impacts on packet forwarding performance. AR causes a stretching of packet service times, while LPI introduces an additional delay in packet service, due to the wake-up times. Our goal is to dynamically manage the engine configuration in order to balance its energy consumption with respect to its network performance. Now, we will introduce the Advanced Configuration and Power Interface (ACPI) specification and how it makes AR and LPI capabilities accessible. In general computing systems, the ACPI specification provides an open standard for device configuration and power management by the operating system. This standard models the AR and LPI functionalities by introducing two sets of energy-aware states, (P) performance and (C) power states. Regarding the C-States, C_0 indicates the operating state where the central processing unit (CPU) executes instructions, while C_1 to C_x is processor LPI states. As (X) value becomes higher, less power is consumed, because the pipeline will be in sleeping state. But the transition between active and sleeping states requires longer time and more power consumption during transition process. i.e., C_0 is active mode and $C_{(1\dots x)}$ are sleep modes. In particular, C_1 is a state where the processor is not executing instructions, but can return to the C_0 state essentially instantaneously. All processors must support this power states. The number of LPI states is considered optional excluding C_0. In addition, the transition times and the power consumption compared to C_0 depend on the specific platform implementation [7]. Regarding the P-states, they allow modifying the operating energy of a processor by altering the working frequency or voltage. So by using P-states, processor can consume different amounts of power while providing different processing performance at the C_0 state. P_0 is the highest performance state with P_1 to P_Y being successive lower performance [7]. The higher index of P and C, the less power will be consumed. Transition between different P-states is generally very slow with respect to packet processing times.

IV. POWER CONSUMPTION OF ROUTER INTERFACE

We begin our investigation of power consumption of the router interface caused by packet sizes with the increment of link utilization. We analyze the power consumption of router interfaces with each L2 frame size 64, 256, 512, and 1518 bytes as the increase of the link utilization. We empirically found that the power consumption of the router interface is directly proportional to the link utilization, as well as reverse proportional with the packet sizes. The power consumption increases dramatically when the traffic with 64 bytes L2 frame size [8]. The power consumption of the router interface increases more than 5 watts and this value can't be ignored because a router which has n interfaces consumes more than 5n watts caused by just router interfaces. It is because the router utilizes electricity for processing packets pass through the router. The more the frames passing through the router; the more the power used in the router [8].

V. ANALYTICAL MODEL

In this section, a relation between the packet size, the packet processing power and interface power is proposed in our study based on the adaption of two models presented in [7][8]. The case of single pipeline is chosen in this research. For simplicity, we adopt the ACPI representation of power management primitives and refer to AR and LPI configurations in terms of P and C states. Most of the previous studies presented in the literature didn't take into account the relation between the internal packet processing power and router interfaces power. There are some researches to measure power consumption of packet processing engines. We adopted the model in [7], because the model evaluation shows an acceptable accuracy. Service rate μ represents the device capacity in terms of packet headers that can be processed per second. Moreover, we assume all packet headers requiring a constant service time. The selection of different P and C states is supposed to impact on the forwarding engine performance in terms of both packet service capacity and wake-up times of the servers. The model notation is introduced in Table I. The overall power equation for packet processing driven in [7] is illustrated in (1)

$$\tilde{\phi} = \left[1 + \frac{(\rho - 1)\,(1 + \lambda\,\tau_{on})}{1 + \beta\,\lambda\,\tau_s}\right]\phi_a + \frac{\lambda\,(1-\rho)\,\tau_{on}}{1 + \beta\,\lambda\,\tau_s}\phi_t + \frac{1-\rho}{1 + \beta\lambda\,\tau_s}\phi_{idle} \quad (1)$$

The average packet delay (latency) is defined as the average waiting time of the packet inside the processing engine and can be calculated according to [7] as in (2)

$$\bar{W} = \frac{\bar{L}}{\lambda\,\beta} = \frac{2\tau_s + \lambda\beta{\tau_s}^2 - \frac{1}{\lambda} + \frac{1}{\lambda\beta}\sum_{j=1}^{j_{max}}\beta_j\,j^2}{2(1 + \lambda\beta\tau_s)} + \frac{\rho^2 - \beta + \sum_{j=1}^{j_{max}}\beta_j\,j^2}{2\,\lambda\beta(1-\rho)} \quad (2)$$

In addition, as stated in [8], the power consumption of the router interface is directly proportional to the link utilization, as well as reverse proportional with the packet sizes. So, the power consumption of a router interface can be defined as the following equation:

$$P_{interface} = \left(E_{HP}\frac{\rho \times R}{s}\right) + E_{PT} \times \rho \times R = \rho \times R\left(\frac{E_{HP}}{s} + E_{PT}\right) \quad (3)$$

In order to obtain the total power consumption of the router, we will consider the switching fabric power and buffer management power are constants. The packet processing power and the interface power are presented in (1) and (2), respectively. So the total power equation will be,

$$\phi_{total} = \left[1 + \frac{(\rho - 1)\,(1 + \lambda\,\tau_{on})}{1 + \beta\,\lambda\,\tau_s}\right]\phi_a + \frac{\lambda\,(1-\rho)\,\tau_{on}}{1 + \beta\,\lambda\,\tau_s}\phi_t + \frac{1-\rho}{1+\beta\lambda\,\tau_s}\phi_{idle} + \rho \times R\left(\frac{E_{HP}}{s} + E_{PT}\right) \quad (4)$$

where ρ is the link utilization factor of the pipeline and can be calculated from (5)

$$\rho = \frac{\lambda\,\beta}{\mu} \quad (5)$$

TABLE I NOTATION

Symbol	Description
μ	Packet service rate of the pipeline in P_y state
β	Average number of packets in the incoming batch
ρ	Link utilization factor of the pipeline
λ	Rate of batch arrival to the pipeline
τ_{on}	Time needed to wake up the HW of the pipeline from C_x sleeping state
τ_{off}	Time needed to put the active HW of the pipeline into C_x sleeping state
τ_s	Setup time of the pipeline in the transition from C_x to P_y
ϕ_a	Power consumption when pipeline is active in P_y state
ϕ_{idle}	Power consumption when the pipeline is sleeping in C_x state
ϕ_t	Power consumption during τ_{on} and τ_{off}
$\tilde{\phi}$	Power consumption for packet processing
R	The maximum link utilization of the router interface (Const)
E_{HP}	Energy consumption for header processing
s	Packet size
E_{PT}	Energy consumption for packet transferring
$P_{interface}$	Power consumption for router interface
$\bar{L}$	Mean value of packets in one burst
j	Number of received packet groups
β_j	Probability that an incoming burst to the pipeline contains j packets
$\bar{W}$	Average packet delay inside the processing engine
ϕ_{total}	Total power consumption of the router

VI. MEASUREMENTS AND ANALYSIS

Firstly, we begin our investigation of power consumption of the router by measuring real world traffic traces between real ISPs in Egypt and Italy. First measurement was based on the inbound traffic profile of core gateway network router in TE Data (Egypt), which is peering with Telecom Italia Sparkle (Italy) and connecting together via STM-16 fiber link (2.4 Gbps). The edge router is Juniper M320 with switching capacity 320 Gbps, and the interface type is serial interface. As shown in Multi Router Traffic Grapher (MRTG) figures. Figure 2 (a) shows the daily traffic pattern, and Figure 2 (b) shows the weekly traffic pattern. The evolution of the incoming traffic load follows the classical night-and-day profile with high similarity between days.

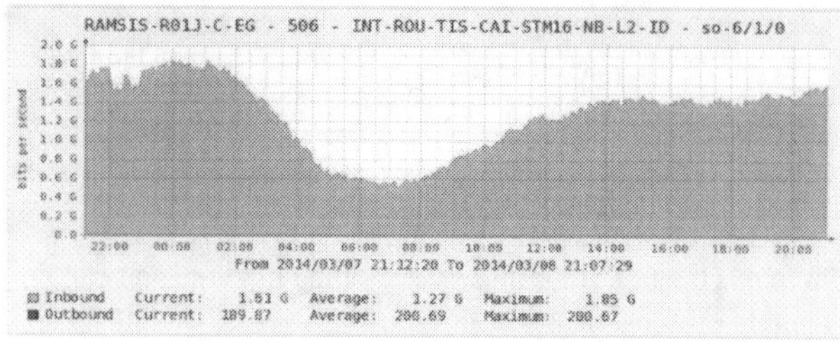

Figure 2. (a) Daily traffic profile of core TE Data network router peering with TIS.

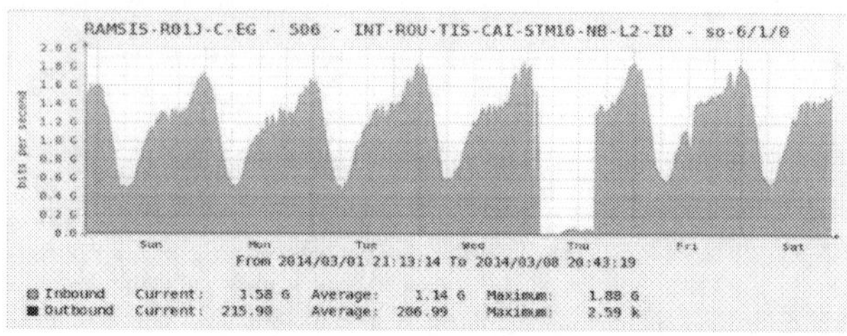

Figure 3. (b) Weekly traffic profile of core TE Data network router peering with TIS.

Second measurement was performed on the inbound traffic profile of other gateway network router in TE Data (Egypt), which is peering with Vodafone (Egypt) and connecting together via STM-16 fiber link. The edge router is also Juniper M320, and the interface type is Giga Ethernet (GE) interface. Figure 3 (a) shows the daily traffic pattern, and Figure 3 (b) shows the weekly traffic pattern.

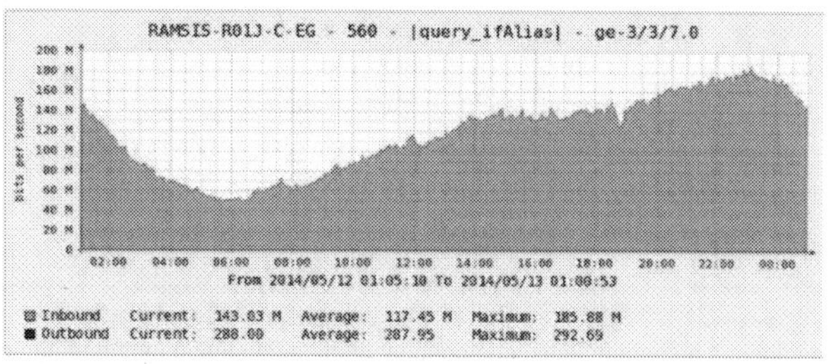

Figure 3. (a) Daily traffic profile of core TE Data network router peering with Vodafone.

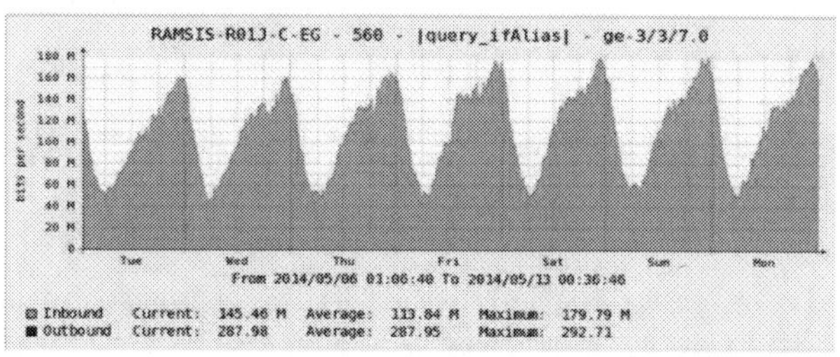

Figure 3. (b) Weekly traffic profile of core TE Data network router peering with Vodafone.

Other traffic distributions are described in Measurement and Analysis on the Wide Internet (MAWI), which is Japanese research group focuses on traffic measurement analysis for long term measurement on Internet, and its real-world traffic traces are publicly available [10] and part of "A Day in the Life of the Internet" [11]. In [7], the experimentations were based on multicore Linux SW Router (SR) and the proposed model estimation was validated by using real-world traffic traces [10][11], and the model evaluation shows an acceptable accuracy. The previous traffic profiles show the regular daily cyclic patterns with traffic dropping at night and growing during the day. In addition, we can figure out that the minimum of the traffic typically appears during the first hours of the morning, while rush hours are during the day. Hence, we can conclude that the traffic distributions are nearly identical regarding different types of edge router platforms, regardless the router architectures, edge router type and interface type.

Secondly, we begin our investigation of the power consumption of packet processing engines using the analytical model of [7], which is validated by the multi core Linux SW Router (SR). This choice is mainly due to the fact that current commercial routers do not include AR and LPI capabilities, and only their nominal and/or maximum power consumptions are reported in the datasheets [7]. By studying the power consumption of packet processing with various configurations of P and C states. The results in Figure 4 show that selecting too deep standby C-states may cause a rise in power consumption. This is simply caused by the wake up τ_s from the deepest C-state. We realized that for high P and C indexes, the packet processing capacity will decrease; also the power consumption of packet processing will be decreased. For low P-C indexes, the packet processing capacity will be increased and the power consumption of packet processing will be increased accordingly.

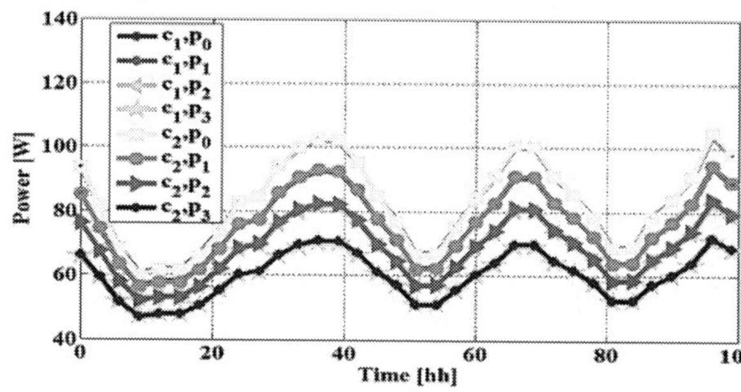

Figure 4. Power consumption of packet processing according to various configurations of P-and C-states.

To figure out the best suitable power states of the pipeline during normal traffic and rush hours, we have to measure the average absolute packet delay, i.e., the average waiting time of the packet inside the processing engine of the pipeline. As shown in Figure 4 and Figure 5, P_3-C_2 state indicates the minimum power consumption (lowest performance) with maximum delay during the minimum volume of traffic loads, while P_3-C_1 state indicates almost the same power consumption (P_3) but with minimum delay during the same minimum value of traffic loads. As a result of that, we suggest reducing the power consumption of the system with P_3 performance (power) state, while not using the deepest sleeping state C_1.

Accordingly, for the maximum traffic volume (rush hours), both P_0-C_1 and P_0-C_2 states indicate the maximum power consumption (highest performance) with minimum delay. As both states have almost the same performance which is P_0, so we suggest using P_0-C_1, as it will lead to a minimum delay in case of rush hours. Table II illustrates the power consumption and average packet delay using different P-C states during the maximum and minimum traffic load. By taking into consideration the effect of the power consumption of router interfaces, CISCO 7609 router is used. It is composed of a routing engine, a line card, and one power supply unit. Environment around the router is very important for the precise measurement of the power consumption. The router should be evaluated at temperature of 25 ℃ ± 3 ℃ and the relative humidity of 30% to 75%. In addition, the router should be evaluated at a barometric pressure between 1020 and 812 mbar. In the AC power configuration, the router should be evaluated at 230 VAC ± 1%, 50 or 60 Hz ± 1% [8]. We measure the power consumption of router interfaces with each L2 frame size 64, 256, 512 and 1518 bytes. Figure 6 shows the power consumption of the router when the generated traffic is injected to each router interface. We empirically found that the power consumption of the interface is in the direct proportional to the link utilization ρ, as well as in the reverse proportional to the packet sizes. The power consumption increases dramatically when the traffic with 64 bytes L2 frames size. In the other cases, it also increases considerably because the more frames passing through the router, the more power used in the router.

TABLE II POWER CONSUMPTIONS AND AVERAGE PACKET DELAY OF THE DEVICE'S P-C STATES DURING MAXIMUM AND MINIMUM TRAFFIC VOLUME

Value of traffic	Power / Delay	P-C states			
		P_0-C_1	P_0-C_2	P_3-C_1	P_3-C_2
Maximum (Rush Hours)	Power Consumption	Low	High	Low	High
	Average Packet Delay	Low	High	Low	High
Minimum	Power Consumption	High	Low	High	Low
	Average Packet Delay	High	Low	Low	High

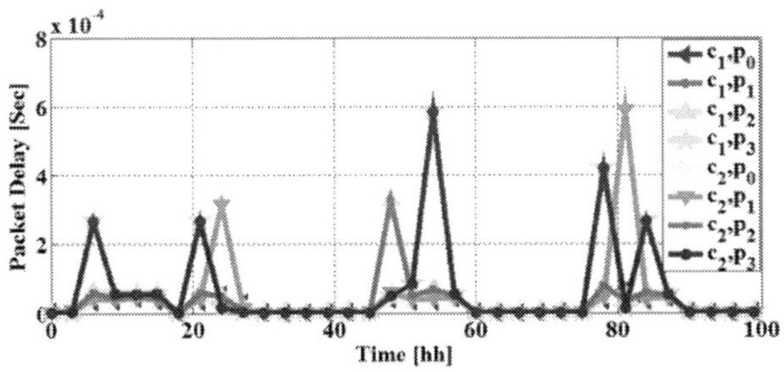

Figure 5. Average absolute packet delay according to various configurations of P-and C-states.

As stated in (5), the packet processing capacity μ is indirect relation to the link utilization ρ. As the packet processing capacity increases, the link utilization factor decreases. Also, as the packet size increases, the link utilization factor will be increases as recited in (3). So there is indirect relation between the packet size and the packet processing capacity as shown in Figure 7. As the packet size increases, the packet processing capacity decreases [12]. Accordingly, the power consumption of the packet processing will be decreased.

As a result, the total power consumption of the router will be decreased.

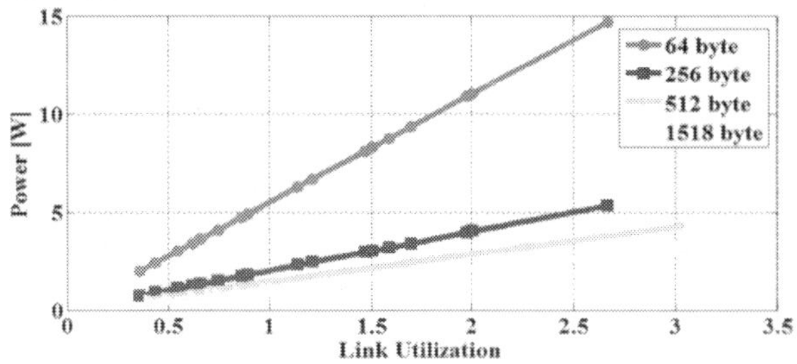

Figure 6. Power consumption of router interface with different packet size.

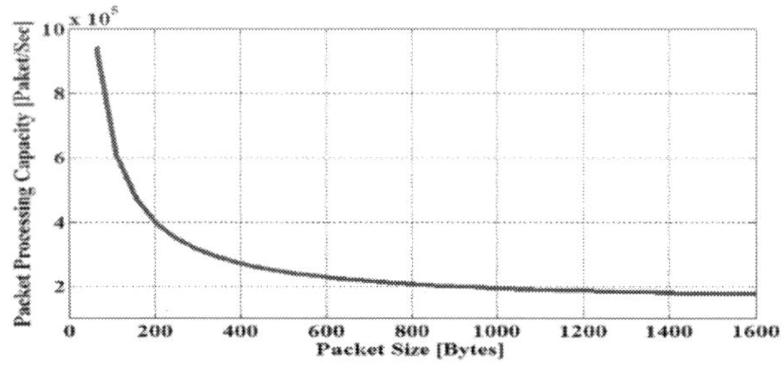

Figure 7. The relation between packet processing capacity and packet size.

Figure 8 and Figure 9 show the total power consumption of the router as stated in (4) for each P_0-C_1 and P_3-C_1 states respectively. As stated previously in section VI, it is obviously shown from Figure 8 that the chosen P_0-C_1 state will lead to high power consumption (highest performance) with minimum possible delay during the maximum volume of traffic loads (rush hour).

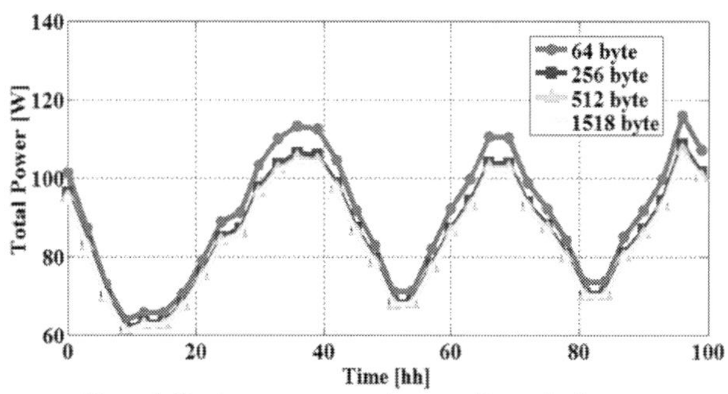

Figure 8. Total power consumption according to P_0-C_1 state.

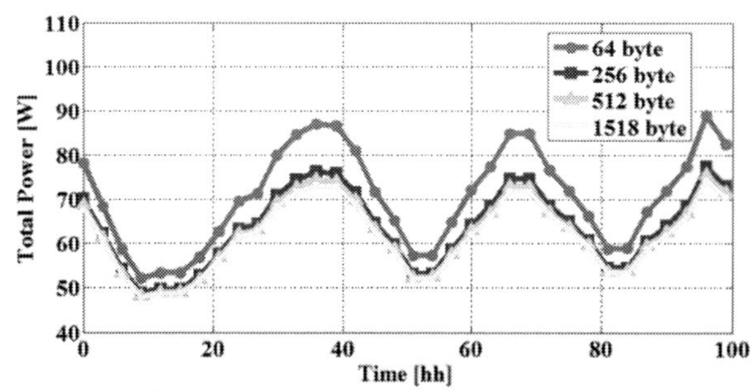

Figure 9. Total power consumption according to P_3-C_1 state.

On contrary for the case of P_3-C_1 state shown in Figure 9 the minimum power consumption (lowest performance) with maximum possible delay during the minimum volume of traffic loads. The values of ϕ_{idle} , τ_{on}, ϕ_a and μ used for numerical calculation of the total power equation stated in (4) for different P-C states were adopted from [7][12], and are illustrated in Table III and IV.

TABLE III POWER CONSUMPTIONS AND TRANSITION TIMES OF THE DEVICE'S C-STATES

C_x state	ϕ_{idle}	τ_{on}
C_0	Active	Active
C_1	10 Watt	10 ns
C_2	8 Watt	100 ns

TABLE IV POWER CONSUMPTIONS AND FORWARDING CAPACITIES OF THE DEVICE'S P-STATES

P_y state	ϕ_a	μ
P_3	50 Watt	650 kpkts/s
P_2	60 Watt	770 kpkts/s
P_1	70 Watt	890 kpkts/s
P_0	80 Watt	1010 ts/s

VII. CONCLUSION

We proposed an analytical model able to capture the impact of packet size on the packet processing capacity, which will affect the total power consumption of edge router. We found also the best suitable power configuration of pipelines in both high traffic volume (rush hours) and low traffic volume, and achieve the best way to optimize the tradeoff between energy consumption and network performance indexes (delay) using different packet sizes.

Firstly, we considered energy aware network devices able to trade their energy consumption for packet forwarding. We proposed an analytical model able to capture the impact of power management capabilities on network performance. This study is based on the analytical models represented in [7][12]. We focused on the packet processing, which generally represents the most energy consuming components of network devices (60%), as well as the power consumed in router interfaces (13%). Our goal was to find the best suitable power configuration of pipelines in both high traffic volume (rush hours) and low traffic volume; and to achieve the best way to optimize the tradeoff between energy consumption and network performance indexes using different packet sizes.

Secondly, we analyzed and drawn an analytical power consumption model of a router interface. We analyzed it against the packet size. According to the results, we can find that the power consumption of the router interface is in the direct proportion to the link utilization as well as in the reverse proportion to the packet size. Also, we deduced that the packet size is in reverse proportion to the packet processing capacity, which will lead to decrease the power consumption of packet processing inside data plane as well. The obtained results show that for low traffic volumes, it is recommended to use a P-state corresponds to the minimization of energy consumption constrained to low packet latency with high packet size. For high traffic volumes, it is recommended to use a P-state corresponds to the maximization of energy consumption constrained to low packet latency with high packet size. Also, it is suggested not to select too deep standby C-state as it may cause a rise in power consumption to make the transition from the sleeping state C_x to the active C_0 state.

Our future work will study the power consumption of the router taking into consideration the buffer management which consumes 8.5% of the total power inside the data plane. Also, we will study the effect of different routing protocols on the total power consumption besides more practical results by setting a practical test bed to validate the analytical model using Network Performance Monitor (NPM) and edge routers support the energy wise feature.

REFERENCES

[1] C. Bianco, F. Cucchietti, and G. Griffa, "Energy consumption trends in the next generation access network—a telco perspective," in Telecommunications Energy Conference, 2007. INTELEC 2007. 29th International, Rome, 2007, pp. 737-742.

[2] M. Webb, "Smart 2020: Enabling the low carbon economy in the information age," The Climate Group. London, vol. 1, no. 1, 2008, pp. 1-1.

[3] S. Nedevschi, L. Popa, G. Iannaccone, S. Ratnasamy, and D. Wetherall, "Reducing Network Energy Consumption via Sleeping and Rate-Adaptation.," in NSDI, 2008, pp. 323-336.

[4] R. S. Tucker,et. al. "Evolution of WDM optical IP networks: A cost and energy perspective," Journal of Lightwave Technology, vol. 27, no. 3, 2009, pp. 243-252.

[5] D. T. Neilson, "Photonics for switching and routing," IEEE Journal of Selected topics in quantum electronics, vol. 12, no. 4, 2006, pp. 669-678.

[6] R. Bolla, R. Bruschi, F. Davoli, and F. Cucchietti, "Energy efficiency in the future internet: a survey of existing approaches and trends in energy-aware fixed network infrastructures," IEEE Communications Surveys & Tutorials, vol. 13, no. 2, 2011, pp. 223-244.

[7] R. Bolla, R. Bruschi, A. Carrega, and F. Davoli, "Green networking with packet processing engines: modeling and optimization," IEEE/ACM Transactions on Networking, vol. 22, no. 1, 2014, pp. 110-123,.

[8] J. Ahn and H.-S. Park, "Measurement and modeling the power consumption of router interface," in Advanced Communication Technology (ICACT), 2014 16th International Conference on, Pyeongchang, 2014, pp. 860-863.

[9] W. Zouaoui, Y. Labit, and C. Albea, "Buffer dynamic management for energy-aware network," in 10th International Conference on Network and Service Management (CNSM) and Workshop, Rio de Janeiro, 2014, pp. 352-355.

[10] Working Group, WIDE MAWI, "Mawi working group traffic archive," 2016. [Online]. Available: http://mawi.nezu.wide.ad.jp/mawi/samplepoint-F/2016/. [Accessed 2016].

[11] "A day in the life of the Internet project," [Online]. Available: https://www.caida.org/projects/ditl/. [Accessed 2016].

[12] T. Meyer, F. Wohlfart, D. Raumer, B. E. Wolfinger, and G. Carle, "Measurement and Simulation of High-Performance Packet Processing in Software Routers," Leistungs-, Zuverlässigkeits- und Verlässlichkeitsbewertung von Kommunikationsnetzen und verteilten Systemen, vol. 7, 2013.

Securing Vehicle's Electronic Control Units

Kevin Daimi
Computer Science and Software Engineering
University of Detroit Mercy
Detroit, USA
email: daimikj@udmercy.edu

Mustafa Saed, Scott Bone, John Robb
HATCI Electronic Systems Development
Hyundai-Kia America Technical Center
Superior Township, USA
email: {msaed, sbone, jrobb }@hatci.com

***Abstract*— Electronic Control Units (ECUs) are essential for controlling many functions and systems in current and future vehicles. Modern vehicles incorporate over seventy ECUs. Those ECUs are vulnerable to security attacks. A number of these attacks can be fatal and can result in casualties. Undoubtedly, there is a critical need for protecting the ECUs infrastructure. This paper proposes an approach to secure vehicle's ECUs based on a grouping principle. Four groups are introduced. Each group is controlled by a Master ECU, and the Master ECUs are controlled by a Super Master ECU. Public key cryptology is adopted. Furthermore, the possibility of applying symmetric key cryptology, Elliptic Curve Cryptology (ECC), and One-Time Pad are investigated.**

Keywords*— *ECUs; Security Architecture; Security Protocols; Security Requirements

I. INTRODUCTION

Modern vehicles deploy a number of busses in their networks. Among these are the Local Interconnect Network (LIN), Controller Area Network (CAN), Media-Oriented System Transport (MOST), and FlexRay. LIN is used for the lowest data-rate functions, such as door locks, climate control, and mirror control. CAN is suitable for medium speed applications including body systems, engine management, and transmission. MOST lends itself to the high-speed data rates, and therefore, it is convenient for multimedia and entertainment. Finally, the FlexRay is suitable for safety-critical applications, such as steer-by-wire, stability control, and brake-by-wire. Connected to these buses are various Electronic Control Units (ECUs). ECUs are embedded systems controlling one or more of the vehicle's systems and subsystems. They play a crucial role in controlling many functions in vehicles. ECUs are made up of both hardware and firmware. They are named and differentiated based on what they are used for. For example, the Engine Control Module (ECM) controls various engine functions such as fuel injection, ignition timing and idle speed control system, the Electronic Brake Control Module (EBCM) is used in the anti-lock braking system (ABS), and the Powertrain Control Module (PCM) monitors and controls speed control, A/C, and automatic transmission [1]-[9]. It is critical to protect these ECUs for proper functioning of the vehicle and for safety purposes.

Nish [10] introduced a number of security issues in modern automotive systems. The communication of Tire Pressure Monitoring System (TPMS) with its sensor is unsecure and missing encryption and signature in the data protocol. As a result, the tire pressure warning lights can be turned on and off causing the driver to worry about the tire pressure when there is nothing wrong with it. Another issue regards the keyless entry systems. The passive keyless entry in modern cars can be subject to relay attack by intercepting and relaying the radio signal from the smart keys to the cars. The attackers can break into and steal the valuables left in the vehicle. Further issue that has a safety nature involves the On-Board Diagnostic port (OBD-II). This interface provides direct access to the vehicle for diagnosing and updating the firmware of ECUs. By connecting to this port through a USB or WiFi, some software on the attacking computer can re-program the ECUs causing considerable and possibly fatal damage.

Othmane, Weffers, Mohamad, and Wolf [11] proposed a taxonomy for vehicle security and privacy aspects. They stressed the security of communication links, data validity, devices security, identity, and access control. They attempted to provide an initial repository of threats to vehicle network. Security threats and the possibility of attacks can arise when drivers try to control the lights, windshields, wipers, air flow and the heater of their vehicles through Bluetooth or exercise remote starting or unlock doors using their PDA [12]. Any attack on the Bluetooth or the PDA will impact security of the vehicle and drivers safety. A vehicle's ECUs communicate through the in-vehicle network and it communicates with Service Providers through cellular network [13]. All the possible attacks on cellular networks will find their way to the vehicle and can impact the ECUs.

A security approach to protect the CAN protocol from masquerade and replay attacks was proposed by Lin and Sangiovanni-Vincentelli [14]. They provided a software-only solution with no additional hardware needed. The focus was on run-time authentication after ignition key is turned on and the security secret keys have been distributed to the ECUs. Han, Potluri, and Shin [15] introduced a security architecture to deal with the potential security attacks infiltrated by mobile devices, such as smart phones and tablets, interfacing with the vehicle to send/receive information to/from the vehicle. Three parties were adopted, the user device, the gateway, and the ECUs. Patsakis, Dellios, and Bouroche [16] stressed that the standards for in-vehicle security are distant from deploying long-established security policies and procedures. They analyzed the current auto industry policies and procedures with regards to security, and highlighted a number of vulnerabilities. In an attempt to overcome these vulnerabilities, they introduced a security architecture to support mutual authentications of ECUs and various access rights for users.

Several attempts have focused on grouping ECUs for various purposes. In one of these attempts, ECUs were divided into four groups; Powertrain Master Control Unit, Chassis Master Control Unit, Cabin Master Control Unit, and Infotainment Master Control Unit [17]. Nilsson, Phung, and Larson [18] indicated five categories: Powertrain, Vehicle Safety, Comfort, Infotainment, and Telematics. The groups; Comfort Systems, Body Control, Real Time Systems, and Safety-Critical systems were suggested by Seo, Kim, Hwang, Kwon, and Jeon [8]. Powertrain Gateway, Body and Comfort Gateway, Chassis Gateway, and Infotainment Gateway were advocated in [4]. ECUs were also grouped as Powertrain, Safety, Comfort, and Infotainment and Telematics [2]. A further approach adopted by Cho, Bae, Chu, and Suh [19] proposed User-Friendly Diagnostic Unit, Engine-Transmission-Chassis-Body Unit, Safety Unit, and Telematics-Information-Entertainment Unit.

This paper proposes a security architecture for secure transmission of ECUs' messages. The ECUs are divided among four groups. Each group is controlled by a Master ECU (MECU). The resulting four MECUs are supervised by the Super Master ECU (SMECU). Public Key cryptology is adopted. Furthermore, the paper investigates the possibility of applying symmetric key cryptology, Elliptic Curve Cryptology, and stream ciphers. The security requirements are examined. The remainder of the paper is organized as follows: Section II introduces the proposed security architecture. Securing the ECUs using public key cryptology is dealt with in section III. Other possible approaches for securing a vehicle's ECUs are briefly introduced in section IV. These include symmetric key cryptology, Elliptic Curve Cryptology and stream ciphers. Finally, the paper is concluded in section V.

II. PROPOSED SECURITY ARCHITECTURE

In in-vehicle network, buses have ECUs connected to them. Three busses are shown in Figure 1 above; high speed CAN (CAN-HS), medium speed CAN (CAN_MS) and a LIN bus. To these buses various ECUs are connected. ECUs broadcast messages. In other words, messages are received by all ECUs, but only acted upon if the message concerns the receiving ECU. The Body Control Module (BCM) and the Instrument Cluster (IC) are connect to both buses; CAN-MS and CAN-HS. These will act as gateways to gate the messages received from one bus to the ECUs connected to the other bus. Table 1 provides the notations used in the hypothetical in-vehicle network.

The security architecture used in this paper is based on the principle of grouping ECUs. The grouping could be based on any subdivision approach. For example, ECUs may be grouped based on their location, functionality, or collaboration. The number of groups is not limited. In Figure 2 below, the ECUs are distributed among four groups of Master ECUs, $MECU_1$, $MECU_2$, $MECU_3$, and $MECU_4$. A number of ECUs are attached to each Master ECU. MECUs do not necessarily contain the same number of ECUs. For this reason, the subscript of the last ECU in each group has different letters. In other words, the use of one subscript letter was avoided to indicate possibly different number of ECUs. There is no direct connection between the ECUs of each group with the other groups.

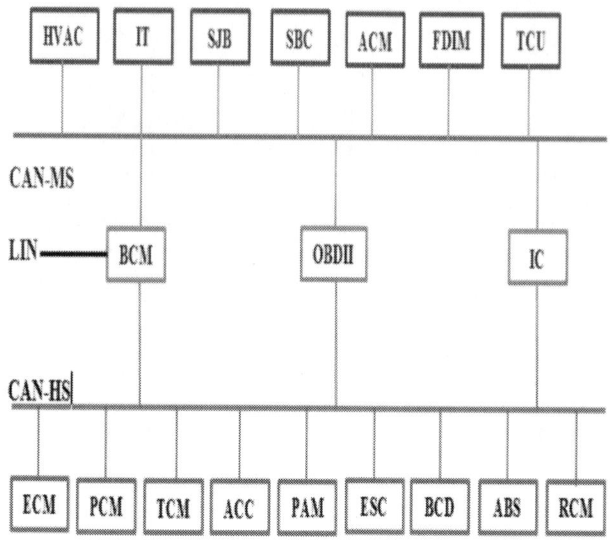

Figure 1. Hypothetical In-Vehicle Network

TABLE I
NOTATIONS USED IN IN-VEHICLE NETWORK

Symbol	Role
ECM	Engine Control Module
PCM	Powertrain Control Module
TCM	Transmission Control Module
ACC	Adaptive Cruise Control
PAM	Parking Aid Module
ESC	Electronic Stability Control
BCD	Blind Spot Detective
ABS	Anti-Lock Brake System Module
IC	Instrument Cluster
BCM	Body Control Module
HVAC	Heat, Ventilation, and Air Conditioning System
IT	Intrusion Detection
SJB	Smart Junction Box
SBC	Seat Belt Control
ACM	Audio Control Module
FDIM	Front Display Module
TCU	Telematics Control Unit
OBD-II	On-board Diagnostic System II

The four master ECUs are connected to the Super Master ECU. The SMECU is the heart of the security architecture. It is the only component connected to the outside word through the security architecture for manufacturer-vehicle communication, which secures various areas, such as Firmware On-The-Air (FOTA), Software On-The-Air (SOTA), and on-board diagnostics. Therefore, SMECU will be protected by that security architecture, which is beyond the scope of this paper.

The SMECU manages the security of the four MECUs. When a message is broadcasted, it will not reach all the ECUs as shown in Figure 1 above. Only the MECU that controls the broadcasting ECU and the ECUs of the same group will receive it. The MECU of that group will then forward it to the SMECU. To broadcast to the ECUs of the other groups, the SMECU will decide which MECU will receive this message, by checking the message ID. Once received by the MECU, it will broadcast it to its members. By observing the message ID, the individual ECUs will decide to either ignore the message or act upon it. The security approach adopted by the proposed architecture does not allow any direct communication between the MECUs. This will prevent threats to the ECUs of one group from propagating to the ECUs of other groups.

The Super Master ECU manages key creation and distribution for the four MECUs. The individual MECUs manage key creation and distribution for their members (ECUs). The broadcasted messages are short. This implies that public key cryptology is appropriate here. However, the symmetric key cryptology can also be used.

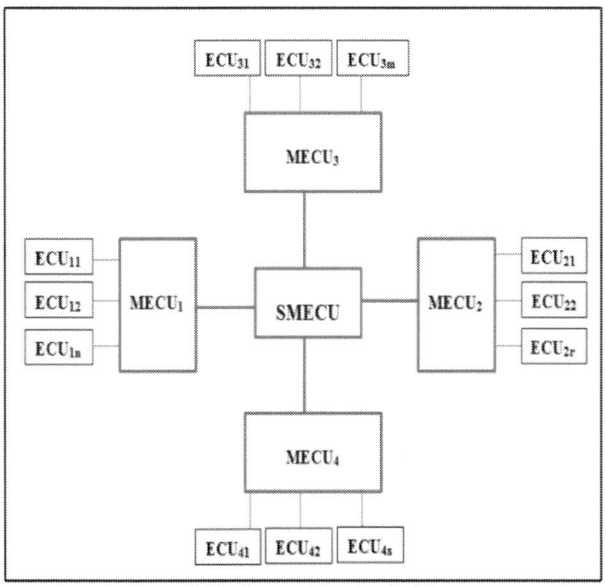

Figure 2. The Proposed Security Architecture

III. ECUs Security

Due to bus frame limitation, an ECU message (payload) will be broken down into three messages. Each frame will contain the ECU ID, ECU_{ID}, Message ID, MSG_{ID}, and the Message, MSG. Messages not exceeding the size of the framework will be sent in one communication. To facilitate following the security protocols, Table 2 provides the protocol notations.

A. Initialization

All nodes will have their initial public and private keys pre-installed at manufacturing time. In addition, each MECU will have the public keys and IDs of its members and its members will have their MECU's public key and ID pre-installed. Further pre-installation include a shared secret value S_i between MECU i and its members, and a shared secret value Vj between each MECU and the Super MECU. Finally, the public keys and IDs of the four MECUs will be pre-stored at the SMECU's memory and the public key and ID of SMECU will be stored in each of the four MECUs.

TABLE II PROTOCOL NOTATIONS

Symbol	Meaning
MSG	Message
$SMECU$	Super Master ECU
$MECU_i$, $i = 1\text{-}4$	Master ECU i
ECU_{ij}	ECU j of MECU i
PU_{ECU}, PR_{ECU}	Public & private key of ECU
PU_{MECU}, PR_{MECU}	Public & private key of MECU
PU_{SMECU}, PR_{SMECU}	Public & private key of SMECU
ID_{ECU}	ID of ECU
ID_{MECU}	ID of MECU
ID_{SMECU}	ID of SMECU
S_i	Secret value shared between MECU i & its ECUs
V_j	Secret value shared between MECU j & SMECU
K_{ECU}	Key shared between ECU and MECU
K_{MECU}	Key shared between MECU and SMECU
KM_{ECU}	MAC Key shared between ECU and MECU
KM_{MECU}	MAC Key shared between MECU and SMECU
$C(KM_{ECU}, MSG)$	MAC function for ECU and MECU
$C(KM_{MECU}, MSG)$	MAC function for MECU and SMECU
T	Time stamp
-O	Used after a subscript to indicate old
-N	Used after a subscript to indicate new
K_{ij}	Symmetric key shared between $MECU_i$ and ECU_j
K_i	Symmetric key shared between $MECU_i$ & SMECU
Gi	Group key shared between $MECU_i$ and its ECUs
H(X)	Hash code of X
$SIG(X)$	Signature of X
N_X	Private key of X in Elliptic Curve Cryptology
P_X	Public key of X in Elliptic Curve Cryptology

B. Keys Generation and Distribution

The pre-installed keys will be used once to distribute the newly created keys and then ignored. Each ECU will create its own public and private keys. The MECUs and the SMECU will also create their public and private keys.

Each ECU will send its public key to its MECU. The new public key, $PU_{ECU\text{-}N}$, will be encrypted by the current public key of the MECU, PU_{MECU}, and then by the old private key of the ECU, $PR_{ECU\text{-}O}$. In other words, the encrypted new public key is signed before sending it to MECU:

ECU → MECU: E[$PR_{ECU\text{-}O}$, E(PU_{MECU}, $PU_{ECU\text{-}N}$)].

Note that here only one message is needed. After carrying out the needed decryptions, the MECU will capture the new public key and store it.

The MECU will use a similar approach and send the encrypted and signed new key to the ECUs belonging to it.
MECU → ECU: E[$PR_{MECU\text{-}O}$, E(PU_{ECU}, $PU_{MECU\text{-}N}$)].

Each MECU sends its new public key to SMECU, and the SMECU will provide its new public key to the four MECUs after receiving theirs following the above style

MECU → SMECU: E[$PR_{MECU\text{-}O}$, E(PU_{SMECU}, $PU_{MECU\text{-}N}$)].
SMECU → MECU: E[$PR_{SMECU\text{-}O}$, E(PU_{MECU}, $PU_{SMECU\text{-}N}$)].

Having done that, all the old public and private keys are discarded. This approach is also used when the keys need to be changed periodically or when needed.

C. Secret Value Generation and Exchange

The new shared secret value, S_i, between $MECU_i$ and its ECU_s is generated as follows:

1) Zero the odd bits of S_i to get S'_i
2) Select an ECU_j at random to get its ID, ID_j.
3) Compute $X = S'_i$ XOR ID_j
4) Encrypt X with the public key of $MECU_i$ to get Y
   $Y = E(PU_{MECUi}, X)$
5) Zero the even bits of Y to get Z
6) Select an ECU_j at random to get its public key, PU_{ECUj}.
7) Encrypt Z with this public key to get the new S_i
   $S_{i\text{-}N} = E(PU_{ECUj}, Z)$

The same algorithm is used for generating the shared secret value, V_j, between MECU j and the SMECU after replacing ECU with MECU, and MECU with SMECU.

D. ECU's Public Key and ID Exchange

Each MECU is in charge of ensuring its members have the public keys and IDs of all other members. The MECU will send messages containing the public key, ID, and time stamp to each ECU. The messages are encrypted with the private key of the MECU and then with the public key of the ECU in question. For example, MECU4 will send the following two messages to ECU4s (refer to Figure 2 above):

$X_1 = E(PR_{MECU4}, PU_{ECU41} \| ID_{ECU41} \| T)$
$X_2 = E(PR_{MECU4}, PU_{ECU42} \| ID_{ECU42} \| T)$
$MECU_4$ → ECU_{4s}: E[PU_{ECU4s}, X_1)
$MECU_4$ → ECU_{4s}: E[PU_{ECU4s}, X_2)

An alternative would be to have the MECU issue certificates. However, certificates will require more communication traffic in this case.

E. Securing ECU Messages

An ECU message, MSG, includes the payload, ECU ID and message ID (MSG = Payload || ID_{ECU} + ID_{MSG}). There are other contents that fulfill other ECU or bus requirements. However, these will not be included in the security protocol. The broadcasting ECU carryout the following:

1) Encrypt MSG with its private key
2) Calculate the cryptographic hash for MSG || S_i, H(MSG || S_i)
3) Sign the cryptographic hash using an agreed upon digital signature algorithm. This signature will be denoted by SIG [H(MSG || S_i)]

It then broadcasts the following three protocol messages to its MECU and members of its group:

$M_1 = E(PR_{ECUij}, MSG \| T]$
$M_2 = E(PR_{ECUij}, H(MSG \| S_i) \| T]$
$M_3 = E(PR_{ECUij}, SIG[H(MSG \| S_i)] \| T]$

ECU_{ij} → X: M_1
ECU_{ij} → X: M_2
ECU_{ij} → X: M_3

Here X is used to denote other ECUs in the group and $MECU_i$. The second and third protocol messages need to be padded to make them the same length as the first message.
Upon receiving these messages, the $MECU_i$ will broadcast a message to its members indicating which ECU broadcasted the message. The message contains the ID of the broadcasting ECU. This will allow the ECUs to use the right public key to decrypt each message. Assuming ECU_{11} from the group controlled by $MECU_1$ is broadcasting, $MECU_1$ broadcasts the following message:

$MECU_1$ → ECU_{1}j: E (PR_{MECU1}, ID_{ECU11} || T).

At this point, each ECU is ready to decrypt the first message with the public key of the sender to get the message, MSG. It then checks the message ID, ID_{MSG}, to see if it needs to do anything. If the message does not concern it, there is no need to decrypt the other two messages. Otherwise, the receiving ECU calculates the hash of MSG || S_i and compares it to the received hash code in message two. Then, the signature received in message three is verified. If either the hash code or the signature cannot be verified, the message is ignored and $MECU_i$ is informed. This could imply a hardware or software issue at the sender site, or a possible attack.

$MECU_i$ will recover MSG from message M1, encrypt it first with its private key and then with the public key of SMECU. It then computes the hash of the message and V_j (H(MSG || V_j), and signs the resulting hash code.

The resulting messages will be sent to SMECU. The SMECU will perform the needed decryptions, and verifications of the hash code and signature. Based on message ID, ID_{MSG}, SMECU will make the decision on which MECUs should receive it. A similar approach will be used to create three different messages for each MECU that needs this MSG. Once these messages are received by the MECU and MSG is recovered, the MECU will broadcast the received message to its ECUs.

F. Fulfilling Security Requirements

Most of the sent messages are encrypted with the public key of the receiver. This ensures confidentiality because no one can decrypt the message but the one who owns the related private key. When a message is broadcasted, it cannot be encrypted by the public key of the receiver due to the fact that a number of simultaneous receivers exist. However, encrypting it with the private key of the sender will ensure only the members of the group can decrypt. It could be argued here that the message is confidential for other members of the group because only those members know the public key of the sender.

To ensure message integrity, all the messages have their hash code added. Furthermore, the hash code is signed with the private key of the sender. The receiver can verify the integrity of the received message by calculating the hash code and comparing the two hash codes. If there is a mismatch, the message has been modified.

To ensure that parties (ECUs, MECUs, and SMECU) are communicating with the right parties, the messages are encrypted with the private key of the sender. In addition the hash code also serves as the authenticator.

IV. Other Possible Security Approaches

A. Using Symmetric Keys

Symmetric key cryptology can also be used to secure the proposed security architecture. The initialization step will be the same as for the public key cryptology. The public and private keys are removed, and symmetric keys K_{ij} are shared between the MECUs and ECUs. Furthermore, symmetric keys K_i are shared between MECUs and SMECU. Each $MECU_i$ creates a group key, G_i to be shared with its ECUs. The SMECU generates four session keys and shares a unique one with each MECU. Encryption with symmetric key provides confidentiality and authentication. The three messages above will be re-written as:

$M_1 = E\ (K_{ij}, MSG \parallel T]$

$M_2 = E\ (K_{ij}, H(MSG \parallel S_i) \parallel T]$

$M_3 = E\ (K_{ij}, SIG\ [H(MSG \parallel S_i)] \parallel T]$

B. Utilizing Elliptic Curve Cryptology

Elliptic curve cryptology (ECC) is also effective in securing the above-mentioned architecture. The initialization will include pre-installing the global public elements $E_q(a, b)$, G, and n. Here, $E_q(a, b)$ is an elliptic curve with parameters a and b, q is a prime integer, G is a point on the elliptic curve whose order is a large value n.

Each group including the MECU and its ECU members will create their private keys, N_X, and calculate their public keys, P_X, where X indicates any ECU, or MECU. To illustrate this, the group of $MECU_1$ (refer to Figure 1 above) is selected. The following procedure is used:

1. $MECU_1$ selects its private key N_1 and calculates its public key P_1, $P_1 = N_1 \times G$
2. ECU_{11} selects its private key N_{11} and calculates its public key P_{11}, $P_{11} = N_{11} \times G$
3. ECU_{12} selects its private key N_{12} and calculates its public key P_{12}, $P_{12} = N_{12} \times G$
4. ECU_{1n} selects its private key N_{1n} and calculates its public key P_{1n}, $P_{1n} = N_{1n} \times G$
5. The MECU and ECUs broadcast their public keys. Therefore, each one of them will have all the public keys: P_1, P_{11}, P_{12}, and P_{1n}.
6. The messages M_1, M_2, and M_3 will be represented as points on the curve $E_q(a, b)$ when broadcasted.
7. The MECU will send the ID of the broadcasting ECU to allow the ECUs to use the right public keys.

The same procedure of generating and exchanging keys applies to MECUs and the SMECU but without the broadcasting of step 5. Instead the SMECU and each MECU will exchange their public keys. At the end, each MECU will have the public of the SMECU only, but the SMECU will receive the public key of the four MECUs. Step 7 will be deleted, as there is no broadcasting between the MECUs and the SMECU.

With elliptic curve cryptology, only the signature will be used. No hash code or message authentication code will be employed.

C. Employing Stream Cipher

Another approach would be using One-Time Pad (OTP). The keystream $S = \{S_0, S_1 \dots S_n\}$ will be generated using a True Random Number Generator (TRNG), such as Intel Digital Random Number Generator (DRNG) [20], or the full-hardware implementation of a true number generator suggested by Schaumont [21]. For this purpose, the MECUs and the SMECU should encompass the hardware needed for generating true random numbers. Initially, all the shared key streams need to be pre-installed at manufacturing time.

The SMECU will create four different keystream using the installed hardware for TRNG, one for each MECU. The generated keystream will be encrypted with the old keystream (initially, the pre-installed one and later the current one) shared with each MECU and sent to MECUs. Likewise, each MECU creates a keystream using its TRNG hardware, encrypts it with the old keystream and send it to its members

(ECUs). Once these keystreams are established, the pre-installed ones are discarded.

To broadcast a message, that message should be encrypted with the keystream prior to broadcasting it. If the bus frame is full, another a frame will be used to transmit what is left of the message. The MECU in charge of the broadcasting ECU will forward it to the SMECU encrypted with the shared keystream. Once received by SMECU, it will be analyzed and sent to the MECUs that need the broadcasted message for their members (ECUs). Once the decryptions are performed, all used keystreams will be discarded and new keystreams will be generated.

V. CONCLUSION AND FUTURE WORK

The Electronic Control Units (ECUs) play a critical role in controlling many of the functions of current day's vehicles. Because these ECUs are part of the in-vehicle networks, the possibility of security attacks is inevitable. To protect the vehicle ECUs against various network attacks, a security architecture based on the notion of master and super master ECUs to ensure ECUs' secure message broadcasting was proposed. This architecture was implemented using public key cryptology. The master and super master ECUs also simulated the role of a Key Distribution Center (KDC) through being in charge of generating keys for the units under their control. The super master ECU controlled the broadcasting of ECUs' messages from one group of ECUs to the other groups. Furthermore, the paper showed that other security approaches are reasonable. To this extent, symmetric key cryptology, Elliptic Curve Cryptology, and stream ciphers were investigated.

Future work will concentrate on the implementation phase. During this phase, the optimal grouping of ECUs will be determined. A comparison of the four approaches; public key cryptology, symmetric key cryptology, stream ciphers, and Elliptic Curve cryptology will be carried out to select the most suitable approach for securing the ECUs. Furthermore, the most convenient algorithm that takes into consideration the computing resources limitations of the ECUs will be adopted.

REFERENCES

[1] CCS, "Electronic Control Units (ECUS)," 2014, http://www.ccs-labs.org/teaching/c2x/2014s/05-ecus.pdf, pp. 1-27, [retrieved: April 2016].

[2] L. Delgrossi, "The Future of the Automobile Vehicle Safety Communications," 2014, https://cache.freescale.com/files/automotive/doc/white_paper/BODYDELECTRWP.pdf, [retrieved: April 2016].

[3] ETAS GmbH, "Electronic Control Unit (ECU) – Basics of Automative ECU," 2014, http://www.scribd.com/doc/268828296/20140121-ETAS-Webinar-ECU-Basics#scribd, pp. 1-30, [retrieved: April 2016].

[4] Freescale, "Future advances in Body Electronics" https://cache.freescale.com/files/automotive/doc/white_paper/BODYDELECTRWP.pdf, 2013, pp. 1-18, [retrieved: April 2016].

[5] Freescale, "In-Vehicle Networking," https://cache.freescale.com/files/microcontrollers/doc/brochure/BRINVEHICLENET.pdf, 2006, pp. 1-11, [retrieved: April 2016].

[6] National Instruments, "ECU Designing and Testing Using National Instruments Products," http://www.ni.com/white-paper/3312/en, 2009, [retrieved: April 2016].

[7] On Semiconductor, "Basics of In-Vehicle Neworking (INV) Protocols," http://www.onsemi.com/pub_link/Collateral/TND6015-D.PDF, pp. 1-27, [retrieved: April 2016].

[8] S. Seo, J. Kim, S. Hwang, K. Kwon, and J. Jeon, "A Reliable Gatway for In-Vehicle Networks Based on LIN, CAN, and FlexRay," ACM Transcation on Embedded Computing Systems, vol. 4, no. 1, Article 7, 2012, pp. 1-24.

[9] T. Tomonari, "EMC Countermeasures for In-Vehicle Communication Networks," TDK Corporation, https://product.tdk.com/en/products/emc/guidebook/eemc_practice_09.pdf, pp. 1-7, [retrieved: April 2016].

[10] P. Nisch, "Security Issues in Modern Automative Systems," 2012, pp. 1-7, http://www.panisch.com/wp-content/uploads/2012/06/Security_Issues_in_Modern_Automotive_Cars.pdf, [retrieved: April 2016].

[11] L. B. Othmane, H. Weffers, M. M. Mohamad, and M. Wolf, "A Survey of Security and Privacy in Connected Vehicles," in Wireless Sensor and Mobile Ad Hoc Networks, Part III, Springer, New York, 2015, pp. 217-247.

[12] S. Mahmud and S. Shanker, "In-Vehicle Secure Wireless Personal Area Network (SWPAN)," IEEE Transcations on Vehicular Technology, vol. 55, no. 3, 2006, pp. 1051-1061.

[13] K. Koscher, A. Czeskis, F. Roesner, S. Patel, T. Kohno, S. Checkoway, D. Mccoy, B. Kantor, D. Anderson, H. Shacham, and S. Savage, "Experimental Security Analysis of a Modern Automobile," in Proc. IEEE Symposium on Security and Privacy (SP), Oakland, CA, USA, 2010, pp. 447–462.

[14] C. Lin and A. Sangiovanni-Vincentelli, "Cyber-Security for the Controller Area Network (CAN) Communication Protocol," in Proc. International Conference on Cyber Security, Washington, DC, USA, 2012, pp. 1-7.

[15] K. Han, S. D. Potluri, and K. Shin, "On Authentication in a Connected Vehicle: Secure Integration of Mobile Devices with Vehicular Networks," in Proc. the 2013 ACM/IEEE 4th International Conference on Cyber-Physical Systems (ICCP'13), Philadephia, PA, USA, 2013, pp. 160-169.

[16] C. Patsakis, K. Dellios, and M. Bouroche, "Towards a Distributed Secure In-Vehicle Communication Architecture for Modern Vehicles," Computers and Security, vol. 40, 2014, pp. 60-74.

[17] Continental Automotive GmbH, "Electronic Vehicle Management - New Options for Commercial Vehicle Controllers," http://www.continental-automotive.cn/www/download/automotive_cn_cn/general/contact_services/downloads/commercial_vehicles/flc_vcu_cvam_en.pdf, [retrieved: April 2016].

[18] D. K. Nilsson, P. H. Phung, and U. E. Larson, "Vehicle ECU Classification Based on Safety-Security Characteristics," in Proc. the 13th International Conference on Road Tarnsport Information and Control (RTIC'08), Manchester, England, UK, 2008, pp. 1-7.

[19] K. Y. Cho, C. H. Bae, Y. Chu, M. and W. Suh, "Overview of Telmatics: A System Architecture Approach," International Journal of Automative Technology, vol. 7, no. 4, 2006, pp. 509-517.

[20] Intel Digital Random Number Generator (DRNG), May 15, 2015, https://software.intel.com/sites/default/files/managed/4d/91/DRNG_Software_Implementation_Guide_2.0.pdf, [retrieved: April 16].

[21] S. Schaumont, "True random Number Generation," Circuit Cellar, No. 268, 2012, pp. 52-58.

Wireless Ticket Exchange Boosts Telecommunication Sector

Wieslawa Wajda
Bell Labs
Nokia
Stuttgart, Germany
e-mail: Wieslawa.Wajda@nokia.com

Abstract— **Telecommunication Market evolution poses challenges for future mobile networks. On one side, pressure on network operators regarding technology investments and decreasing revenue; while on the other side, changes in customer behavior and perception give rise to the quest for structural re-organization and for new business strategies in the telecommunications business. This paper gives attention to the telecommunication market from the microeconomic perspective and describes a solution for a near perfect telecommunications market where the market innovation and the efficiency of underlying telecommunication system are optimized by forces of demand and supply. The author envisions a pervasive telecommunication market based on the marketplace concept proven over 200 years' combined with advanced wireless network architecture.**

Keywords- ***Wireless Ticket Exchange; multi-tenancy; telecommunications market; marketplace.***

I. INTRODUCTION

The telecommunication market evolution poses challenges to future mobile networks. There is an enormous pressure on the network operators to reverse the trend of decreasing revenues, to adopt new cloud infrastructure, to provide broadband, delay and reliability stringent services, as described in [1] and to ensure necessary technological investments as discussed in [2] and [3]. On one hand, higher transmission peak capacity is required and on the other, networks are highly underutilized, as stated in [4]. From the user perspective, rapid changes in customer behavior (and perception) set special requirements for network and new service categories force redefinition of the provider-to-customer relationship [5].

A promising approach towards network cost reduction is sharing of radio resource. The pure infrastructure sharing can be realized, but at the expense of suboptimal profits. In contrast, radio resource sharing between "equal" partners is very challenging - interoperability and responsibility in management decisions are the main problems to solve. The literature proposes a lot of strategies for sharing of physical radio resources, e.g. game theoretical approaches, but the strategies deal with some potential sharing ideals and concern mostly single aspects reduced to one specific problem, which do not help to solve short term realistic multi-dimensional situation in radio resource sharing, as discussed in [6] and [7]. There is also a well known concept concerning "non-equal" cooperating partners, on one side the Mobile Virtual Network Operator (MVNO) and on the other the Mobile Network Operator (MNO). MVNO does not dispose of own radio infrastructure and has to cooperate with an incumbent network operator by leasing radio resources within the condition of a service level agreement (SLA). Since the SLA contrasts are long-lasting contracts, they are not adaptable to changing situation during the contract time. So, they are not dynamic to readjust for real capacity need in terms of location and time needed and not flexible for fast reaction to global market changes. Furthermore, the MNO dominance makes impossible for upcoming 3rd parties to enter the telecommunication market. With other words, the telecommunication market does not meet all conditions for flexibility, business dynamicity and price discrimination. Therefore we propose Wireless Ticket Exchange (WTE) a solution which makes possible, that the telecommunication market will be:

- Open for and transparent to all market players,
- Flexible and dynamic,
- Can quickly respond to rapid market changes,
- Guarantees easy entry to the market for newcomers,
- Decision freedom and independence of network and service providers will retain,
- Service providers have the possibility to address targeted consumer groups rapidly, and
- Contracts between providers as well as between providers and users are flexible with regard to contract subject, price, and duration.

Our approach does not focus only on technology as such, but also on integration of economic and user aspects into a holistic framework realized by the WTE approach.

The rest of this paper is organized as follows. Section II provides economic background and introduces basics of market mechanisms in user–provider interaction. Section III addresses necessary changes towards a future telecommunication market. Section IV goes into details of the idea of the Wireless Ticket Exchange. Section V addresses the user integration into the upcoming pervasive telecommunications market. Section VI concludes the paper.

II. MARKET MECHANISMS

To understand the issues arising in telecommunication network economics, we focus first on some basic microeconomics market mechanisms.

Due to market mechanisms, demand and supply balances towards an optimum. The higher the price of a product the more the supplier is willing to produce and sell. As seen in Figure 1, product demand follows the inverse of the product price. The market clears at the equilibrium price p* and the quantity q*. The variation of the price and quantity over time depends on the way in which supply and demand respond to economic variables such as demander's income, production costs, etc. If the price p* is regulated to p_1, the quantity supplied decreases and a demand shortage develops [8].

Above mentioned mechanisms show the native market feedback balancing demand and supply to the optimum. Any external influence violates market forces [9].

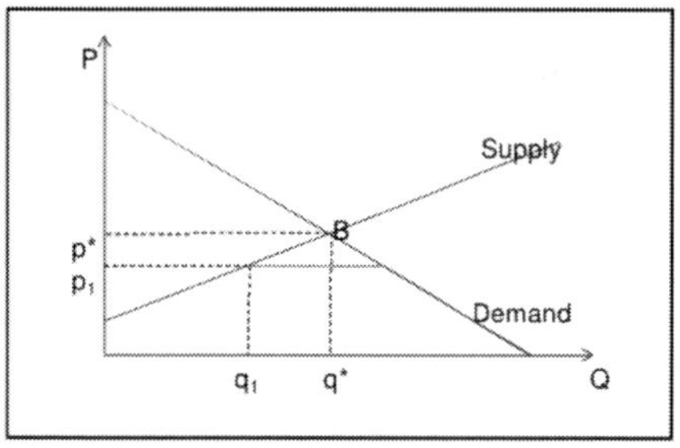

Figure 1. Market mechanisms.

As shown in Figure 2 the number of potential customer base *C*, as given in (1) depends on users' affordability *A*, defined as the relationship between the disposable incomes *I* and price *p*, as shown in (2), where *k* is a constant.

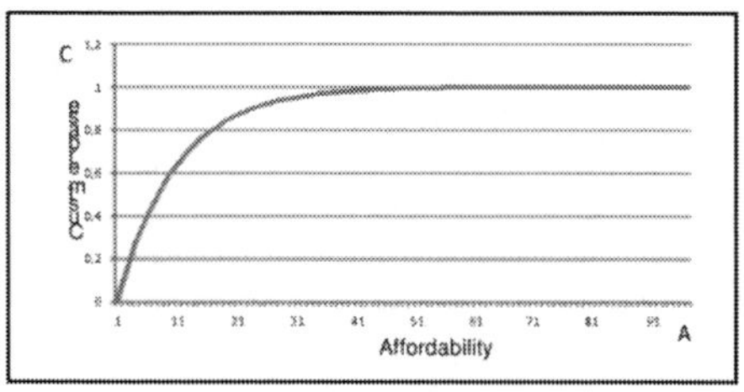

Figure 2. Normalized customer base vs. product affordability.

$$C = 1 - e^{-A}, \quad (1)$$

$$A = k\frac{I}{p}. \quad (2)$$

Price changes of a product affect the affordability and so the number of potential customers in such way that the higher the product's affordability the higher the market size. Also, the lower the product price, the more price-sensitive users will be attracted [10]. Besides the price, user's non-monetary preferences must be taken into account in strategic decisions of a provider.

A. Users utility

The preferences of a user i using a telecommunication service can be therefore represented by a utility function U_i which is an abstract concept in economy and which represents the satisfaction or benefit that a user gains from consuming a given amount of resources. The utility maps the set of outcomes q, e.g., Quality of Service (QoS), access time to the network, etc., to the set of real values, as e.g. proposed in [11]. Usually, the utility function strictly decreases in price p_i, which means, the user prefers to pay as little as possible. The reference utility we can define as $U_i(q_0,0)$, i.e., a utility without monetary outcome, and then the valuation function for the outcome q is the maximum price the user is willing to pay for the preferred outcome over the reference utility:

$$V_1(q) := \sup\{p_i : U_i(q, p_i) - U_i(q_0, 0) \geq 0\}. \quad (3)$$

Now we assume, the user would like to stream a video with a high quality ϱ and his utility function $U_i(\varrho, p_i)$ is increasing in ϱ. Additionally, we suppose that the user is willing to pay an additional fee β for a higher streaming quality and will not pay for the service with a lower quality than defined as ϱ_{min} even if the service is for free. In this case for all $0 \leq \rho_{\min} \leq \rho_{\min} + x$ the utility function is defined as

$$U_i(\rho_{\min} + x, p_i + \beta x) = U_i(\rho_{\min}, p_i)$$

Applying $q_0 = \rho_{\min}$ and concerning (3)

$$V_i(\rho) := \sup\{p_i : U_i(\rho, p_i) \geq U_i(\rho_{\min}, 0)\} = \sup\{p_i : U_i(\rho, p_i) \geq U_i(\rho, \beta(\rho - \rho_{\min})\} = \beta(\rho - \rho_{\min}).$$

If $\rho < \rho_{\min}$, the user is not willing to pay for the service improvement, hence the user gets the same utility as $\rho = \rho_{\min}$. The valuation function

$$V_i(\rho) = \beta[(\rho - \rho_{\min})]^{+}.$$

reflects the maximum price the user will be willing to pay. Therefore the utility function

$$U_i(\rho, p_i) = \beta[(\rho - \rho_{\min})]^{+} - p_i.$$

can be used by the operator to compute an equivalent price for a service with quality ϱ. The above model indicates the importance of the effects of user preferences on product, in this case, on service design. Operator has the opportunity to create an extensive service portfolio to measure the demand structure, and to calibrate the service parameters according to users' valuation. The wider the service portfolio, the higher the probability that certain services comply with users' requirements and the faster an operator can optimize services and the revenue.

B. Operators revenue

Building on the above observation we construct a business valuation function representing operator's revenue from transactions at the time services are sold. In general, the revenue R is the quantity of the sold product times the selling price p.

The number of sold products results from the number of customers C who bought a number N of the product. The number of sold products results from the number of customers C who bought a number N of the product snd so the revenue R can be defined

$$R = C * N * p\,. \tag{4}$$

Considering (1) we define

$$C = \lambda(1 - e^{-\eta A}), \tag{5}$$

where $\lambda \geq 0$ is the fraction of users who bought the service, and $\eta > 0$ is a constant. We define product demand as

$$N = k * e^{-(\Gamma - \mu)^2}, \tag{6}$$

where k>0 is number of transactions per user, $\Gamma > 0$ is the parameter describing service characteristics, and $\mu > 0$ the most demanded service. Hence with (4), (5) and (6) we can define the total revenue R_{tot} from service:

$$R_{tot} = \sum_{i=1}^{n} (k_i * e^{-(\Gamma - \mu)^2} * \lambda(1 - e^{-A_i}) * p_i)\,. \tag{7}$$

In summary, a telecommunication market model, as shown in Figure 2 and Figure 3 can be characterized by a number of potential customers interested in a specific telecommunication product and by a number of units of this product, the potential customer efforts in dependence on product embodiment.

As shown in Figure 2 the higher the product affordability the more customers will probably buy this product. It is advantageous to have cheap products due to higher customer base. Furthermore cheap product have better profit margin. Figure 3 shows, that the better product's embodiment fulfills customer demand the more product units will be sold per customer. Services (see Figure 3) described by the service depiction value considering affordability, price, QoS, duration time, target group, etc. have to be carefully designed in order to attract users and to maximize the demand.

The telecommunication market today does not have a mechanism which guarantees that a general demand/supply balance can be maintained on the market. This entails a need for information on market conditions and its capacities.

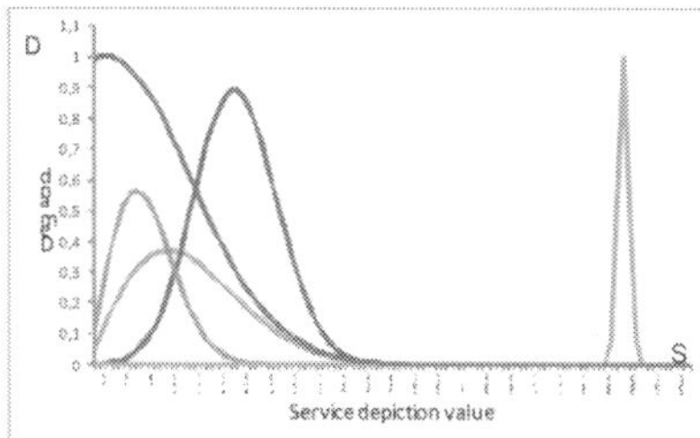

Figure 3. Different services and their normalized demand on the market.

Conventional distribution channels such as shops or provider's own internet platform are cost intensive and address to low customer base. Therefore, the provider is forced to maximize products volume, e.g., to create complex and expensive product packages and/or to force the customer to accept a long-term contract. This is in turn contradictive to above findings. As a result, the provider cannot exhaust the market potential and let business opportunities unexploited. If the provider would get the opportunity to reduce distribution costs and to adopt contract volume and duration to customers' needs more closely he would increase its revenues significantly.

A remedy can be a marketplace that integrates all customers having demand for telecommunication products. Such marketplace is provided online and so marketing and customer assistance in dedicated shops is not needed. Purposive provider's internet pages are superfluous too. In addition, contrary to provider's web pages, offers provided on a marketplace are transparent and help customers to understand the presented service and price plan. An online marketplace provides the product presentation and the trading for every provider and will therefore reduce the unit costs.

To enable the telecommunication market fulfilling the mentioned requirements in Section I we propose a telecommunication marketplace empowering natural market forces. Such a marketplace can be represented by an auction or an exchange.

C. Auction and Exchange

Economics know different embodiments of competitive markets, depending on traded artifacts and trading rules. Auction and exchange are examples of marketplaces. For example, Google proposed recently a concept, where a user pings service providers for their best offers while placing a call [12]. Then, either the user or an appropriate application evaluates the bids and completes the call. In a traditional auction there are usually many prospective buyers and one auctioneer conducting the auction process which lasts for a defined time period. Auctions are in general appropriate for unique objects and in telecommunication markets often used to trade licensed radio spectrum [13]. Unlike auctions, an exchange is a marketplace with many sellers and many prospective buyers, where the prices are posted [14]. Trades are made directly between the buyers and the sellers and the clearing process is conducted immediately if there is a call. Sellers compete by submitting offers to the exchange or, in a simplified way, directly to the user.

Therefore, in order to decide whether auction or exchange is more preferable as a trading concept for telecommunication products by considering criteria, inter alia, transaction duration, dynamicity, openness and transactions simplicity, we decided that an exchange is better suited as a platform for trading of telecommunication artifacts than the auction.

III. NEW ARCHITECTURAL AND BUSINESS MODEL

The above theoretical analysis shows that mentioned requirements on the telecommunication sector can be fulfilled by creation of a flexible operating platform, the marketplace. Marketplace architecture implies multitenancy and network virtualization, as claimed in [13]. This opens the value-chain of the telecommunication sector and so leads to separation of telecommunication provider roles. As a consequence, previously closed proprietary interfaces are turned into non-proprietary interfaces and thus offer infrastructure facilities to upcoming 3rd parties.

Therefore, in the next generation wireless network a possible business model can be based on increased specialization of the market players towards:

- Mobile Network Infrastructure Providers (MNIP).
- Mobile Virtual Network Operators (MVNO).
- Service Providers (SP), Content Providers (CP), etc.
- Marketplace Operator.

Mobile Network Infrastructure Provider offers network infrastructure and technologies as well as connectivity service. To make physical resources multi-tenant scalable, a MNIP transforms its network resources into logical resources by virtualization and wraps them to telco artifacts targeted to different customers. Telco artifacts are described by a number of parameters as QoS, traffic volume, location, radio access technology, contract duration, price, etc. The MNIP is obligated to guarantee the complete performance of the telecommunication artifacts.

Networks created and managed by *Mobile Virtual Network Operator* are based on virtual resources purchased from MNIPs on a marketplace. Note that the proposed MVNO differs from the today's defined MVNO. Since the MVNO does not own its own network, no customers can roam to that operator. However, all the customers of the MVNO have roamed to the networks of the MNOs. This makes the situation asymmetric, and this is not the case in our concept. MVNO can purchase connectivity services to expand its virtual network by additional area. Thanks to the flexibility given by the marketplace, MVNO can freely design spacial extend of its network and dynamically adopt resource volume to predicted traffic load. The calculation of needed resource in respect of amount, contract duration time and price is in its own responsibility.

Service Provider cooperates with MVNOs and offers services targeting current customer needs. Depending on the business model the services can be either integrated into existing virtual network or can be offered to the customer separately.

Marketplace Operator provides marketplace platform where the MNIPs, MVNOs, and other players offer their products and make business.

Besides providers and operators also *users* will play an important role on the changing telecommunication market. Users will have the possibility to adopt contracts to their needs, preferences and actual location and ask for means supporting the creation of individual service bundles. Furthermore users expect also to have access to networks of different operators in order to get the specified service.

IV. WIRELESS TICKET EXCHANGE – THE MARKETPLACE

The envisioned telecommunication market is based on well defined and straight trading rules and creates a trading environment transparent to all parties. Each bidder knows the offerings by competitors and the asked prices. The proposed telecommunication market comprises the platform WTE, the WTE Operator, various telco artifact providers and users.

On the WTE market players meet one another and conduct transactions by trading telco artifacts. Telco artifacts can be any telecommunication object provided by telecommunication players. This can be hardware such as a Base Station, Small Cells, Backhaul as well as spectrum, bandwidth, service, etc. The telco artifacts are described in a form of standardized Telco Tickets whereby the structure of Telco Ticket can differ for commercial and private users. In general, Telco Tickets describe details of the offer

As already indicated, the WTE is provided by the WTE Operator. He has a broker role and provides an exchange infrastructure supporting the execution and fulfilling of transactions. The broker role comprises in getting Telco Tickets from the telco artifacts provider and managing the transaction process. A transaction is executed in real-time. Since demand and supply interact in a closed-loop, the price level and service characteristics have important effect on quantity demanded and inversely, the demand influences supply. We would like to emphasize, that the future networks will be definitely dominated by solutions allowing ***m:n*** customer to provider relationships. Assuming so, customers are not necessarily bound to long term contracts and can choose between multiple providers according to user's specific demand. This will be an opportunity for providers to create innovative products and so to differentiate from each other. Broad base services in terms of technology, service type, service quality and price will in turn generate positive stimuli for the market success of the market players. The WTE is separated into the Commercial Ticket Exchange and the End User Ticket Exchange. The Commercial Ticket Exchange covers trading between business companies trading with business addressed artifacts, i.e., Business-to-Business (B2B) market. They have the possibility to sell and to buy network resources, different services, network nodes, etc. Furthermore, the companies offer services to the users. Their offers are traded on the End User Ticket Exchange serving users demand i.e., a Business-to-Customer (B2C) market. Furthermore, services such as Machine-to-Machine (M2M) are also provided at the WTE.

A. *WTE functions*

The WTE has to perform three tasks:

- Admission as a trader.
- Telco Ticket presentation.
- Transaction processing and fulfilling.

Admission as a trader is performed in a registration procedure where the applicant data is collected. The application procedure is different for commercial and for end user applicants.

Telco Tickets will be exposed by a WTE service application presenting submitted bids and asks to the customers and allowing the customers to purchase selected artifacts. The WTE provides exchange facilities with interfaces for human interaction and machine type communication.

B. *WTE functional architecture*

The main functional entities of the WTE architecture are the *Trading Facility*, the *Communication Facility*, the *Service Register*, the *Root Home Register*, the *Trader Register*, the *Subscriber Name Server (SNS)*, and the *Authentication Center* (AuC) (see Figure 4).

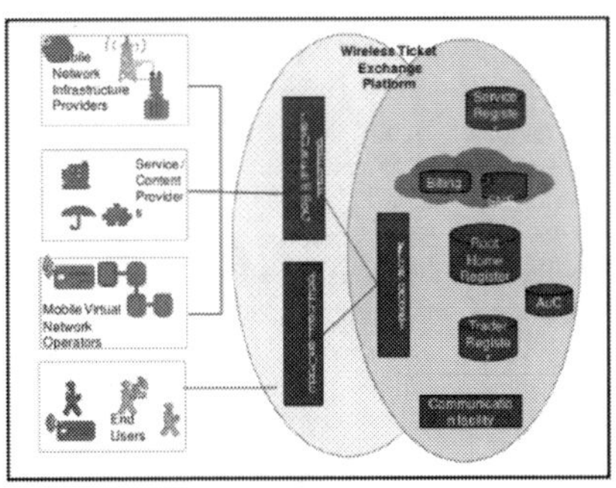

Figure 4. WTE functional architecture.

The *Trading Facility* allows users to access the WTE as a visitor or as a subscriber. Rights a granted to a visitor to see the offered bids and asks, but without the privilege to close transactions. The WTE subscriber may be the end user as well as a commercial user, a commercial company. After the registration as a WTE subscriber, the End User gets a Subscriber Identity Module (SIM) card authorizing to trade on the WTE. Registration data of both, commercial as well as non-commercial users' are stored in the *Trader Register*. The *Service Register* stores Telco artifacts to be traded. The content of the Service Register, bids and asks uploaded from the contractors, is presented in a human readable form to allow traders to choose and to select services they need, and to buy corresponding tickets. The *Communication facility* supports internal communication between the Registers, between the Registers and Trading Facility, and external communication between the Wireless Ticket Exchange and subsystems of the network. The *Root Home Register* (RHR) receives data from the Trading Facility and stores the data and sends it to the Home Service Server of the involved network. The *Subscriber Name Server* (SNS) guaranties that the call is routed directly to user's current location.

C. *Integration of marketplayers infrastructure into WTE*

Trading of products on the WTE requires an integration of the infrastructure belonging to market players into the WTE functionality, as shown in Figure 5.

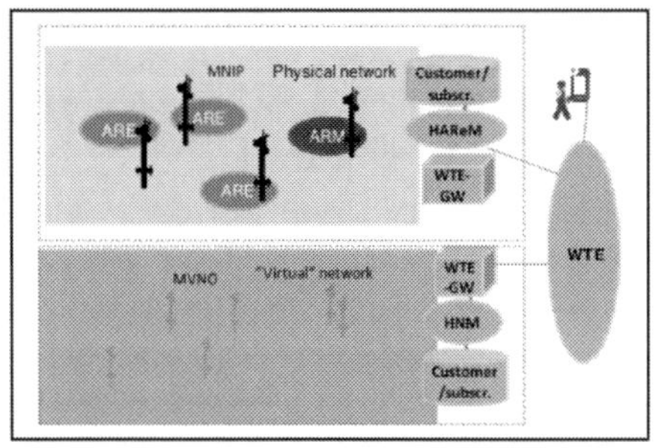

Figure 5. WTE extensions to the network.

This can be achieved by means of a specialized gateway, the WTE-Gateway, which is able to translate heterogeneous interfaces into WTE standard. The WTE-Gateway is moreover connected to other specialized nodes on the MNIP, MVNO or SP side. Figure 5 depicts an example of MNIP and MVNO. MNIP is equipped with a logical entity called Heterogeneous Atomic Resource Manager (HAReM) and a customer database. HAReM combines Atomic Resource Entities (ARE) collected by Atomic Resource Manager (ARM) to larger data transport entities, and creates Telco Tickets that will be delivering to the WTE in order to sell. Additional architectural entities on the MVNO side are Heterogeneous Network Manager (HNM) and Customer & Supplier database. HNM is responsible for virtual network creation, management of the virtual network, forecasting the network capacity due to subscriber's requirements, and foreseen traffic load in respect of considered user demands on throughput. The HNM includes also creation and management of Telco Tickets.

V. USERS CENTRIC APPROACH

To enjoy the benefits of the WTE user has to register to WTE service as a trader. After the registration procedure the user becomes a trader who can benefit from different offers of various MVNOs and Service Providers. The user can purchase telco services on the WTE and (in exceptional case) the user can sell acquired Telco Tickets back. Every WTE subscriber is equipped with a SIM card identifying him as a trader. The SIM card storing user's identification number (WTE identifier) allows him to access the network of MVNOs registered on the WTE. It is quite evident, that the trader has to possess Telco Tickets from one or more MVNOs before he can do calls in corresponding network. When a subscriber buys a service on the WTE, the subscriber's data is automatically transferred to MVNOs Home Subscriber Server or corresponding facility in such a way that the buyer becomes the status of native subscriber of the seller for the time covered by closed transaction. If required, transaction procedure can be repeated by any number of times with different network operators. As a result a user has access to networks belonging to those MVNOs.

In case off Telco Tickets containing combine services, as for example content service and corresponding streaming service, both providers are informed about conducted transaction.

At the time the user enters a network of a MVNO that has an agreement with the user the MVNO provides the user with a MVNO local identifier. The telecommunication system uses the local identifier to route the call to the destination address. The user gets the status of a native subscriber of the seller for the time covered by the closed transaction.

VI. CONCLUSIONS

We conclude that separation of telecommunication players' roles is necessary to fulfill actual and future market requirements. By opening the value chain more business opportunities for traditional and new players will be available. The results will be welfare in maximizing market equilibrium by the forces of supply and demand. From this point of view we did not restrict our research to pure engineering on technological solution but we integrate economic and user perspectives, as well. As a consequence we draw the idea of WTE where various telecommunication providers, network operators, business customers and end users trade telecommunication artifacts in a free, dynamic, transparent environment with associated functional network and marketplace architecture. The many-to-many customer to provider relationship forces competitive advantage and boost performance in product differentiation and innovation. In opposite to known business models, we propose that providers retain their independence and freedom of decision in issues: which, with whom and how much resource to share. Due to flexible and dynamic contracts the WTE operators can cope with rapid changes in customers' behavior, attitude and requirements. Again, due to market transparency users will generate immense dynamics and leverage expected assets.

From the regulation point of view, WTE allows an easily entering the market for upcoming 3rd parties. However, putting such an approach into practice reduces dominancy of today players in the mobile radio communication. Since the market offers new possibilities too, they can expect additional value by developing their commercial creativity. To this end, we are confident, trading of telecommunication artifacts addressed to commercial companies, as well as to private consumers opens new streams of revenue, brings opportunity for network monetization, radically improves cost structure and increases users' satisfaction.

In future works we will provide numerical methods and SON market driven algorithms applied to WTE service.

ACKNOWLEDGMENT

I would like to give thanks to my colleagues Dr. Lutz Ewe and Osman Aydin for the outstanding discussions.

REFERENCES

[1] METISII White Paper, see https://metis-ii.5g-ppp.eu/wp-content/uploads/5G-PPP-METIS-II-5G-RAN-Architecture-White-Paper.pdf, 2016.

[2] Forbes Trefis Team, "Verizon's Wireless Margins Under Pressure, Still Has Network Advantage", http:/www.forbes.com/sites/greatspeculations/2014/12/12/verizons-wireless-margins-under-pressure-still-has-network-advantage, 12/12/2014.

[3] A.-M. Kovacs, "Telecommunications competition: the infrastructure-investment race", Study, Internet Innovation Alliance, October 2013.

[4] W.Wajda," Insights into Cellular Networks_ Anatomy of traffic profiles" The Tenth International Conference on Wireless and Mobile Communications (ICWMC 2014), IARIA, June 2014, pp.192-198, ISSN: 2308-4219, ISBN: 978-1-61208-347-6

[5] A. Drury and P. M. Olmstead, "Media Metamorphosis", White Paper of Ovum and Research & Innovation, Atos 2013.

[6] H.Zhang et al, "Resource Allocation in Spectrum-Sharing OFDMA Femtocells With Heterogeneous Services", IEEE Transactions on Communications, volume 62, Issue 7, pp. 2366 – 2377, DOI: 10.1109/TCOMM.2014.2328574.

[7] O. Aydin, EU Project FP7-ICT-248001 SAPHYRE, D7.4, 2011

[8] K. Ahlersten, "Essential of microeconomics", ISBN 978-87-7681-410-6, Krister Ahlersten & Ventus Publishing ApS, 2008.

[9] J.-J. Laffont and J. Tirole, "Competition in Telecommunications", The MIT Press, 2000.

[10] M. Andrews, G. Bruns, M.a Dogru, H. Lee. , "Understanding quota dynamics in wireless networks", ACM Trans. Internet Technol. 14, 2-3, Article 14, Oct. 2014, doi:http://dx.doi.org/10.1145/2663494

[11] P. Maillé and B. Tuffin, "Telecommunication Network Economics", Cambridge University Press, ISBN 978-1-107-03275-0, February 28, 2014.

[12] S. Baluja, M. Chu, M. Matsuno "Flexible Communication Systems and Methods" Google Inc., Patent US 20120036035 A1.

[13] S. Vassaki, M. I. Poulakis, A. D. Panagopoulos, P. Constantinou, "An Auction-based Mechanism for Spectrum Leasing in Overlay Cognitive Radio Networks", IEEE 24th International Symposium on Personal, Indoor and Mobile Radio Communications (PIMRC), IEEE Conference Publications, 2013, pp. 2733 - 2737, doi: 10.1109/PIMRC.2013.6666611.

[14] H. Bidgoli," The Internet Encyclopedia- Band 1", published by John Willens & Sohns, ISBN 0471222011, 2004.

An Automated Approach for Selecting Web Services

Alysson Alves, Gledson Elias
Informatics Center
Federal University of Paraíba
João Pessoa, Brazil
e-mail: a.alvesdl@gmail.com, gledson@ci.ufpb.br

Abstract—**The task of selecting web services is one of the main challenges for successfully exploring the Service-Oriented Architecture (SOA) approach in software development processes. Whereas the availability of web services tends to increase rapidly in the software industry, it is impractical to adopt ad-hoc manual approaches for selecting web services. Thus, considering a very large and complex search space, it is required an automated approach for selecting web services. In such a direction, exploring Search Based Software Engineering (SBSE) techniques, this paper proposes an automated approach for selecting web services, whose optimization strategy is based on functional and structural metrics that evaluate the functionalities provided by candidate web services, as well as their dependencies in the architectural level. As main contribution, experimental results show that the proposed approach represents an extremely complex problem in a systematic and structured way, discovering good-enough or even optimal solutions among the candidate web services.**

Keywords-Web Services; Service-Oriented Architecture; Search Based Software Engineering.

I. Introduction

The advancements in software engineering approaches have contributed for increasing productivity in software development processes [1]. As a promising approach, software reuse has the potential to reduce development time, cost and risk during the development of a software product [2]. In such a context, Service-Oriented Architecture (SOA) has emerged as one of the main software reuse approaches, in which software systems can be developed reusing services available in the internet. Note that, SOA is an architectural style for building software systems, while Web Services (WS) are the preferred standards-based way to realize SOA [3].

Ideally, web services are perfectly connected and integrated without additional adaptation efforts for composing a software system or even a new web service. However, in practice, web services can be developed by different software providers, and, generally, such services can only be integrated with additional adaptation efforts for resolving incompatibilities among their required and provided functionalities [4]. As a consequence, such incompatibility issues must be already considered during the selection of the candidate web services, trying to choose more compatible candidates as a mean to reduce adaptation efforts, and consequently integration time and cost.

The selection of web services has proven to be a phase of major complexity in SOA-based development processes. Most processes for selecting web services take into account only quality attributes or non-functional requirements of the candidate web services, such as availability, reliability, response time and price. However, functional requirements also have significant impact in the quality of a SOA-based software product. Indeed, functional requirements make possible to assess the effectiveness of the integration of all candidate web services, minimizing integration mismatch issues. The higher the integration effectiveness, the lower the amount of incompatibilities that arise from the integration, and consequently the lower the adaptation efforts for integrating candidate web services.

Therefore, the selection of web services for a given architectural specification is a pivotal task that is more complex than traditional products selection [5]. Besides, taking into account that the availability of web services tends to rapidly increase in software industry, it is impracticable the adoption of ad-hoc manual approaches for selecting web services. In fact, considering a SOA-based architectural specification, several candidate implementations can exist for each web service specification included in the architectural specification. The amount of possible solutions creates a very large search space with exponential complexity, in which the base is the average number of candidate implementations and the exponent is the number of web service specifications included in the architectural specification.

As a consequence, considering a very large and complex search space, it is required an automated approach for selecting web services. Even adopting an automated approach, the search space is typically too large to be explored exhaustively, suggesting the adoption of metaheuristic search techniques explored in Search Based Software Engineering (SBSE), in which software engineering problems are reformulated as optimization problems that can be tackled with metaheuristics, such as Genetic Algorithms [6].

In such a direction, exploring SBSE techniques, this paper proposes an automated approach for selecting web services, in which from a SOA-based architectural specification, web service specifications are contrasted against their correspondent candidate implementations, which are selected by evaluating the effectiveness of their integration, minimizing integration mismatch issues, and consequently, reducing adaptation efforts for integrating them. In the proposed approach, the optimization strategy is based on functional and structural metrics that evaluate the functionalities provided by candidate web services, as well as their dependencies in the architectural level. As main contribution, experimental results show that the proposed approach represents an extremely complex problem in a systematic and structured way, discovering good-enough or even optimal solutions among the candidate web services.

The remainder of this paper is structured as follows. Section II introduces the main concepts and fundamentals related to the approach proposed herein. Then, Section III briefly discusses related work, evincing the contribution of the proposed approach. In Section IV, the proposed approach is presented, defining the metrics adopted in the optimization strategy. Thereafter, Section V presents an experimental evaluation in three case studies. Finally, concluding remarks and future work are discussed in Section VI.

II. Concepts and Fundamentals

According the OASIS consortium, SOA is a paradigm for organizing and utilizing distributed services that may be under the control of different ownership domains [2]. SOA has emerged as a means to promote software reuse, in which software systems can be developed reusing services available in the internet. On the one hand, SOA is an architectural style for building software systems, which can be implemented using different strategies or technologies. On the other hand, Web Services are the preferred standards-based way to realize SOA. Thus, while SOA is conceptual and abstract, WS-based architectures and technologies are specific and concrete.

Web Services technologies are built on top of XML based open standards, which abstract details related to network protocols, operating systems and programming languages. Among such standards, Web Services Description Language (WSDL) has a fundamental role in the context of the approach proposed herein. WSDL is an interface definition language that is used for describing the functionality offered by a web service, including the provided operations and their input and output parameters. Thus, its purpose is roughly similar to that of a method signature in a programming language.

SOA concepts and WS-based architectures and technologies support intra and inter-provider service integration. However, as already discussed, integration mismatch issues can arise and must be treated adopting automated approaches during the selection of the candidate web services. In such a context, considering a very large and complex search space, automated approaches for selecting web services have been proposed in the literature adopting metaheuristic search techniques explored in the SBSE field.

According Harman and Jones [6], in SBSE, software engineering problems are reformulated as optimization problems that can be tackled with metaheuristics, such as Genetic Algorithms and Simulated Annealing, facilitating automated and semi-automated solutions in situations typified by large complex problem spaces with multiple competing and conflicting objectives. Complementarily, in [7], Harman argues that software engineering provides the ideal set of application problems for which SBSE techniques are supremely well suited, once the virtual nature of software makes it ideal for search-based optimization.

In order to reformulate a given software engineering problem as an optimization problem, SBSE-based approaches ought to define: *(i)* a representation of the problem, which must be amenable to symbolic manipulation; *(ii)* a fitness function defined in terms of the adopted representation; and *(iii)* a set of manipulation operators, which are applied in the search algorithm for transforming candidate solutions.

The fitness function is the characterization of what is considered to be a good solution, imposing an ordinal scale of measurement upon candidate solutions. By contrasting the value of the fitness function for each candidate solution, metaheuristic search techniques can find good-enough or even optimal solutions. Although eventually possible, search techniques do not guarantee to find the optimal solution. Besides, due to their non-determinist aspects, they can find different solutions in different executions.

In the proposed approach, the adopted search technique is genetic algorithms, which is a class of evolutionary algorithm that mimics the biological natural evolution process as a problem-solving strategy, including operators such as crossover, mutation and selection [8]. In summary, a set of candidate solutions, represented as chromosomes, are quantitatively evaluated using the fitness function. Then, promising candidates are kept and allowed to reproduce using genetic operators, creating the next generation of candidates. The process repeats during several generations, making them into better, more complete or more efficient solutions.

III. Related Work

Selection of web services is a key research field in SOA-based development processes. As a consequence, it is possible to find several proposals in the literature [5][9][10][11][12][13], proving different strategies for selecting web services in more effective ways in order to reduce development time and cost. Despite their pivotal contributions, in general, such available proposals deal with criteria related to non-functional requirements only, more specifically those related to Quality of Service (QoS), including availability, reliability, execution cost and time, reputation, location and price. Few proposals can be found that deal with criteria directly related to functional requirements and structural properties, which clearly is the main contribution of the approach proposed herein, as will become clear in the following.

Briefly, this section presents and discuss six approaches identified in the literature which are related to our work to some extent. In [9], Fetthallah and coworkers propose a QoS aware service selection approach based on genetic algorithm. The Fetthallah's proposal has the aim of optimizing the composition of web services based on criteria, such as response time, availability, reliability, price and reputation. Lifeng and colleagues [10] define a penalty-based genetic algorithm for QoS-aware web service composition with service dependencies and conflicts. The Lifeng's proposal also considers QoS criteria only, such as response time, price, reputation, availability and reliability.

Vescan [11] presents an evolutionary approach for component selection. Based on genetic algorithms, it adopts QoS-aware metrics such as cost and reusability, but also includes a functional metric. Although adopts a functional metric, unlike the proposed approach, it does not try to identify mismatch issues among dependent components, but tries only measuring the ratio of functionalities provided by each component in relation to functionalities required in the whole system. Clearly, the functional and structural metrics adopted in the proposed approach are much more precise in evaluating mismatch issues.

Adopting similar QoS-aware criteria, Maamar and his fellows [12] have discussed the selection of web services for composition based on the criteria of execution cost, execution time and location of provider hosts. Besides, Tang and Cheng [13] analyzed the optimal location and pricing of web services from the view of web services intermediary, whose criteria can contribute to companies for making selection decisions.

Lastly, Feng and associates [5] examine an approach for web service selection based in six criteria (functional, price, location, integration and reputation). The functional criterion takes a rough-grain keyword-based search in a service repository considering required functionalities that the web services must fulfill. In contrast, instead of evaluating keywords related to functional requirements, the proposed approach evaluates the signature of operations provided and required by candidate web services, which represents a much more precise strategy than simple keyword-based search.

IV. Proposed Approach

By exploring SBSE techniques, the proposed approach has the goal of automating the web service selection process. In the proposed approach, the metaheuristic search algorithm is based on functional and structural metrics that evaluate the functionalities provided by candidate web services, as well as their dependencies in the architectural level. Together, both metrics evaluates the integration effectiveness among candidate web services. As a result, it is expected to find a near optimal architectural configuration, which minimizes integration mismatch issues, and consequently, reduces adaptation efforts for integrating its constituting web services. Figure 1 illustrates the stages of the proposed approach.

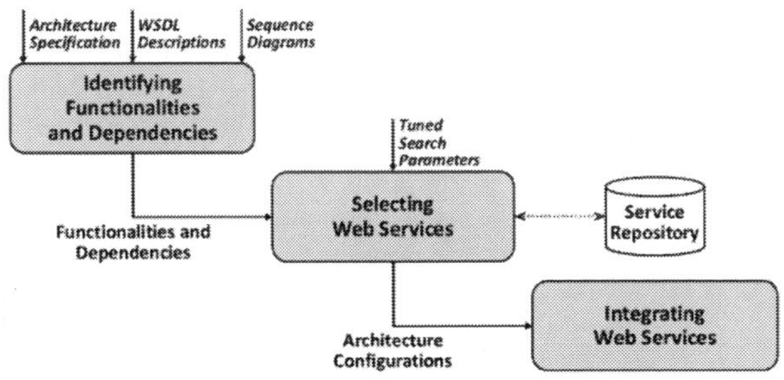

Figure 1. Stages of the Proposed Approach

The first stage, called *Identifying Functionalities and Dependencies*, has the purpose of identifying provided and required functionalities, as well as services dependencies. To do that, the first stage adopts as inputs three types of artifacts: the architecture specification, WSDL descriptions and sequence diagrams. As explained later, all of them are produced during the architectural design phase.

Upon identifying functionalities and dependencies, the second stage, called *Selecting Web Services*, represents the core of the proposed approach in which candidate web services are evaluated and then selected for composing near optimal architectural configurations that reduce adaptation efforts for integrating constituting web services. Note that several architectural configurations can be recommended, allowing the software development team to choose one that best meets the needs of the project and organization.

After selecting web services, in the third stage, called *Integrating Software System*, the software development team can integrate and adapt the set of web services included in the selected architectural configuration.

In this paper, the focus is on the first two stages of the proposed approach. Due to that, the next subsection introduces some notes about the identification of functionalities and dependencies. Then, in a succeeding subsection, the mathematical representations of the functional and structural metrics are presented in details.

A. Functionalities and Dependencies

Considering a SOA-based software development process, the architectural design phase must come before the service selection phase. In the architectural design phase, the software architect ought to identify the functionalities provided and required by each specified service, together with their dependencies. Such functionalities are specified as interfaces. When adopting Web Services technologies, interface specifications are explicitly described using WSDL, allowing to indicate the set of operations provided by each interface for each specified web service. Thus, in the proposed approach, provided functionalities are effortlessly extracted from WSDL descriptions evaluating a set of XML elements, including *portType*, *operation*, *input*, *output* and *message*.

Differently, required functionalities and dependencies cannot be explicitly represented in WSDL specifications. Instead, required functionalities and dependencies can be implicitly modeled using sequence diagrams associated with each operation provided by each specified web service. Thus, in the proposed approach, required functionalities and consequently service dependencies are extracted in a more elaborated way, evaluating sequence diagrams that show how web services collaborate and work together, revealing the set of operations required by one web service but provided by other ones. For instance, in Figure 2, it is possible to note that the *getPackage* operation, provided by the *TravelSrv* service, requires the *getFlight* operation, provided by the *FlightSrv* service. As a conclusion, the *TravelSrv* service requires the *getFlight* operation. Besides, the *TravelSrv* service depends on the *FlightSrv* service.

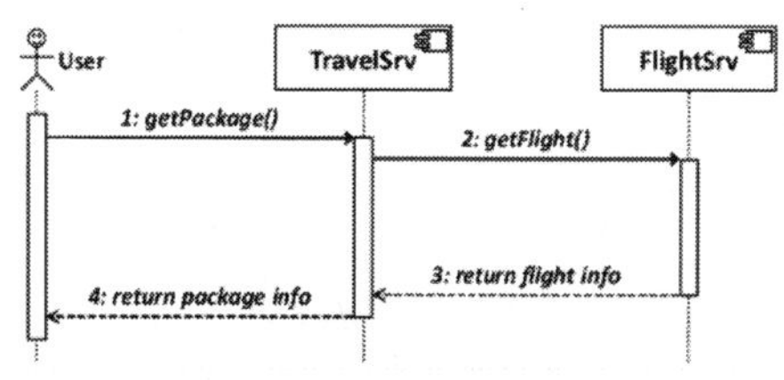

Figure 2. Service Dependency in a Sequence Diagram

After identifying provided and required operations, it is possible to generate an architecture specification that shows all constituting web services together with their dependencies (Figure 3). To do that, provided and required operations are respectively organized in provided and required interfaces, making the architecture specification to appear like those adopted in component-based development processes [14]. As can be noted, each service dependency is characterized by connecting the related services through their provided and required interfaces.

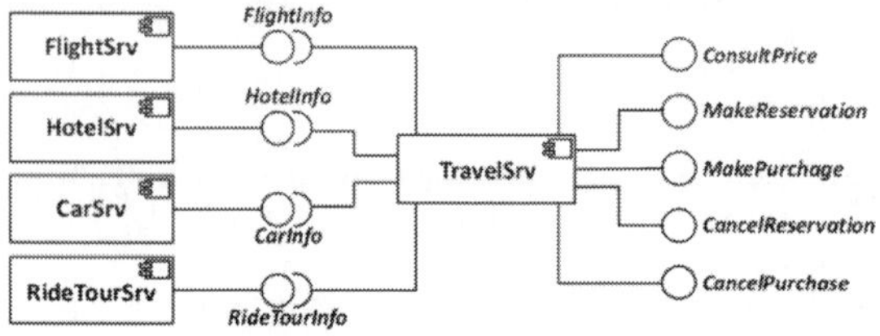

Figure 3. Architectural View for Service Dependencies

B. Functional and Structural Metrics

As already discussed, the proposed approach selects candidate web services by evaluating integration effectiveness through functional and structural metrics that evaluate the functionalities associated with candidate web services, as well as their dependencies. On the one hand, the structural metric evaluates how effective is the link between each pair of dependent services. On the other hand, the functional metric evaluates how similar are the specification and the implementation of web services.

In order to measure the structural metric, it is necessary to evaluate how effective is the integration between the required interface of the requester service and the provided interface of the provider service. Figure 4 characterizes a link, including associated services and interfaces, which together define all entities to be considered in measuring the structural metric.

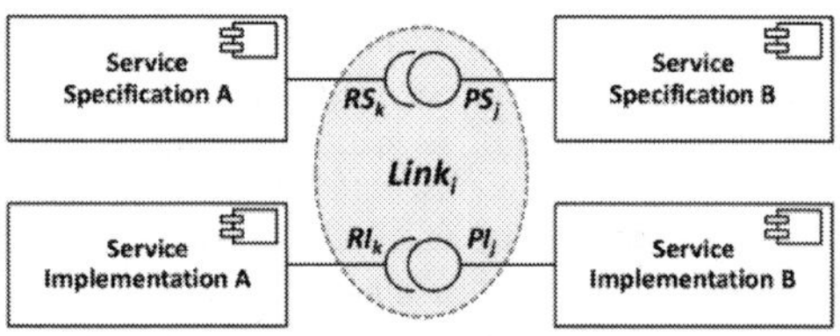

Figure 4. Characterization of a Link

As can be observed, each link is characterized in terms of two interfaces in the architecture specification and two interfaces in the candidate architecture configuration: RS_i - required interface of the requester service specification; PS_i - provided interface of the provider service specification; RI_i - required interface of the requester service implementation; and PI_i - provided interface of the provider service implementation.

Taking into account such interfaces, it is important to note that the greater the number of operations in common in such interfaces the better the integration effectiveness. Consequently, as indicated in (1), the value of the structural metric for a link can be defined by the relation between the number of operations in common in the related interfaces and the total number of operations in the required interfaces of both the requester service specification and implementation. As defined, the value of the structural metric for a link is in the interval [0, 1], where the closer to 1 is the value, the better is the integration effectiveness, and so, the lower is the adaptation effort.

$$L_i = \frac{|(RS_i \cap PS_i) \cap (RI_i \cap PI_i)|}{|(RS_i \cup RI_i)|} \qquad (1)$$

As can be observed in (1), the denominator includes operations in required interfaces only. The reason for that is the premise adopted in the proposed approach which states the following: *superfluous operations in provided interfaces do not represent extra adaptation effort*. In other words, non-used provided operations in the provider service do not impose adaptation effort in the requester service.

Now, considering all links in the architecture specification, as indicated in (2), the value of the structural metric for the whole architecture is defined by the relation between the total sum of the structural metric for each link and the total number of links in the architecture (L). Thus, the value of the structural metric for the architecture is also between [0, 1], where the closer to 1 the value, the better the candidate architectural configuration.

$$A_x = \sum_{i=1}^{L} \frac{L_i}{L} \qquad (2)$$

Unlike the structural metric that evaluates dependencies among services, the functional metric contrasts web service specifications against their correspondent candidate implementations, evaluating their similarity in terms of provided and required interfaces. In other words, a candidate service implementation imposes a lesser amount of adaptation effort when its provided and required interfaces are more similar in relation to the corresponding interfaces in the service specification.

In order to measure the functional metric for a given service, as illustrated in Figure 5, it is necessary to evaluate the functional metric for each provided and required interface of the service.

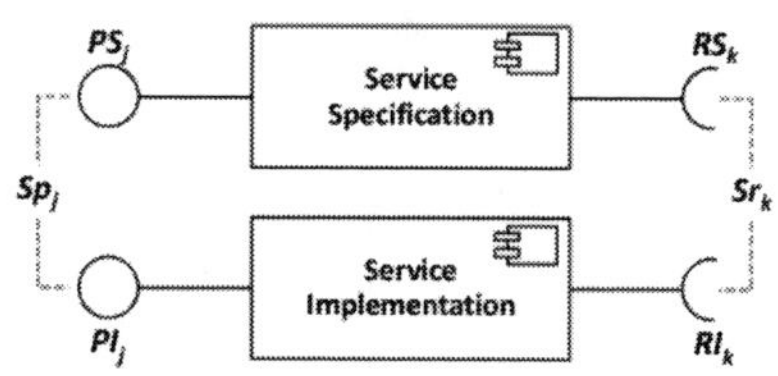

Figure 5. Characterization of Similarity

Considering correspondent provided interfaces in the service specification and implementation, it is important to note that the greater the number of operations in common in such interfaces the better the integration effectiveness. Thus, as indicated in (3), the value of the functional metric for a given provided interface can be calculated by the relation between the number of operations in common in the provided interfaces in the service specification and implementation divided by the number of operations in the provided interface in the service specification. Here, once again, the proposed approach assumes that superfluous operations in provided interfaces do not represent extra adaptation effort, and so, the denominator in (3) does not consider operations in the provided interface in the service implementation.

$$Sp_j = \frac{|PS_j \cap PI_j|}{|PS_j|} \quad (3)$$

Now, considering correspondent required interfaces in the service specification and implementation, the greater the number of operations in common in such interfaces the better the integration effectiveness. Thus, as indicated in (4), the value of the functional metric for a given required interface can be calculated by the relation between the number of operations in common in the required interfaces divided by the total number of operations in such interfaces conjointly.

$$Sr_k = \frac{|RS_k \cap RI_k|}{|RS_k \cup RI_k|} \quad (4)$$

Equations (3) and (4) evaluate individually each provided and required interface in a given service. As defined, the values of the functional metrics Sp_j and Sr_k are also in the interval [0, 1], where the closer to 1 the value, the better the provided or required interface.

Now, it is needed to derive the functional metric for the service as a whole, revealing how similar are provided and required operations in the service specification and implementation. Thus, considering all provided and required interfaces of a given service specification, as indicated in (5), the value of the functional metric for the service is defined by the relation in which the numerator is the total sum of the functional metric for each required and provided interface of the service, while the denominator is the total number of required and provided interfaces of the service. As defined, the value of the functional metric for a given service is also in the interval [0, 1], where the closer to 1 the value, the better the candidate web service.

$$S_i = \frac{\sum_{k=1}^{|RS \cup RI|} Sr_i + \sum_{j=1}^{|PS|} Sp_j}{|RS \cup RI| + |PS|} \quad (5)$$

As can be seen in (5), in terms of required interfaces, the functional metric comprises the number of required interfaces in both the service specification and implementation conjointly ($|RS \cup RI|$). However, in terms of provided interfaces, the functional metric for the service comprises the number of provided interfaces in the service specification only ($|PS|$). Note that, once more, it is supposed that superfluous provided interfaces in the service implementation do not represent extra adaptation effort, and so, the terms in (5) do not account for provided interfaces in the service implementation (PI).

At this point, considering all candidate services in the architecture configuration, as indicated in (6), the value of the functional metric for the whole architecture is defined by the relation between the total sum of the functional metric for each service and the total number of services in the architecture (S). Thus, the value of the structural metric for the architecture is also between [0, 1], where the closer to 1 the value, the better the candidate architectural configuration.

$$C_x = \sum_{i=1}^{S} \frac{S_i}{S} \quad (6)$$

Finally, functional and structural metrics should be combined together in order to derive the fitness function adopted in the metaheuristic search technique, more specifically a genetic algorithm. In such a direction, the fitness function is defined in (7) as a normalized weighted mean of the functional and structural metrics, in which the terms w_c and w_a represent their respective normalized weights. As can be noticed, the value of the fitness function is in the interval [0, 1], where the closer to 1 the value, the better the candidate architectural configuration in terms of adaptation effort.

$$F_x = w_c . C_x + w_a . A_x \begin{cases} 0 \leq w_c \leq 1 \\ 0 \leq w_a \leq 1 \\ w_c + w_a = 1 \end{cases} \quad (7)$$

V. Experimental Evaluation

In order to conduct an experimental evaluation, the proposed approach was implemented in the Java platform. In such experiments, the genetic algorithm is parametrized as follows. For each generation, the population is equal to 300 candidate architecture configurations. The stopping criterion is reached when the highest ranking solution's fitness becomes stable in a plateau during 25 successive iterations and no longer produce better results. The selection of candidate solutions to breed a new generation is based on the tournament method. For breeding a next generation, the uniform crossover method is adopted, together with a mutation ratio of 20%. Finally, the normalized weights w_c and w_s included in the fitness function adopt both the value 0,5, representing an equal contribution for the functional and structural metrics.

The experimental evaluation was performed using a typical architecture specification composed of five web service specifications and six dependencies among them. Each web service specification has 30 candidate implementations, generating a search space size equal to 30^5. The evaluation takes place in three different scenarios, varying the number of specifications that have perfect implementations: *(i)* all specifications with perfect candidates; *(ii)* three specifications with perfect candidates; and *(iii)* absence of perfect candidates. Such scenarios make possible to evaluate the proposed approach in the presence or absence of perfect candidates, including something in the middle.

For each scenario, the proposed approach was compared against the exhaustive search and the random search. In such a comparison, the proposed approach and the random search have been executed 1000 times, and the mean value of the highest ranking solution's fitness is computed. Besides, the exhaustive search has been executed just one time for discovering the optimal solution. As show in Figure 6, experimental results reveal that, in all scenarios, the proposed approach has always found the optimal solution, which is confirmed by the exhaustive search. Due to that, in such experiments, standards deviations are equal to zero, and so, confidence intervals are not estimated.

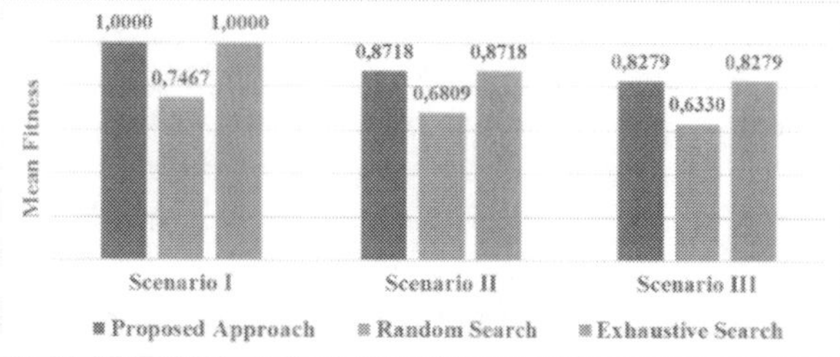

Figure 6. Experimental Results

Besides, in relation to random searches, in the first scenario, in which all specifications have perfect candidates, the solutions recommended by the proposed approach are around 33,92% more efficient than those recommended by random searches, according to the fitness function in (7). In the second scenario, in which three specifications have perfect candidates, the efficiency of the proposed approach in relation to random searches is reduced to approximately 28,04%. Finally, in the last scenario, in which there is an absence of perfect candidates, the efficiency of the proposed approach becomes stable around 30,79%. It is important to stress that, in the best cases, the efficiency ratios turned to 50,56%, 42,85% and 51,35%, respectively.

As another interesting outcome, it must be highlighted the low processing cost of the proposed approach, which can be perceived by its fast convergence around 0,3 seconds, against the exhaustive search that takes around 300 seconds. In all scenarios, the genetic algorithm has converged on average between 5 and 7 generations, ranging from 2 generations in the best cases to 19 generations in the worst cases.

VI. Concluding Remarks

Considering the relevance of web service selection in the context of SOA-based software development, this paper represents an interesting contribution by presenting an automated approach based on functional and structural metrics. The approach provides measures that evaluate the functionalities provided by candidate web services, as well as their dependencies at the architectural level. Besides, the approach proposes a heuristic selection algorithm based on Genetic Algorithms, which has low processing cost and mitigates the chances of suggesting a local optimum.

Despite their key contributions, previous work has largely been concerned with non-functional requirements. Differently, the proposed approach deals with functional and structural properties, which clearly represents its main contribution. As an additional contribution, the proposed approach represents an extremely complex problem in a systematic and structured way, discovering good-enough or even optimal solutions among candidate web services.

Experimental outcomes demonstrate the effectiveness of the proposed approach not only in terms of the quality of the recommend solutions, but also in terms of low processing cost in all evaluated scenarios. Despite contributions and benefits, as future work, the proposed approach needs to be evaluated in more complex scenarios, composed by a large number of highly interconnected services. It is important to note that, in such future experiments, the expectation is to find more interesting results, once that, generally, metaheuristic-based approaches can find better results in contrast with random search in scenarios with large search spaces.

Acknowledgment

This work was supported by the National Institute of Science and Technology for Software Engineering (INES – www.ines.org.br), funded by CNPq, grants 573964/2008-4.

References

[1] I. Sommerville, "Software engineering", 9th edition, Addison-Wesley, 2011.

[2] OASIS, "Reference model for service oriented architecture 1.0", Committee Specification 1, 2006.

[3] Q. H. Mahmoud, "A service-oriented architecture (SOA) and web services: the road to enterprise application integration (EAI)", 2005. http://www.oracle.com/ technetwork/articles/ javase/soa-142870.html [retrieved: May, 2016].

[4] S. Becker, A. Brogi, I. Gorton, S. Overhage, A. Romanovsky, and M. Tivoli, "Towards an engineering approach to component adaptation", Springer-Verlang. 2006.

[5] G. Feng, C. Wang, and H. Li, "Web services based cross-organizational business process management", 7th Asia-Pacific Web Conference, 2005, pp. 548-559.

[6] M. Harman and B. F. Jones, "Search-based software engineering", Information and Software Technology, vol. 43, 2001, pp. 833-839.

[7] M. Harman, "Why the virtual nature of software makes it ideal for search based optimization", 13th International Conference on Fundamental Approaches to Software Engineering, 2010, pp. 1-12.

[8] R. Linden, "Genetic algorithms: an important tool for computational intelligence", 2nd edition, Brasport, Rio de Janeiro, 2008 (in portuguese).

[9] H. Fetthallah, M. A. Chikh, and D. Y. Mohammed, "QoS-aware service selection based on genetic algorithm", 3rd International Conference on Computer Science and its Applications, 2011, pp. 291-300.

[10] A. Lifeng and M. Tang, "A penalty-based genetic algorithm for QoS-aware web service composition with inter-service dependencies and conflicts", 3rd International Conference on Computational Intelligence for Modelling Control and Automation, 2008, pp. 738-743.

[11] A. Vescan, "A metrics-based evolutionary approach for the component selection problem", 11th International Conference on Computer Modeling and Simulation, 2009, pp. 83-88.

[12] Z. Maamar, Q. Z. Sheng, and B. Benatallah, "Selection of web services for composition using location of provider hosts criterion", CAiSE Workshops, 2003, pp. 67-76.

[13] Q. C. Tang and H. K. Cheng, "Optimal location and pricing of web services intermediary", Decision Support Systems, vol. 40, issue 1, 2005, pp. 129-141.

[14] J. Cheesman and J. Daniels, "UML components: a simple process for specifying component-based software", Addison-Wesley, 2001.

Simulation of Real Time Multi Radar Data With a Non-Real Time Simulator

Atakan Simsek, Dr. Ahmet Murat Ozdemiray, Dr. Alper Yildirim
TUBITAK BILGEM Advanced Technologies Research Institute, Ankara, Turkey
Email: {atakan.simsek,murat.ozdemiray,alper.yildirim}@tubitak.gov.tr

Abstract—**Radar Warning Receiver is a type of Military Airborne Radar system, which works based on a predefined scheduling algorithm that uses Radar Scan Table. In real life, these tables' time measurement unit is milliseconds (could be less than one millisecond for specific radar types). When Radar Warning Receiver System is part of a Radar Defense System, determinism and time accuracy become vital properties to have. To satisfy these properties, a real-time simulation environment is necessary. Since real-time simulator development process is challenging and time-consuming, we propose a technique which simulates real-time multi-radar data using non-real time radar simulator. Our technique achieves this by managing simulation network.**

Keywords–Simulation Network; Radar Simulator; Network Management

I. INTRODUCTION

Radar Warning Receiver (RWR) systems are widely used for detecting signals from other radar systems [1][2][4]. These systems warn the pilot if there are emitters in the range of the RWR. These warnings are handled by, manually or automatically based on the usage type. Military RWR systems are more complicated than the commercial RWR systems, since the latter only use specific radar bands [5]. More sophisticated systems can classify emitter type by using signal strength, phase, waveform and other signal properties.

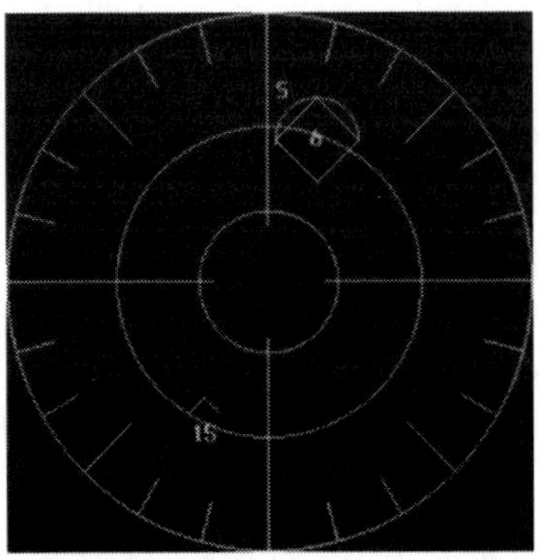

Figure 1. Threat Warning Indicator [8]

In military domain, RWR systems generally have a Threat Warning Indicator (TWI) display, depicted in Figure 1 [8], in the cockpit. Pilot uses this display to track friend or enemy emitters (threats). Airborne RWR system consists of different band antennas placed around the air platform. A receiver uses these antennas for scanning different frequency bands periodically [4].

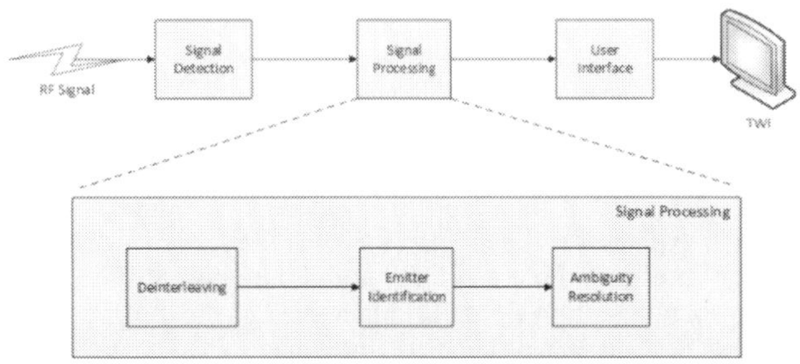

Figure 2. RWR Flow

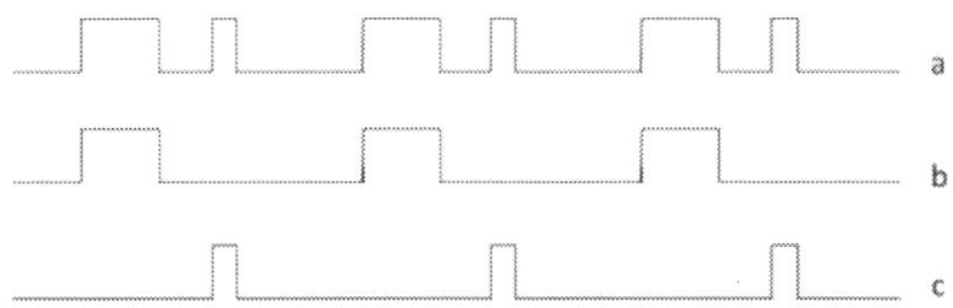

Figure 3. Deinterleaving

An RWR system can be defined by three major modules: Signal Detection, Signal Processing and User Interface. At Signal Detection Module, receivers sense the emitter signals and determine emitter parameters such as frequency, time of arrival, direction of arrival, pulse repetition frequency, pulse repetition interval, etc. These parameters are combined to define Pulse Descriptor Word (PDW). PDWs are analyzed and deinterleaved to infer emitter radar characteristics. Figure 3 'a' illustrates combined pulses of 2 emitters. Figure 3 'b' and 'c' depicts separated pulses after deinterleaving operation. Deinterleaved PDWs are used for Threat Identification process. PDWs are matched with previously known emitter records. If matching process results in only one emitter, the emitter is identified. If it results in more than one emitter, the ambiguity problem is solved by intelligent algorithms. The identified emitters are shown on the TWI and the pilot is warned with predefined icons on the display.

RWR systems can be defined as passive systems because they only receive frequency signals from emitters and do not emit any signals. RWR systems can be used for tracking the threats in order to take some counter measures [3].

The functionality of RWR Systems can be summarized as:

- Radio Frequency signal detection
- Radar type signal identification

Figure 4. Signal Bands

TABLE I. SIMPLE SCAN SCHEDULE

Band ID	Dwell Time (millisecond)
0	10
1	50
2	60

- Detected signal management
- Visual and audio warning generation

The rest of this paper is organized as follows. Section II will explain real time requirements in RWR domain. Section III will present problem definition and our approach to solve this problem. Section IV will explain network flow of our solution and Section V will conclude the paper.

II. Real-Time Conditions

An RWR system needs look-up tables in order to prepare scan schedule algorithm and identify emitter types. Radar Scan Table (RST) is used for defining scan steps and Mode Table is used for defining emitter specific parameters. These tables are defined in the Mission Data File (MDF) and loaded into RWR before the operation. Therefore, RWR is a configurable system according to mission specific needs. The "Dwell Time" field of the RST represents 'sensing time of a specific target on that frequency band'. One important requirement of RWR systems is to produce enough number of PDWs in an exact Dwell time (these PDWs will be used to analyze and identify the emitter type correctly). Dwell time can be changeable according to mission requirements but its time measurement unit is milliseconds for military RWR systems. RWR management software (RWR-MS) should accomplish these dwells in millisecond time resolution. Moreover, in some cases this value may be decreased to microseconds.

In Figure 4 there are three different signal bands (2GHz - 3GHz, 3GHz - 6GHz, 6GHz - 18GHz). Basic scan schedule can be constructed as seen in Table I. A more realistic scan schedule can be seen in Table II.

It should be emphasized that, producing enough number of PDWs, which will be used for emitter identification, in exact dwell time is the most important requirement of an RWR. Therefore, RWR Management Software should be developed with a simulator or an environment, which ensures that at specific dwell time an emitter emits within a specified frequency band and the emitter should stop emitting exactly at the end of the dwell time. Non real time operating systems cannot supply this requirement, because they cannot guarantee the determinism. Radar Scan Tables are constructed based on tight scheduling and determinism assumption. Therefore, a real time operating systems should be used in RWR systems. "PDW production count in exact dwell time" requirement can be tested only by intersecting the emitter and receiver schedules in exact time accuracy. Therefore, a real time simulator should be used to test the RWR system capability. In our study, we prepared a network environment, which satisfies real time scheduling requirement and employs standard emitter simulator instead of a real time emitter simulator. It is achieved by looking the problem from a different perspective. In our solution, emitter and receiver schedules are not intersected. Instead, emitter schedule covers the receiver schedule for each dwell.

TABLE II. MORE REALISTIC SCAN SCHEDULE

Band ID	Dwell Time (millisecond)
0	5
1	25
2	30
1	10
0	5
2	15
1	15
2	15

III. Proposed Solution

In this section, we will define the problem and propose our solution. Moreover, we will discuss the concepts and components needed to understand our approach.

A. Problem Definition

In military research and development projects, commercial products usually cannot be used for security reasons. Therefore when a new project starts, its development environment also should be developed parallel with main project (especially in the projects requiring state of the art technologies). If simulators or other development environment elements are complex products, their developments may last nearly half or full time of the main project development period. At that situation, main projects cannot use these elements in development period. In our case, same situation happens and we cannot use real time radar simulator in development phase of main project. Therefore, we simulates real time radar simulator with existing simple radar simulator. In this paper, we introduce a solution which solves an industry problem by managing network components and network flow. The novel approach of this paper is setting up a complex development environment by using existing products and network components. The purpose of this solution is achieving the functionality of real time simulator. Performance comparison with other real time simulators is beyond the scope of this paper because these simulators are military specific products and their technical specifications are not publicly reachable.

B. Our Solution

The proposed system can be divided into two sub units: RWR Unit and Simulator Unit. They are deployed into different hardwares (Figure 5).

- *Threat Warning Indicator*: This component represents the graphical components of RWR. The pilot can see the emitters and send commands by using this component.

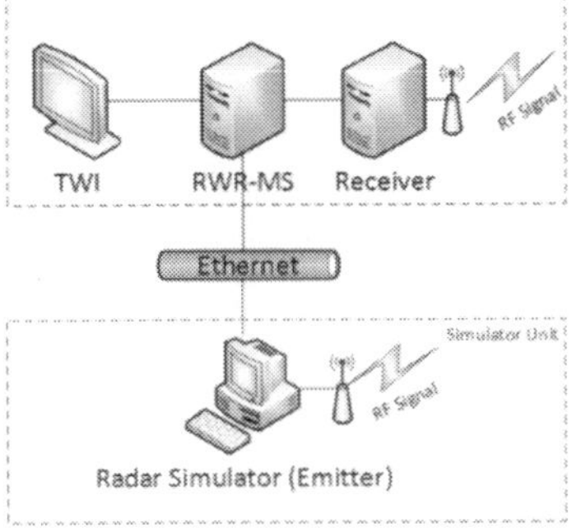

Figure 5. System Components

TABLE III. RST

RST ID	Dwell Period	Dwell Time	Freq Band Min	Freq Band Max
0	150	10	2000	3000
1	1200	50	3000	6000
2	500	60	6000	18000

- *RWR Management Software*: It is the main software which, manages RWR states and operations. It interacts with all of the RWR system to send commands and receive responses. RWR-MS gets PDW data from the Receiver and detects the emitter identity. "ScanControl" is a class which manages scan operations among TWI, Receiver and Radar Simulator. It works on a Single Board Computer. In order to supply determinism, time accuracy and other real time conditions, VxWorks 6.9 Real Time Operating System is used.
- *Receiver*: This component receives emitter signals and converts them into PDWs. It consists from the Radar Receiver Antenna and a Curtiss Wright FPGA hardware board.
- *Radar Simulator (RadSim)*: This is an existing Multi-emitter simulator. It can simulate up-to 4 different emitter simultaneously. It consists from Intel architecture single board computer and FPGA hardware unit. Radar parameters can be entered via graphical user interfaces. Radar parameters are deployed to its hardware unit via previously developed "Windows Forms Application". This unit has signal generating and emitting property. In this solution, its application was modified to communicate with RWR-MS software.

RWR-MS "MDF-Reader" class reads Mission Data File from hard disc and serves RST and Mode Tables to the related classes (Table III and Table IV):

Table III fields are as follows:

TABLE IV. MODE TABLE

Mode ID	Emit ID	Freq Min	Freq Max	PRI Min	PRI Max	PW Min	PW Max
1	1	2500	2600	5000000	5600000	1200	1400
2	1	3300	3400	4500000	4900000	1400	1700
3	2	2700	2750	7500000	7700000	3500	3550

- *Dwell Period*: RWR receiver should sense this Frequency Band at least one "Dwell Time" in this period.
- *Dwell Time*: Exact time required to scan on that specific band.
- *Freq Band Min-Max*: Frequency range minimum/maximum value.

Table IV fields are as follows:

- *Emitter ID*: This id identifies Mode belongs to which emitter.
- *Freq Min-Max*: These fields identify frequency range.
- *PRI Min-Max*: These fields identify Pulse Repetition Interval (PRI) range. PRI is the elapsed time from beginning of one pulse to beginning of the next pulse.
- *PW Min-Max*: These fields identify Pulse Width (PW) range. PW is the length of time between the rise and decay of a pulse.

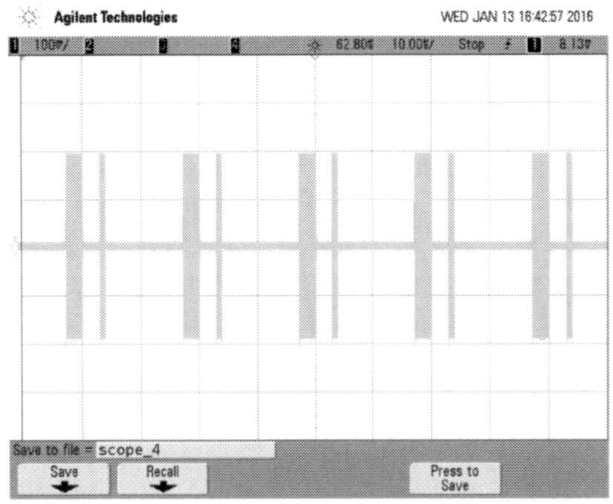

Figure 6. Radar Simulator Output (Oscilloscope Screen)

IV. SIMULATION NETWORK

This section describes the network flow step by step. Figure 7 represents the data flow diagram between components and Figure 8 represents the sequence diagram. At the initialization period of the RWR-MS, ScanControl module starts as a new process and this process runs as a loop until the RWR system is shut down. The "Reader" class reads MDF file into memory; RST and Mode tables are created. At the beginning of each ScanControl loop, dwell data is read from RST and indexes of related Mode (Radar running mode) Table entries are calculated. Next, Ethernet communication class sends indexes of these modes to RadSim. Simultaneously, same MDF file is loaded into RadSim before simulation starts. Using the same configuration files allows us to send only related modes indexes instead of all data in mode table; in order to manage data traffic between RadSim and ScanControl efficiently. As an example, "1,3,-1,-1" is a valid message from ScanControl to RadSim, which represents two valid Radar modes in this Dwell with the mode indexes 1 and 3 respectively. Since RadSim can simulate up-to four different radars at the same time, -1 is inserted in the message to represent the empty radar slot.

TABLE V. DWELL TIME ACCURACY

Experiment Number	Simulated Radar	RST Dwell Time (millisecond)	Look Dwell Time (millisecond)	Extracted PDW Count	Correct Emitter Identification	Ambiguous Property
1	Search Radar 1	5	3	6	No	Unknown PRI Type
2	Search Radar 1	5	4	6	No	Unknown PRI Type
3	Search Radar 1	5	5	23	Yes	Correct
4	Search Radar 2	10	8	37	No	MDF Match Ambiguity
5	Search Radar 2	10	9	51	Yes	Correct
6	Search Radar 2	10	10	54	Yes	Correct

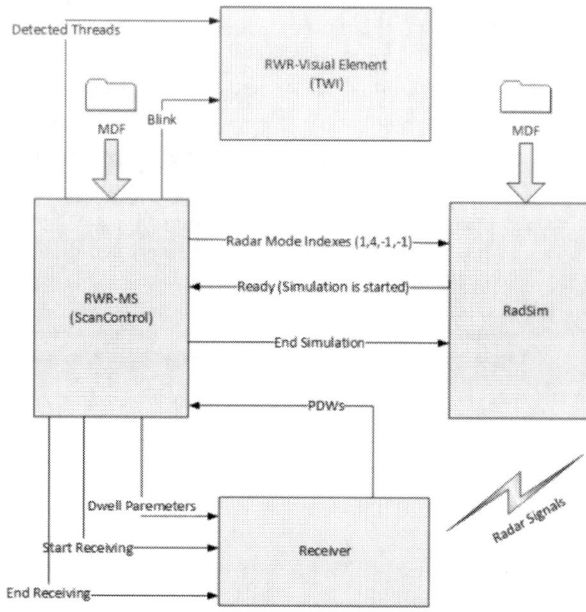

Figure 7. Network Flow

At the start of the simulation, RadSim reads Mode table in MDF and loads radar parameters. After this step is completed, RadSim starts to generate radar signals (Figure 6 shows the Oscilloscope screen of RadSim output) and "Simulation is started" message is sent to ScanContol as an acknowledgment message. At the same time, RWR-MS reads RST to adjust receiver parameters. ScanControl waits for this RadSim acknowledge message when the receiver is ready. When RadSim "Simulation is started" message is received, RWR-MS starts the timer and opens the receiver antennas for the specified dwell time period. The receiver stops when the dwell time is completed. As the sequence diagram shows in Figure 8, RWR-MS opens the Receiver antennas after RadSim starts simulation. Also, the Receiver antennas are closed after exact dwell time while RadSim continues to generate radar signal. This mechanism ensures that Radar Scan Table time accuracy constraint is exactly applied.

Subsequently, the system passes to the next dwell and same operations are repeated. Simultaneously, another process in RWR-MS reads the produced PDWs from the Receiver. These PDWs are used to identify the emitter type and other parameters by related modules. When emitters are detected, they are sent to TWI to warn the pilot (Figure 10). Total full scan time cannot exceed one second, independent from the Dwell count. When a full scan is completed; a blink message is sent to display to warn the pilot.

If we use real time simulator, there will be no interaction between RWR-MS and Simulator modules. Before simulation, both RWR and Real Time Simulator are programmed with predefined Mission Data Files. Simulator only emits data according to its MDF and RWR only sense data according to its MDF. We prepare this network environment and handshake protocol to intersect their schedule exactly for each frequency band. In our solution, we use Gigabit Ethernet and TCP for network communications.

We carried out some experiments to show importance of dwell time accuracy and to validate our simulator (Table V). In this table, our Radar Simulator simulates two different Search Radars. In the 1th and 2nd experiment, receiver should sense 5 milliseconds according to RST but for experimental purpose it senses less than 5 milliseconds between frequency band 2000-3000 MHz. In such situations, search radar frequency band and our receiver frequency band are not intersected. Therefore less than necessary PDWs are extracted from receiver module for 1th and 2nd experiment. The RWR-MS module performs emitter identification operation but the emitter is not correctly identified because of inadequate data. Same situation occurs for 4th experiment. These results show that dwell time accuracy is very important for RWR and it should be developed/tested with a precise simulator. For 3rd and 6th experiment, correct accuracy is supplied and emitter identification is done successfully. Note that, 5th experiment is correctly finished but this situation is undeterministic.

In another experiment, our simulator is tested with a more complex scenario. In this experiment, our simulator simulates two moving emitters. In the first dwell, Emitter A is emitting at frequency 3400 MHz and Emitter B is emitting at 3700 MHz. In the second dwell, our simulator changes frequencies. Emitter A's new frequency is 2600 MHz and Emitter B's new frequency is 2200 MHz. Figure 9 shows the timeline of this experiment. In this figure:

- T0: First dwell, simulator starts simulation
- T1: First dwell, RWR starts sensing
- T2: First dwell, RWR ends sensing
- T3: First dwell, simulator ends simulation
- T4: Second dwell, simulator starts simulation
- T5: Second dwell, RWR starts sensing

Our solution guarantees that, $T_0 < T_1$ and $T_3 > T_2$ intuitively owing to its design characteristic. For a single dwell,

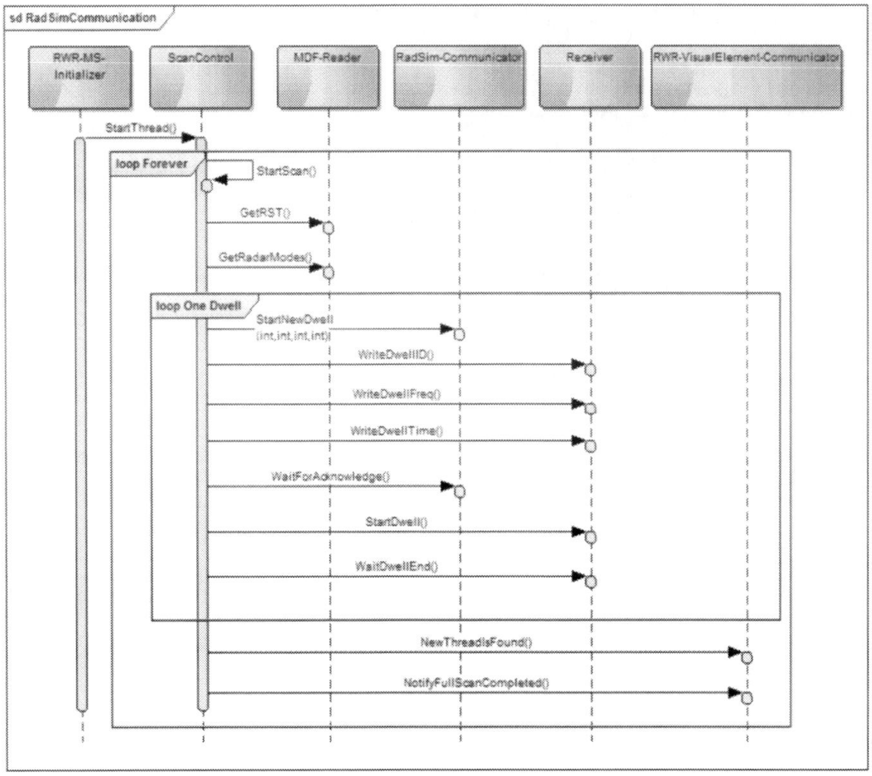

Figure 8. Flow Sequence Diagram

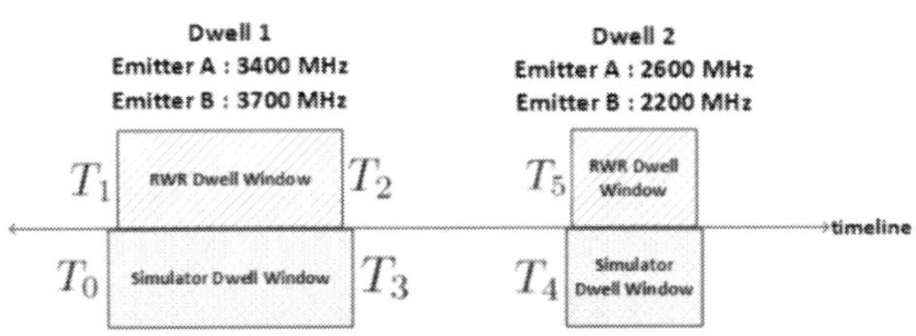

Figure 9. Simulation Timeline

emitting requirement is tested in Table V. Therefore, in this experiment we investigate its dwell switching capability. We have $(T_3 - T_2) + (T_5 - T_4)$ amount of extra latency in dwell switching time. In this experiment we find this value as 0.24 millisecond (average value for 10 runs). Main reason for this loss is TCP overhead and simulator load time. We prepare an experiment to compare Ethernet protocols efficiencies and undeterminism. Table VI shows the result of our experiment. In this experiment 19200 byte data is send from sender to receiver. This experiment repeated 10000 times to find min,max and average values. Result shows that Raw Ethernet protocol can decrease latency but we plan to use 'Discrete Wires' to decrease latency minimum.

In this solution we use an existing simulator that its emitting capability, signal count and signal strength has already been validated in previous projects. For this new configuration, only its scheduling accuracy can be arguable but we do not

TABLE VI. ETHERNET PROTOCOLS

Protocol Name	Min Time (msec)	Average Time (msec)	Max Time (msec)
Raw Ethernet	0.085	0.1271	0.1562
UDP	0.131	0.151	0.234
TCP	0.215	0.284	0.445

change its characteristics. RWR-MS sends only start simulation and end simulation commands to this simulator. However the results in the Table V verify simulator scheduling accuracy because this results match up with our theoretical knowledge in RWR systems. In this experiment, we verify that our simulator works well in the selected single frequency band. Moreover, Figure 9 shows that, our solution has a latency value at dwell switching but our design compensates this. We know this handicap and we plan to solve this issue by changing network protocol as future work.

V. Conclusion and Future Work

In this paper, we present a simulator environment to simulate radar signals. We prepared a set-up which ensures that simulator signal is ready when receiver starts to scan. At the completion of the exact dwell time, receiver stops to collect data. We have shown that receiver collects radar signal in the exact dwell time period as required for successful operation. This enables us to solve RWR real time schedule requirement and simulate in a real time like environment. In our solution,

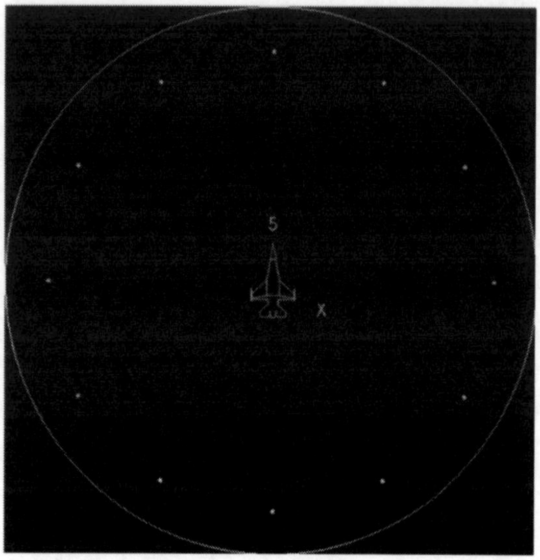

Figure 10. TWI Screen after Emitter Identification

the simulator also compensates the latency while switching is being performed between two dwells. As a future work, we plan to replace Ethernet connection with "Discrete Wires" to decrease network latency and undeterminism. We plan to change the design of RadSim to support Remote Procedure Call (RPC). We expect to decrease system jitter time and to increase determinism by using discrete wires and adding RPC functionality.

REFERENCES

[1] Peinecke, Niklas, Hans-Ullrich Doehler, and B. R. Korn, "Real-time millimeter wave radar simulation." Journal of Aerospace Information Systems 10.7 (2013): 337-347.

[2] C. B. Boettcher and R. Poster, "Object-Oriented Design Of Radar Warning Receiver Application Software", Digital Avionics Systems Conference, 1991. Proceedings., IEEE/AIAA 10th. IEEE

[3] F. Neri, "Introduction to Electronic Defense Systems", 2nd ed, MA, USA:Artech House, 2006

[4] Wikipedia.com, Radar Warning Receiver, 2015 [Online], Available:https://en.wikipedia.org/wiki/Radar_warning_receiver [retrieved 05,2016]

[5] Wikipedia.com, Radar Configurations and types, 2015 [Online], Available:https://en.wikipedia.org/wiki/Radar_configurations_and_types [retrieved 05,2016]

[6] J. W. S. Lui, "Real-Time Systems", Prentice Hall, 2000

[7] M. Dursun and O. Kizilay, "Zaman Tetikli Almac Planlayici Yazilim Bileseni Tasarimi", *UYMS*, 2014, pp.165-176

[8] Wikipedia.com, RWR Example, 2015 [Online], Available:https://en.wikipedia.org/wiki/File:Rwr_example.gif [retrieved 05,2016]

Open Source Tool for Networks Management Communication

Nuno Tiago Louro Simões
School of Technology and Management
Polytechnic Institute of Leiria
Leiria, Portugal
E-mail: 2130967@my.ipleiria.pt

Carlos Manuel da Silva Rabadão
Research Center for Informatics and Communications
Polytechnic Institute of Leiria
Leiria, Portugal
E-mail: carlos.rabadao@ipleiria.pt

Abstract—**Considering the complexity of the networks, one of the solutions for this complexity could be to centralize its configuration. Thus the *Software-Defined Networking* (SDN) concept may be an important solution. This paper suggests the implementation of a tool to support the development and testing of networks and services before they are put into production. The use of a tool that simplifies the configuration of a network service makes the networks and services to be less susceptible to errors and failures by those who set them up, thus allowing telecom operators, among others, to be able to create new services, improve the monitorization of their human resources and, above all, improve their financial results. In the end, success will be achieved because with a simple interaction and basic knowledge we are able to manage network services.**

Keywords - SDN; network services; network programming; NSO.

I. Introduction

The number of electronic devices with Internet access has been increasing in recent years [1]. Nowadays, it is even possible to have Internet access with a simple watch. With the appearance of these devices along with the advances in Information technology (IT), telecom operators need to introduce new features to capture the customer's attention. One of these innovations could be the creation of new services in the network. One of the problems that the creation of new services currently faces is the congestion that the network has. This makes the configuration of networks complex and increases the difficulty in creating new services. Nevertheless, operators have been able to manage both the network and the services, but it is natural that they are susceptible to failure by those who manage and implement them. This process is typically done by a human. Most failures stem from several factors, including pressure caused by the need to put new services quickly on the market or by the routine repetition of processes that limit the potential of the network [2].

We can hardly develop a perfect *software* immune to failures and errors, but there are methods that can be used to try to prevent them, for example, the use of *scripts*. *Scripts* allow us to automate some tasks. As these *scripts* are developed by humans, they will be susceptible to failures and errors, even if they are unintentional.

Taking into account the foregoing considerations, the scientific community has been looking for new approaches that can help to reduce limitations. This area is explained in the next sections. Considering the increasing number of people using devices with internet access and the consequent increase of the network complexity, we are motivated to develop an application to help in the service and network management so that it can be innovated and improved. The aim of this paper is to present the development of a tool, based on the concept of SDN, which allows the testing of a network and the implementation of services before they are produced.

Concerning the management of services, one of the approaches associated to it is the SDN concept. SDN is the basis of this work, which will be introduced in Section II. In this section we will present some SDN solutions existing in the market, as well as some of the technologies used. In Section III, we will present the proposed architecture that supports this work. The architecture contributes to the mitigation of previously presented problems. In Section IV, we will explain the implementation of our proposal. Finally, in the last section, we will present the conclusions and suggestions to work.

II. Software-Defined Networking

This section initially presents some concepts for a better understanding of the article. After, we will introduce some commercial SDN solutions that exist in the market and some technologies used for the implementation of the tool created.

A. Background

According to the *Open Networking Foundation*, the SDN is the physical separation of the control plane and the forwarding plane of the network [3]. With SDN concept, the networks will be configured and managed in a centralized way [4], facilitating the development of new *standards* and services. The SDN concept emerged at the same time as other technological solutions, from which the need motivated by complexity in the network arises. These needs combined with the fact that operators need to put more services in the market, as soon as possible, turn the process more complex and more likely to fail.

The purpose of SDN is to make the management of the network easier and transform the network programmable [5]. Thus, it simplifies the understanding of the network, which means that operators can do their job quicker and easier, according to the *time-to-market's* factor. Consequently, the operators may have good financial profits, which is an advantage.

Now we will present some of the existing SDN solutions: *Virtualized Services Controller* (VSC), by the internal company of Alcatel-Lucent, the Nuage Networks [6] [7] and

Network Control System (NCS) [8] by Tail-f, currently owned by Cisco portfolio.

B. SDN solutions

In this subsection we will make a brief analysis of each SDN solutions studied.

1) Virtualized Services Controller (VSC)

VSC, based on *Alcatel-Lucent Service Router OS* [9], is the SDN solution control panel of Nuage Networks and the most powerful SDN controller in the industry [7] [10]. VSC works in similar way to the network control plane for the data center, because it has a complete view of the network and its services. VSC automatically discovers network parameters, whatever type they are: Layer 2 (*switching*), Layer 3 (*routing*), *Quality of Service* (QoS) or security rules. In the VSC, the connection between the controller and the network routing is established through the communication protocol - *OpenFlow* [11]. This protocol allows the communication between the service controller and the network layer where it should find the hardware, i.e., the *hypervisor* and *vSwitch* [12].

2) Network Control System (NCS)

The NCS is the solution to control the network established by Tail-f. Later Cisco acquired Tail-f Company and the name of the SDN solution set was changed to "*Cisco Network Service Orchestrator* (NSO) *enabled by Tail-f*" [8]. The NSO is nothing more than a transparent layer, or interface, for those who configure the network. The NSO was meant to facilitate the creation and configuration of network services [13]. This solution is independent of brands and network equipment manufacturers, whether it is real or virtual. This SDN solution can be used to interact with both users/network administrators as well as with management applications that are already used in a network.

To sum up, all SDN solutions up to now are more or less similar. They are all are composed by three parts: implementation, monitoring and infrastructure/network equipment. This structure is more or less predictable given the SDN architecture.

C. Technologies used

This subsection will refer briefly to some technologies used or associated with the development of the proposed solution and also related to SDN. These technologies are: YANG, *extensible Markup Language* (XML) and *Network Configuration Protocol* (NETCONF).

1) YANG

The YANG is a data modelling language used for a data state configuration model. This language is used by the network configuration protocol - NETCONF - and is published in the *Request for Comments* (RFC) 6020 of September 2010. The YANG is related to the content and operations in layers of NETCONF [14].

2) XML

The XML is used to describe data. This shape can be easily used to read and write data. XML is adopted in many areas of information technology, including networks. It can be dynamic and it is very similar to the *Hypertext Markup Language* (HTML). We can consider that the construction of XML is done by blocks which are identified by *tags* [15].

3) NETCONF

The NETCONF is generically used to make the management of network devices configuration and it is based on the encoding in XML [16]. This protocol defines basic operations that are equivalent to commands to be executed from the *Command-Line Interface* (CLI). As in XML, NETCONF also uses *tags*. One of the manufacturers that uses NETCONF on its devices is Juniper Networks [17].

III. Architecture Proposal

In order to frame the solution/tool to propose, first we must present a logical structure of the SDN and after we will present the generic architecture of the solution developed.

The logical structure of the SDN, based on the same technology architecture, has three main layers, displayed in Figure 1 that are: *Application Plane*, *Control Plane* and *Data Plane*.

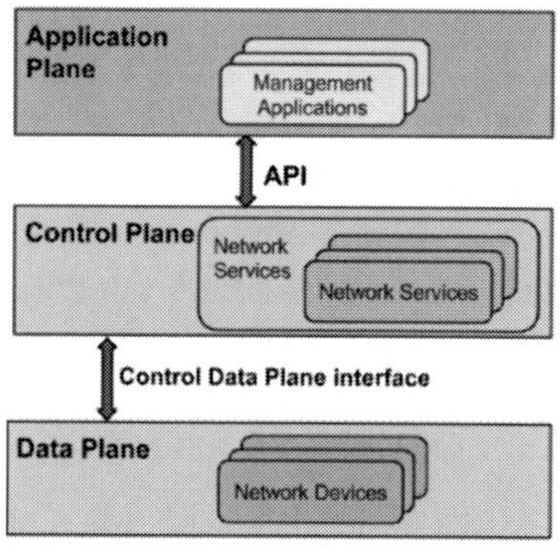

Figure 1. Logical structure of SDN

Next we will explain each layer mentioned above [18]:

- *Application Plane*: it can refer to some *net apps* such as orchestration applications, business applications and SDN applications;
- *Control Plane*: it aims to implement all coordination protocols that are necessary for the proper functioning of the *Data Plane*;
- *Data Plane*: it serves to analyze the headers of incoming packets and forward these packets to their final destination, depending on the routing and switching tables.

After presenting generically the SDN architecture, it is time to present an approach to SDN, more dedicated to network management, adopted to implement this work. The architecture shown in Figure 2 is quite simple, as it is divided into three layers: user, orchestration of the network and, finally, the network itself.

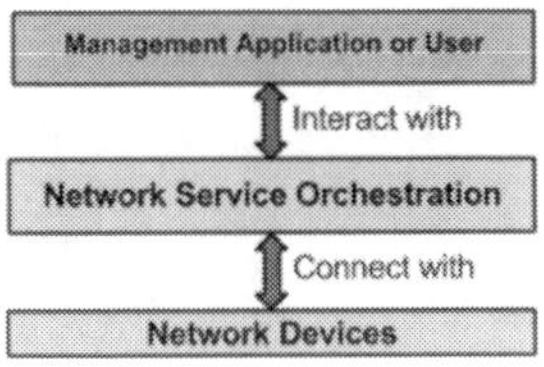

Figure 2. Generic architecture implementation performed

The architecture consists of three layers, described below:

- *Management Application or User:* this layer, as the name implies, is where the user, who will interact with the network, has the primary role and where we think he will spend most of the time;
- *Network Service Orchestration*: this is the "smart" layer of the presented architecture. In this layer the entire process will be unfolded. The Network Service Orchestration will interpret the user's *input* and transform it so that it can be applied to the network, which is the next and last layer to be presented;
- *Network devices*: this last layer is the physical infrastructure of the network. It is composed by the *core* and the access network, where it intends to apply the settings for network management and for the creation of services.

After presenting the generic architecture of the solution implemented, we will make a deeper analysis of the same.

A. Architecture used in the implementation

A more detailed architecture proposed for the development of this work is shown in Figure 3.

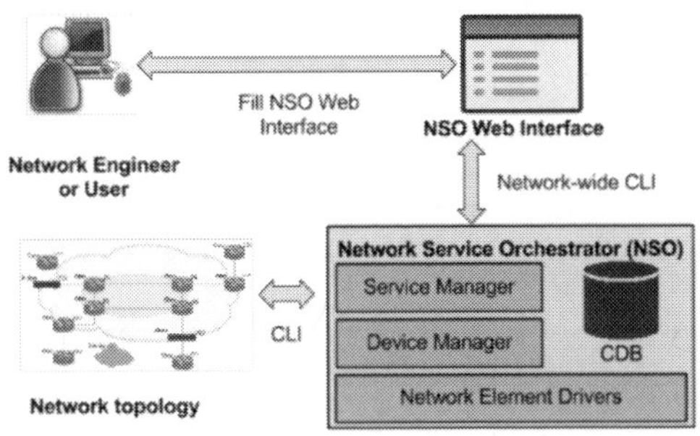

Figure 3. Architecture used in the proposal

In this figure we can observe that from the starting point (*Network Engineer or User*) to the end point (*Network Topology*), the user only interacts with a *WebUI* to configure the network mode as required. The *WebUI* is the point we have recreated, being more intuitive, specific and simpler to use, which is something new, compared to the existing tool. The novelty consists in the communication between the NSO and a *web interface*, as it is made through the Network-wide CLI and, as we can observe in the figure, this communication cam be bidirectional. The necessary mechanisms to convert the high-level user-made settings must be previously configured and implemented, allowing users with low technical level to proceed with the configuration of the network and services. Then the form communicates with the Network Service Orchestrator through the implementation made in *back-end* of *WebUI* and in command line. Note that this process is abstract to the final user. It is in the stage of communication between the NSO and the type of Network that all the fundamental processes for the correct operation of this took are taken. The NSO is divided into four parts (three layers and a part relating to data storage) [13]:

- *Service Manager*: this is where the intelligence of the NSO tool is. This layer enables the operator to manage high-level aspects of the network that are not supported by the devices that are directly connected to it. The services should be defined previously. It is from here that the management (creation, editing or deletion) of network services will be made;
- *Device Manager*: its function is to manage the configuration of transactional devices, supporting the synchronization feature of bi-directionally settings and refined changes in real time;
- *Configuration Database* (CDB): it is here that the information on the device configurations is all stored, so there is data synchronization. It is in the CDB that the synchronization, consistency and reconciliation with respect to the configuration between the services and devices occurs;
- *Network Element Drivers* (NED): they are responsible for the link between the NSO and network devices. The NED uses the concept of atomicity, i.e., the execution of a command is either correct and runs, or if a simple thing is wrong, nothing will be executed. The NSO, according to the device we want to configure, informs the device type (*device-type*) of what to do, independently of the brand/device manufacturer. The device interface is modeled on files, using the YANG, and each file is modeled with the controls - that can be updated – in the respective device. The philosophy of the NED varies from device to device. For Cisco and Alcatel, commands are converted to CLI to run on the device terminal. For the Juniper equipment, that already uses NETCONF - based encoding in XML -, the philosophy is different, i.e., not needing to convert settings.

As it was said before, the communication between NSO and the devices should be done by OpenFlow, NETCONF, XML, CLI or any other. If we do a deeper analysis of the communication, we will notice that the communication between the NSO and the network equipments are the responsibility of the NED or the OpenFlow controllers, as we can see in [19] document. Note that this communication is made by the NSO and it was not changed in the proposed tool.

We finally get to the network and the devices, which may be of different brands and models. In this solution, the NSO gets to know the equipment by means of the communication Secure Shell (SSH) protocol.

After the presentation of the proposed tool architecture, we will explain, in the next section, how it is implemented.

IV. Prototype

The implementation of this tool is based on the architecture presented in Section III. In this section, we will deepen the architecture used, namely the implementation carried out and which ultimately resulted in the presentation of a simple tool that makes the network services management.

A. Prototype implementation

As mentioned above, our aim is to develop an *Open Source* tool where we can test the settings of a network and its services. The network can be either real or virtual. The concept behind the tool is SDN. With this kind of tool, the entire configuration process is centralized and this same configuration does not require in-depth knowledge of computer networks. So we can simplify the configuration and understand a network. From a purely visual point of view, the developed tool is nothing more than a *Graphical User Interface* (GUI) or *WebUI*. Next, we will explain the process of implementing this tool. The solution developed is based upon three main stages:

- Scenario/network topology – where the network equipment is included;
- Development of the intermediate layer – a layer that will make the connection between the configuration and network equipment and which is transparent to the user. The development basis was the use of the platform *"Cisco Network Service Orchestrator enabled by Tail-f"* and this is the platform that connects the network topology to the graphical interface. Cisco NSO is an orchestration technology that is based on the SDN concept, since the Orchestrator Apps are part of the Application Plane, one of the layers that belong to SDN. This phase will be the *back-end* for the user;
- Graphical User Interface - primary site of interaction between the user and the network. *Front-end* for the user.

The implementation of these three stages will be presented in the following subsections.

1) Scenario/network topology

Initially a virtual Linux Ubuntu machine was created to run the 14.4 version. In this machine a network was developed on a network simulation software GNS3 [20], shown in Figure 4, where several different manufacturers were set, including Cisco and Juniper.

In Cisco's *routers* they used the file "c3725-adventerprisek9-mz.124-25d.bin" to virtualize the IOS. This model was the only one to which we had access, although we know that there are more recent models. As for Juniper, we had to use a vSRX *Open Virtual Application* (OVA) image, more specifically a 12.1X47-D15.4 version of JunOS vSRX. The only settings made in this equipment were addressing, routing, the *Open Shortest Path First* (OSPF) in this case, and the communication protocol configuration used – SSH.

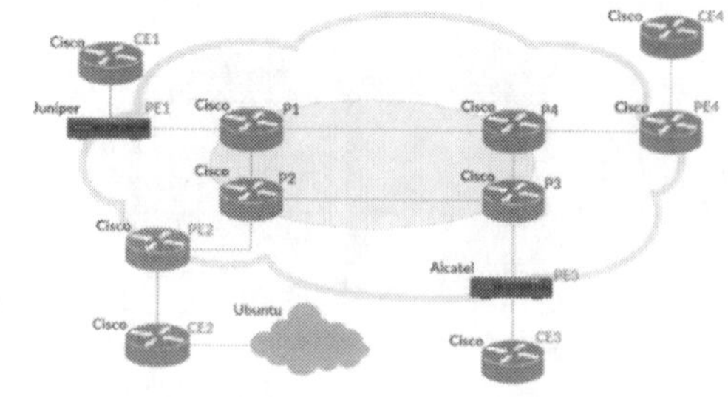

Figure 4. Network topology defined to test developed in GNS3

To bridge the gap between the topology developed and the GUI we used, as mentioned above, the NSO solution that we will explain in detailed in the next subsection.

2) Development of the intermediate layer

After the topology and configuration of the devices is completed, we have defined some services to be implemented and tested on the network. One of the objectives of this tool was that, later, the communication services could be configured using the GUI. The services implemented were QoS, *Virtual Private Network* (VPN) and a basic service of *Virtual Local Area Network* (VLAN), as well as the Hostname configuration of the equipment. One of the aims is to use the developed prototype to manage the referred network services. With this prototype we can, in just a few steps, configure QoS, VPN, VLAN or the hostname in a network. The hostname service would serve as proof of concept. After setting communication services, we have set up the configuration parameters of the service. To do this, we created a "skeleton service" to be implemented. In this "skeleton" there are several files, including the modelling of services, using the YANG. It is in the YANG files' that the fields, or parameters, are defined to be ordered for proper implementation of the services in the network. Figure 5 shows an example of part of a YANG file (*hostname.yang*) for implementing the hostname service, with the purpose of changing the hostname of the required device. This service, as mentioned previously, was created to demonstrate the implementation done and will be reflected in the tested network devices.

```
module hostname {
        namespace "http://com/example/hostname";
        prefix hostname;
        import tailf-ncs {
                prefix ncs;
        }
        container host {
                list hostname {
                        description "Configure
hostname";
                        key name;
                        uses ncs:service-data;
                ncs:servicepoint "hostname";
                leaf name{
                        type string;
                }
                  leaf device {
                        type leafref {
                          path
"/ncs:devices/ncs:device/ncs:name";
                        }
                  }
                  leaf changeto {
                        type string;
                  }
          }
      }
  }
```

Figure 5. YANG file for modelling a service: Hostname (*hostname.yang*)

In Figure 5 we can see the set parameters which will support the data to be filled in the NSO. On the YANG model we can see the name of the device whose hostname we want to change, and the new hostname we want to give it. If we run the command to create the Hostname service, it works, but only on the data storage in NSO CDB. After the change in YANG file, we must define the service mapping so that the command is executed and the service created. As for the mapping setting, this is nothing more than changing the template (*hostname.xml*) that is generated when we create the service in the NSO. In Figure 6 we present an example of Hostname service. the result may be the *template* shown next.

```
<config-template xmlns=http://tail-f.com/ns/config/1.0
servicepoint="hostname">
        <devices xmlns="http://tail-f.com/ns/ncs">
        <device>
                <name>{/device}</name>
                <config>
                        <hostname
xmlns="urn:ios">{/changeto}</hostname>
                        <configuration
xmlns="http://xml.juniper.net/xnm/1.1/xnm">
                                <system>
                                        <host-
name>{/changeto}</host-name>
                                </system>
                        </configuration>
                </config>
                </device>
        </devices>
</config-template>
```

Figure 6. Hostname service's *template* (*hostname.xml*)

In Figure 6 we can also note that the *template* already follows the hostname configuration, either to a Cisco *router*, identified by your operating system (IOS) or to the Juniper *router*, identified by your operating system (JunOS).

In Figure 7 we present a command that is an example of the Hostname service configuration and that may be used for practical implementation of changing of a device hostname, in this case, the *router p0*.

```
admin-ncs(config)# host hostname troca device p0
changeto p0cisco
admin-ncs(config)# commit
```

Figure 7. Example of command for Hostname service creation in NSO

After explaining the NSO, we will explain the creation of the GUI process that, for the network manager, is the only part that will be used for service management, after the network and the service are created, naturally.

3) Development tool

The final stage resulted in the development of a graphical interface where the user is expected to interact most of the time with regard to the service management part. The graphical interface was created in WordPress and is very simple. It is important to note that the main purpose was not the implementation of a high-level *web interface*, but the development of a solution that can serve as a stage prior to the configuration of the network and production service. We tried to create a simple and functional interface to make its use as easy as possible. There are more graphic tools with the function of network configuration, but most of them have many concepts which may not be necessary to those who will manage a network and its services [21]. The Cisco NSO technology is not very used yet but it is property of a big network company so it has potential. We have not found any related work with it, so to the best of our knowledge, our work is the first of its kind.

The implementation of the *WebUI* is divided into two parts: the visible (*front-end*) and non-visible (*back-end*), which are running the most important process. The *front-end* is very simple and it is based mainly on buttons and filling out forms. The *back-end* is where the data, that was previously filled in by the user forms, is read. In the *back-end* of the tool we have done the proper implementation to interpret and process everything the user sees. This reading follows the sequence shown in Figure 8.

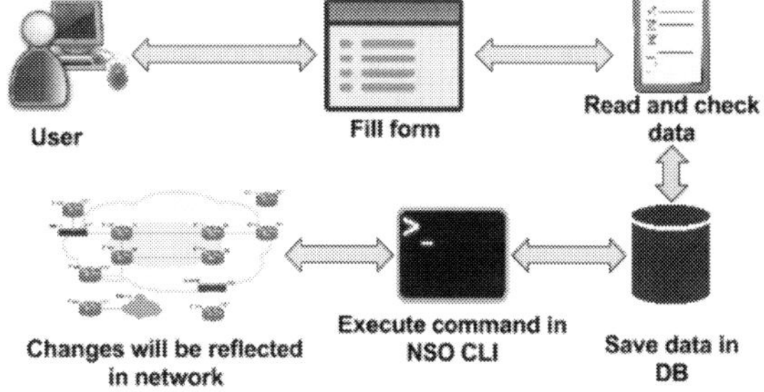

Figure 8. Process execution sequence runs in back-end in graphic interface

In what concerns the database, it is very simple and it is used mainly to synchronize the data to be presented in the form with the data on the NSO. The most important command, through which the connection between the GUI and terminal NSO is made, is shown in Figure 9.

```
$ /home/tail-f/ncs_new/bin/ncs_cli -C -u admin
```

Figure 9. Access command terminal of NSO

Running a *script* with this command is reflected in NSO terminal and later, in the existing network. The communication mode between the prototype and the NSO was the NSO [NCS] CLI Scripts [13], since it was the simplest and quickest way of implementing what we intended to test. Our NSO CLI Script is a solution available by NSO technology itself, thus it is a valid option to be used. There were other communication modes like the Python, REST and Java, depending on the type of solution to the management of network we have or we intend to develop.

To conclude the chapter, we present an example test of the entire process carried out.

B. Test of tool operation

On the graphical interface, the NSO checks the data after the user fills out a form for the hostname change. The form is shown in Figure 10.

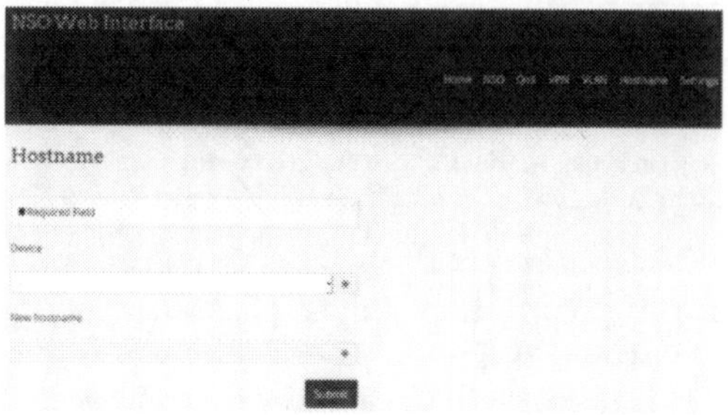

Figure 10. Hostname form, part of the graphic tool developed.

The parameters are validated after they are inserted. Only after their insertion will the commands be executed in the NSO terminal, the data is stored in the CDB and the mapping definition is made. This definition is reflected in the *template* result in the XML file, previously shown in Figure 6. Finally, the NED interprets the received data. The command is executed on the machine and the result is successful, as shown in Figure 11.

Figure 11. Execution of commands sequence in back-end. Transparent process for the user.

All network services were implemented on the prototype. We did not develop all template services, because this work is expected to be done/developed by network or device manufacturers. Although we only present the test for hostname service, for proof of concept of the prototype tool, the results of testing QoS services will also be successful in Alcatel router. The changes were confirmed in this specific router.

We conclude the presentation of the implementation and of the demonstration of this tool execution.

V. Conclusion and Future Work

We proposed and implemented an *Open Source* tool that can be used to manage a network, and especially its services before they are put into production. Using the concept of SDN, the management can be done either in a real network or in a virtual one, whether it already exists or it is created from scratch. Its simple use allows the users to spend less time in the configuration and creation of services and, at the same time, it can be used to optimize both the network and the creation of new services. In practice, the process is simple: add a tool to a network and that tool is ready to be used. The configuration of the equipments, as it is done nowadays, will be maintained, but it will use a graphic tool so that this process becomes more simplistic and abstract to the user.

As future work, we can suggest the implementation of new services and the consolidation of this tool through a more optimized prototype. It would be an advantage to present this prototype to managers or network administrators, who work in this area daily, in order to improve this tool.

References

[1] Cisco Systems, Inc, "Cisco Visual Networking Index: Global Mobile Data Traffic Forecast Update, 2014–2019", 2015.

[2] HP Enterprise Business, "Why SDN... Software-defined Networking?", 2014. Available from: <https://goo.gl/kfclyH>. Accessed on: December 05, 2015.

[3] Open Networking Foundation, "Software-Defined Networking (SDN) Definition. Open Networking Foundation". Available from: <https://goo.gl/hMOCuy>. Accessed on: January 10, 2016.

[4] D. Kreutz, F. M. V. Ramos, P. Verissimo, C. E. Rothenberg, S. Azodolmolky and S. Uhlig, "Software-Defined Networking: A Comprehensive Survey", Proceedings of the IEEE (Volume:103 , Issue: 1), January 2015.

[5] Y. Jarraya, "A Survey and a Layered Taxonomy of Software-Defined Networking", IEEE Communications Surveys & Tutorials (Volume:16 , Issue: 4), April 2014.

[6] Nuage Networks, "Products - Nuage Networks". Nuage Networks. Available from: <http://www.nuagenetworks.net/products/>. Accessed on: December 15, 2014.

[7] Nuage Networks. Virtualized Services Platform, "Nuage Networks VSP Data Sheet", June 2014. Available from: <http://goo.gl/Qj4nqB>. Accessed on: December 15, 2014.

[8] Cisco Systems, Inc., Tail-F Systems, "Cisco Network Service Orchestrator (NSO) enabled by Tail-f". Available from: <https://goo.gl/Oy1BKH>. Accessed on: December 22, 2015.

[9] HP Enterprise Business. "Leverage SDN: Create consumable, programmable, and scalable cloud networks", 2015, pp. 17.

[10] Nuage Networks, "Arista and Nuage Networks: Building Cloud Datacenters with OpenStack", Dec. 01, 2015. Available from: <http://goo.gl/zJ4juN>. Accessed on: January 07, 2016.

[11] N. McKeown, G. Parulkar, T. Anderson, L. Peterson, H. Balakrishnan, J. Rexford, S. Shenker and J. Turner, "OpenFlow: Enabling Innovation in Campus Networks", ACM SIGCOMM Computer Communication Review, Volume 38 Issue 2, April 2008, pp. 69-74, doi: 10.1145/1355734.1355746.

[12] I. M. Kultan and Nuage Networks, "Virtualized Services Platform (VSP) & Network Services (VNS)". Vienna, Austria, pp. 16. 2015.

[13] Cisco Systems, Inc, "Tail-f Network Control System 3.3 Getting Started Guide", 2014, pp. 1; 3; 51-52; 59.

[14] Cisco Systems, Inc., Tail-F Systems, "What is YANG?" Available from: <http://www.tailf.com/education/what-is-yang/>. Accessed on: November 25, 2014.

[15] M. Rouse, "What is XML (Extensible Markup Language)?" TechTarget, Dec. 2014. Available from: <http://goo.gl/v65bZi>. Accessed on: January 10, 2016.

[16] R. Enns, M. Bjorklund, J. Schoenwaelder and A. Bierman, "RFC 6241 – NETCONF Configuration Protocol", Jun. 2011. Available from: <https://tools.ietf.org/html/rfc6241>. Accessed on: December 31, 2015.

[17] Juniper Networks, Inc, "Junos OS NETCONF XML Management Protocol Developer Guide", pp. 3. 2015.

[18] W. Stallings, "Software-Defined Networks and OpenFlow", The Internet Protocol Journal, March 2013.

[19] J. J. Jensen, "Multi-Vendor Service Orchestration & Network automation for today's networks", 2016.

[20] GNS3 Technologies, Inc, "What is GNS3?", 2016. Available from: <https://www.gns3.com/software>. Accessed on: February 21, 2016.

[21] L. D. Vecchio "GUI for Netfloc – An OpenSource SDK for SDN", January 29, 2016.

Island-Based Sensor Relocation in Wireless Sensor Network to Improve Connectivity

Sahla Masmoudi Mnif
National School of Computer Science
University of Manouba
Tunisia 2010
e-mail: sahla.masmoudi@ensi-uma.tn

Leila Azouz Saidane
National School of Computer Science
University of Manouba
Tunisia 2010
e-mail: leila.saidane@ensi.rnu.tn

Abstract—**Wireless sensor networks applications require connectivity between deployed sensors over the region of interest (ROI). We note that the random deployment of sensors, leads to dividing the network in different partitions and makes the communication impossible between deployed nodes. In this paper, we propose to use a mobile robot which will travel through the supervised area and will relocate redundant sensor nodes in order to ensure connectivity. We assume in our work that the mobile robot is not aware of the network topology, so that the robot has to discover the network topology and to enhance the connectivity in the WSN. We propose for this purpose two Island-Based strategies. In the first strategy, the robot walk is made in a random manner; this strategy is called Island-Based Random Walk (IBRW). In the second strategy, called Island-Based Walk with Memorization (IBWM), the robot memorizes the collected information and tries to improve the connectivity in the WSN. Through simulation we evaluate and compare the performances of these strategies.**

Keywords- Sensor; Wireless Sensor network; Connectivity; Mobile Robot; Relocation.

I. INTRODUCTION

Ensuring connectivity in Wireless Sensor Networks (WSNs) is a challenging issue, especially in hazardous areas. Many applications of WSN require an important level of connectivity in the network to detect any abnormal event (e.g., fire, seism, intrusion detection, etc.) and forward an alert to the "sink" node in order to inform users. As examples we can mention, detection instruction application in military fields, the survey of frontiers zones and the control of mountains and forest occupied by terrorists. In fact, to survey this kind of environment, sensors are generally deployed, in a random manner (e.g., dropped from an aircraft). Sensor nodes are expected to detect any given events (intrusion, fire, etc.) and communicate together in order to survey a Region Of Interest (ROI). But nevertheless, the total connectivity between sensors is not guaranteed with random deployment of sensor nodes, which leads generally, in partition of the network.

Upon an initial deployment, the sensors should communicate and maintain this communication between nodes in order to stay reachable to each other.

A. Motivation

In recent years, the mobility has been introduced in WSNs to ensure and improve connectivity and coverage of the ROI. The sensor node using a mobile platform will have the possibility to move and to relocate its position. In our work, we are essentially interested by hazardous areas like inaccessible mountains, forests and deserts or harsh frontiers. Our goal is to survey these areas against any attacks (terrorist attacks). For this kind of areas, the deterministic deployment of sensors is not easy. For this purpose, in this paper we deal with a random deployment of sensors.

In general case, with random deployment the total connectivity is not guaranteed. Sensors need to be relocated to achieve total connectivity. Some existing sensor self-deployment algorithms [4][12][15] are adaptive to node failure and may actually be employed to solve the sensor relocation problem regarding sensing hole healing. A sensor relocation algorithm is proposed in [2]; this algorithm relocates redundant nodes in a cascading manner. However, its assumption, i.e., pre-knowledge about sensor field, makes it less practical in real-world scenario. Noting that, using mobile sensor nodes is expensive, we envision using, in our work, static sensor nodes and a mobile robot to relocate static nodes if necessary. The robot is assumed to be equipped with sensors and moves through the ROI according the given strategies. The robot has to relocate sensors to obtain a connected and covered network. The main task of the mobile robot is to discover disconnected nodes and to try to ensure total connectivity over the network. Different scenarios are envisaged where robot is in short of static sensors and should pick up redundant sensors and relocate them in the ROI. We propose to exploit the redundant nodes resulting in random deployment of sensors rather than adding some new sensors for economic purpose.

B. Problem Statement

We consider a given ROI equipped with a large number of wireless sensors which are deployed randomly in this area. By this deployment of nodes, the connectivity between nodes is not guaranteed. In our work, we propose to use a mobile robot to relocate redundant sensors in order to ensure communication between sensors.

Assumptions: we are assuming the following:

- The deployed nodes are wireless static sensors.
- The number of deployed sensor nodes is very important.
- Each sensor node is characterized by its unique Identity which is computed from its address.
- Each sensor node is able to compute its location by mean of localization technique like the Global Positioning System (GPS).
- Each sensor node has two independent components: sensing and communication units. Both parts are powered from the same limited source of power (battery).
- Each sensor node is able to compute its residual energy.
- The transmission (communication) range of each node is denoted r_c. We suppose that all nodes have the same communication range.
- The sensing range of each node is denoted r_s. We suppose that all nodes have the same sensing range.
- After a random deployment of sensor nodes in the area, they will be redundant nodes in some zones and they will be non- covered zones.
- We use a mobile robot which is a mobile sensor and have a very important storage and computation capacities.
- The robot has a communication range noted R_c and a sensing range R_s larger than the other sensor nodes.
- Initially, the mobile robot is equipped with sensor nodes (which we will call them "Reserve Nodes") that it can use them to enhance connectivity in the network.

The mobile robot should run through the controlled area and decides the appropriate action to do: the robot can discover the network topology (discover the position of deployed sensors), can pick up redundant sensors or can continue its travel in the ROI.

Our paper is structured as follows: We start with a brief review of the existing solutions for the redeployment of sensors in WSN. Then we present our solution and we validate it by means of different experiments and simulations and finally, we close this paper by a conclusion.

II. Related Work

In recent years, sensor relocation has been a challenging matter that was studied by many researchers. Several solutions have been proposed to solve the redeployment issue. One relevant solution was to provide motion capability to all sensors. This way, the sensors can move and relocate themselves in order to adjust the topology and achieve the connectivity and/or the coverage.

The sensors must synchronize their movement to enhance the network topology.

Among the proposed solutions, we mention particularly the cascade motion which is detailed in [2]: instead of moving directly to the target, the sensor nodes adopt a cascade movement which means that the nearest node to the target point will move there, and the location of nearest node is replaced by moving another sensor and so on.

Virtual Forces Aspect has been also proposed as a solution for sensor relocation. In this way, deployed sensors communicate together and compute their new locations in order to ensure connectivity and/or coverage. Then these sensors exercise a repulsive or an attractive force to move to their estimated locations. This strategy was studied and presented in [18].

The mobility of nodes is very efficient and improves the network topology, but it requires an important energy consumption which causes the node depletion and decreases the network lifetime.

Other solutions consist of the use of fixed sensor nodes and the network is assisted by some "actors" like mobile robots.

Some studies proposed to use the robot to carry data between disconnected sensors so that the robot collects the detected event from nodes and then delivers these information to the other nodes. This approach is presented by Zhao et al. [19]. In this way, the event is delayed and a latency time is introduced which can be considered as a shortcoming for critical applications.

Another set of related works include algorithms using DATA MULES [14][15], which are wireless devices integrated on mobile entities (e.g., animals, vehicles, etc.) A DATA MULE is a data collector; it picks up data from nodes and relays it to other nodes, so that, data would not be relayed on long routes and the network lifetime is increased

In other proposed solutions, the actors are mobile sensors that exploit the redundant nodes and relocate them to achieve better connectivity and/or coverage trying to preserve the network lifetime as long as possible. Most of the proposed solutions are grid-based ones like the solution proposed in [2]. For sensor relocation in mobile sensors networks we mention for example ZONER proposed in [20]. This solution presented a distributed zone-based sensor relocation protocol for mobile sensors on the basis of restricted flooding technique. When mobile sensors are cost effective and have critical energy constraints, we try in our work to propose a sensor relocation strategy for static sensor networks using a mobile robot.

III. Proposed Solutions

In this section we present our approach to relocate the sensors using a mobile robot. We start this section by presenting the network modeling and then we define the robot algorithms to relocate the sensors.

We assume that the region of interest is unreachable, making the deterministic deployment impossible. Hence, we consider an initial random deployment of sensor nodes and we scatter a large amount of sensors within the region of interest.

Each node in the network knows its own position by an attached GPS (Global Positioning System) or any other equipment of localization. Sensors have the same communication range r_c and the same sensing range r_s, we note that $r_c >= r_s$.

Using this kind of sensor deployment, connectivity in the resulted network is not guaranteed. Furthermore, the random deployment leads to the creation of disconnected islands.

1) ***Definitions:***

Island: An isolated set of connected sensor nodes.

MainIsland: The Island containing the "Sink" node is called "Main Island".

Redundant sensor: a sensor is said to be redundant if his perception zone is covered by the perception zones of other sensors.

In each island, the connectivity is ensured but the islands are not able to communicate between each other. Generally, each island contains redundant sensor nodes. Figure 1 shows an example of an Island-based network.

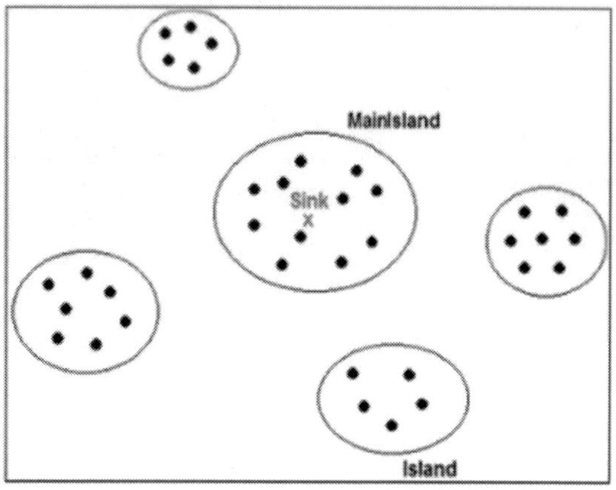

Figure 1. Example of an Island-Based WSN.

2) *Redundant Sensor Identification:* the mobile robot has to identify the redundant sensors in order to use them to connect islands. We use a hexagonal partition of region in order to identify and locate redundant sensors. The structure of hexagon cell is chosen in a manner that sensors belonging to two adjacent cells are able to communicate. A sensor is said to be redundant if its cells (perception zone) is covered by other cells. Tasks of redundant sensors can be made by the neighboring sensors and so that the redundat sensor can be in a passive mode in order to save energy.

3) *Island-Head Identification :* For each Island, a chief is elected, called Island-Head. This island-Head collects all the information about the island (positions of redundant nodes, positions of nodes in the islands, etc.). The Island-Head is elected as the node with the highest level of residual energy and having the largest set of neighbors. In order to select the Island-Head, an election factor noted *f* is defined by (1):

$$f = \frac{1}{2} * \frac{E_{res}}{E_{\max}} + \frac{1}{2} * \frac{Nb_n}{Nb_{nodes}} \quad (1)$$

where E_{res} and E_{max}, represent respectively the residual energy and the maximum level of energy for a given node. Nb_n and Nb_{nodes} refer to the number of neighbors of a sensor node and the number of nodes in a given Island.
The node with the highest value of *f* is elected as an Island-Head. In case of multiple candidates, the node with higher Identity is elected. A backup Island-Head is chosen to replace Island-Head in case of its depletion.

When the Island-Head is elected, it collects the positions and all information concerning the redundant_nodes. After that, the Island-Head orders the redundant sensor nodes go to the passive mode (sleeping mode) to save energy of the whole network.

We assume that the robot knows the position of the sink node. Therefore, it is not aware of the network topology. Hence, the main role of the mobile robot is to discover the topology of the network and simultaneously, it tries to redeploy redundant sensors in order to enhance the network topology and to ensure connectivity between each Island of the network and the "MainIsland" to obtain a connected network.

We notice that, the mobile robot is considered as a sophisticated entity with an important computational capability and a large amount of energy. We suppose also that the robot can be recharged as needed. The robot has also sensing and communication capabilities, we note R_c the communication range of the robot and R_s its sensing range; $R_c >= R_s$. We assume also that the robot is equipped by a number of sensors Nb_{res} that can be used connect disconnected Islands.

Each couple of nodes (whether sensor node or robot) can communicate directly when they are within each other communication range.

In our solution, we will exploit sensor redundancy to enhance the connectivity over the network. We mention that the mobile robot can be in one of these states:

- Discovering topology: it has to discover the position of deployed sensors, Islands, etc.
- Collecting redundant sensors: when encountering redundant nodes, the robot can pick them up.
- Connecting Island: the robot places sensors in order to connect the Islands
- Free: the robot has no task to do.

We propose two strategies for sensor relocation: the first strategy is called Island-Based Random Walk (IBRW) in which the robot walk is made completely in a random manner and the second strategy is called Island-Based Walk with Memorization (IBWM) in which the robot walk is made based on the recently discovered information (about topology, position of redundant nodes, disconnected islands, etc.)

A. *Island-Based Random Walk*

Our first proposed solution is called Island-Based Random Walk (IBRW). In this solution the robot walks in the ROI in a random manner. Periodically, the robot stops (after a distance of 2* R_c) and sends a Hello-Robot Message. Each sensor receiving a "Hello-Robot", forwards this message to its "Island-Head" and the "Island-Head" replies with "Island-information" containing all the information concerning this island (position of nodes, positions of redundant sensors, sensors identities, number of redundant nodes, etc.).

- If the robot does not receive any reply (after a prefixed duration), it continues its walk in a random direction.
- If the robot receives an "Island-information", it computes the position of the nearest node of the "sink" and then it calculates the number of needed sensors to connect the island to the "MainIsland".
  - If this requested number of sensors is available on the robot, it relocates them (the nodes will be relocated according to hexagonal pavement).
  - If this requested number of sensors is not available on the robot, it continues its walk in a random manner.

Figure 2 shows the way that two Islands should be connected using the hexagonal pavement. Green cells are used to connect an Island to the "MainIsland".

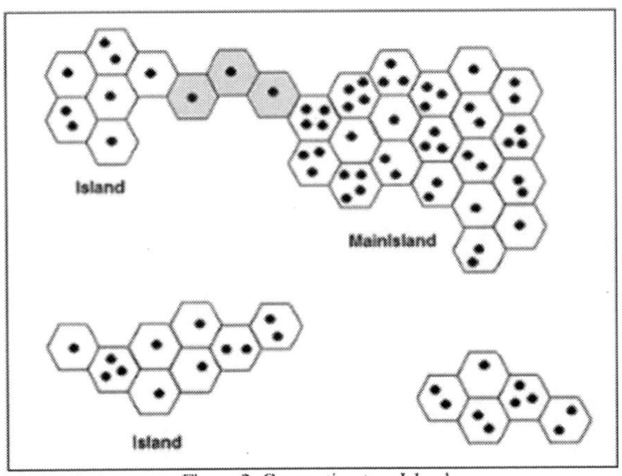

Figure 2. Connecting two Islands

B. *Island-Based Random Walk with Memorization*

In this strategy, the robot adopts the same functioning as the IBRW with some other amelioration. The robot is initially in a free state. The robot starts its travel in Discovering Topology state and it moves through a random direction. The robot, during this state, sends periodically a Hello-Robot Message. When the robot encounters an Island, it receives a reply from the Island-Head. This message contains all information about the considered Island. All received information is saved in the robot and the robot updates its information about the network topology.

- When a robot encounters an Island, it memorizes all the information concerning this Island mainly the locations of redundant nodes.
- When they are no carried sensors on the robot, the robot returns back to the nearest redundant nodes, picks them up and relocates them like in the IBRW algorithm. Then the robot continues its travel in a random direction.

IV. Performance Evaluation

Our proposed solution is implemented under NS2 simulator. Several simulations were established with different scenarios. For all simulations we use a large number of deployed sensors to ensure full connectivity and enhance coverage over the network.

The sensors are initially deployed randomly through a square ROI; we set r_c=25m, r_s=25m and R_c=45m. We set the dimension of the ROI to 500*500. The Initial load of the robot 5Reserve nodes) is fixed to 60 sensors. The number of deployed sensor nodes is set to 200 sensors in the first time. In a second step, we will vary the number of deployed sensors from 100 to 600 sensors.

The number of created islands over the network is an important factor which gives us an idea on the total connectivity in the network. Figure 3 shows that the number of created islands increases when the number of deployed sensors decreases. As a result, the connectivity between nodes increases when the number of deployed sensors increases.

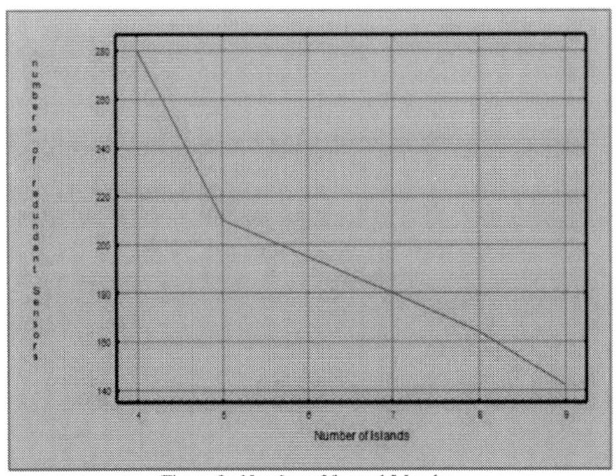

Figure 3. Number of formed Islands

In our work we try to attend a tradeoff between the number of deployed sensors and the connectivity rate. In other terms, we try to determine the optimal number of deployed sensors to achieve a desired connectivity level.

To evaluate our proposed solutions we fixed some metrics like connectivity rate, connectivity Time, the total travelled distance by robot and the average consumed energy by static sensors.

A. *Connectivity Time*

Connectivity time (CT) is the time needed by the robot to ensure connectivity over the entire network. This metric should to be minimized.

Figure 4 shows that when the number of deployed sensors increases, the connectivity time decreases for the two proposed strategies IBRW and IBWM. This can be explained by the important number of redundant sensors when the number ofdeployed sensors number increases. In this case the number of Islands to connect to the "MainIsland" decreases.

We remark also that IBWM outperforms IBRW in terms of connectivity time which can be explained by the optimization of functioning of robot for IBWM compared to IBRW.

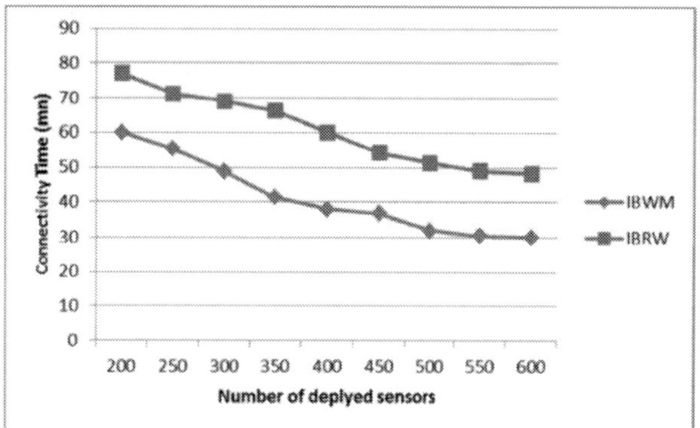

Figure 4. Connectivity Time

B. *Connectivity Rate*

The connectivity rate (CR) is the rate of connected sensors in the network; this metric can be given by (2)

$$\frac{\text{The number of connected sensors}}{\text{The number of deployed sensors}} \qquad (2)$$

This metric should be maximized to enhance the performance of the tested algorithms. We modify the number of deployed sensors and we compute the CR to show the impact of the numbers of the deployed sensors on the connectivity rate.

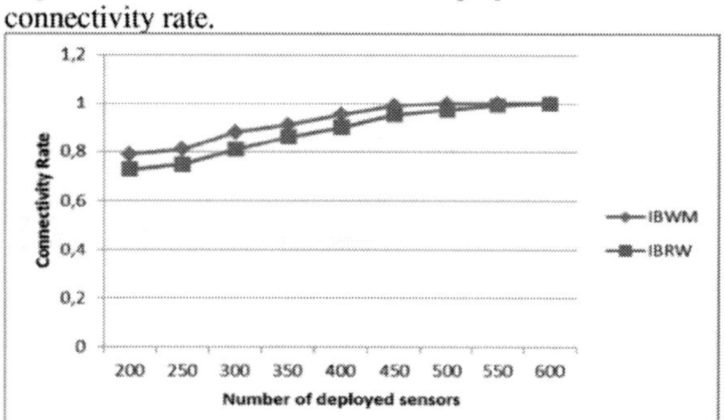

Figure 5. Connectivity Rate

Figure 5 shows that CR increases with the number of deployed sensors. Figure 5 illustrates also that IBWM algorithm outperforms IBRW in terms of connectivity rate. In fact, the walk of robot is more optimized in IBWM strategy making the connectivity process easier.

C. *Total Travelled Distance*

We compute for each proposed algorithm the total travelled distance by the robot. Figure 6 shows that the travelled distance decreases when the number of deployed sensors increases. In fact, in this case, the robot had to connect more Islands to the "MainIsland" and is obliged to travel more long distances. Figure 6 shows also that IBWM outperforms the IBRW in terms of the total travelled distance. In fact, compared to IBRW, the IBWM algorithm exploits the nearest discovered redundant sensors.

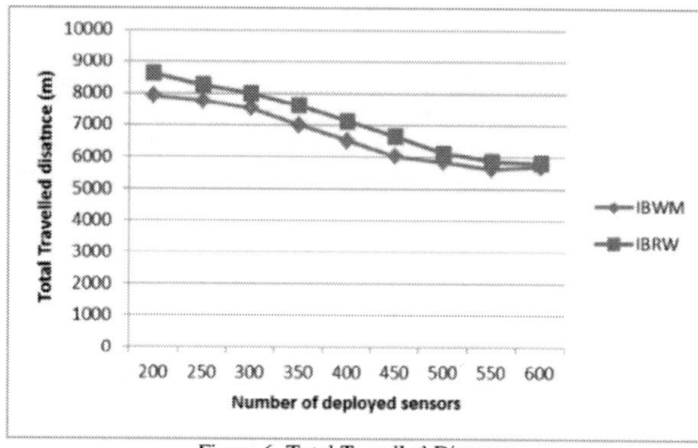

Figure 6. Total Travelled Distance

D. *Energy Consumption*

The high energy consumption driven by mobile sensors is an important criterion which justifies the use of static sensors and a mobile robot to redeploy them. We compute for our proposed solutions the average consumed energy by all static sensors. Figure 7 represents the mean consumed energy according to the number of deployed sensors.

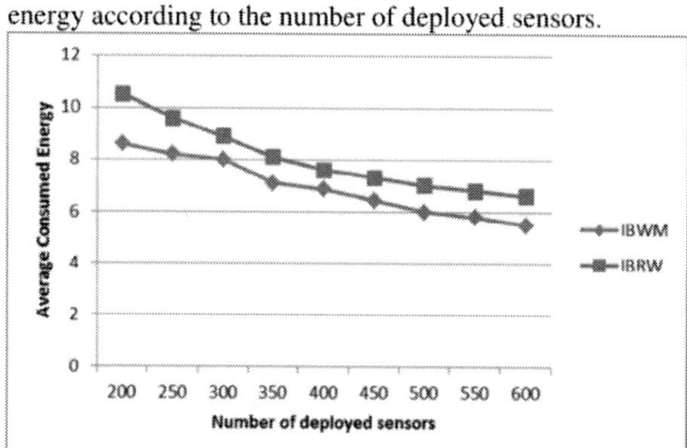

Figure 7. Average Consumed energy by static sensors

We note that the energy consumption decreases with the number of deployed sensors. In fact, when the number of deployed sensors increases, the number of resulted islands decreases and so the number of redundant sensor nodes increases within each island; the redundant nodes will be in sleeping mode. We note also that IBWM outperforms IBRW strategy in terms of consumed energy. In fact, in IBRW strategy, the robot does not memorize any information about the topology. Each time the robot is obliged to communicate with encountered sensors.

E. *An illustrative Example:*

Our proposed solutions can be used to insure connectivity in WSN applications. We mention mainly agriculture precision, where a set of sensor nodes is randomly deployed on a zone and a mobile robot can be used to ensure connectivity in this network. From Figure 4, we can know the minimum number of needed deployed sensors to ensure connectivity in a given time. We can also determine the minimum number of needed sensors to have connectivity lower than a given threshold. For example in our example the CR is greater than 0.96 when the number of islands exceeds 7.

Detection Intrusion in hazardous areas is an example which can use our work. A robot can be used to redeploy sensors in order to achieve total connectivity. The optimal number of deployed sensors to achieve a given level of connectivity in a given time can be determined from curves and figures resulting from our simulations.

V. Conclusion and Future Work

In this paper we proposed a robot-based sensor relocation to ensure connectivity in the Wireless sensors networks. We proposed to model our network by a set of disconnected islands that are formed due to a random deployment of nodes. We proposed also to use a mobile robot to relocate redundant nodes in order to connect the islands of the networks.

We defined two strategies; in the first one IBRW, the mobile robot makes a random travel. In the second one the robot memorizes the locations of encountered redundant nodes and uses the nearest ones when needed. Through several simulations we validated our work.

We show that our work can be used to determine a tradeoff between the required connectivity rate or time and the number of deployed sensors.

As a further work we propose to enhance these solutions by the use of a large number of robots and we propose also to compare our proposed solutions to other relevant proposed solutions in literature.

References

[1] R. Kershner, The number of circles covering a set, American Journal of Mathematics, 1939.p665-671,

[2] T.La Porta, G.Wang, G.Cao and W.Wang, Sensor Relocation In Mobile Sensor Networks, Infocom 2005.

[3] F.Wang, M.Thai and D.Du, on the construction of 2-connected virtual backbone in wireless networks, IEEE Transactions on Wireless Communications 2009.

[4] A.Abbasi, M.Younis and K.Akkaya, Movement-assisted connectivity restoration in wireless sensor and actuator networks. IEEE Transactions on Parallel Distributed Systems 2009.

[5] G.Wang, G.Cao and T.Laporta, A Bidding Protocol for Deploying Mobile Sensors, The 11th IEEE International Conference on Network Protocols (ICNP) 2003.

[6] G.Wang, G.Cao and T.Laporta, Movement-assisted sensor deployment, Infocom 2004.

[7] G. Fletcher, X.. Li, A. Nayak and I.Stojmenovic, Carrier-based sensor deployment by a robot team, IEEE SECON, 2010.

[8] Y. Mei, C. Xian, S .Das, Y. C.Hu and Y. H.Lu, sensor replacement using mobile robots, computer communication 30(13) 2007.

[9] D.Xuan, Z.Yun, X.Bai, S.Kumar and Ten H. Lai, Deploying Wireless sensors to achieve both coverage and connectivity, Mobile Ad Hoc Networking and Computing,2006.

[10] X.Li and N.Santoro, ZONER: a zone-based sensor relocation protcol for mobile sensor networks, IEEE WLN, 2006.interface," IEEE Transl. J. Magn. Japan, vol. 2, August 1987, pp. 740–741, [Digests 9th Annual Conf. Magnetics Japan, p. 301, 1982].

[11] X.Li, N.Santoro and I.Stojmenovic, Mesh-based sensor relocation for coverage maintenance in mobile sensor networks, UIC 2007.

[12] A.Howard, M.J.Mataric and G.S.Sukhatme, Mobile Sensor Networks Deployment Using Potential Fields: A Distributed, Scalable Solution to the Area Coverage Problem, the 6th International Symposium on Distributed Autonomous Robotics Systems, 2002.

[13] E.Egea-López, J.Vales-Alonso, A.S.Martínez-Sala, P. Pavon-Mariño and J.García-Haro, Simulation Tools for Wireless Sensor Networks, Summer Simulation Multiconference - SPECTS,2005.

[14] I.F.Akyildiz, W.Su, Y.Sankarasubramaniam and E.Cayirci, A Survey On Sensor Networks, IEEE Communications Magazine,2002.

[15] T.Watteyne, Using Existing Network Simulators for Power-Aware Self-Organizing Wireless Sensor Network Protocols, INRIA,2006.

[16] G. Chalhoub, Réseaux de capteurs sans fil, Clermont Université,2009.

[17] A.Gallais, J.Carle and D.Simplot-Ryl , La k-couverture de surface dans les réseaux de capteurs, AlgoTel, 2007.

[18] X.Wang, Sh.Wang andD.Bi, Virtual force-directed particle swarm optimization for dynamic deployment in wireless sensor networks, ICIC, 2007.

[19] W. Zhao, M.Ammar, and E. Zegura, A message Ferrying Approach for data deliveryin sparse mobile adhoc networks, Mobihoc 2004.

[20] A.M. Khedr and H. Ramadan, Effective Sensor Relocation Technique in Mobile Sensor Networks, IJCNC Vol3, No.1, january 2011.

Layer-2 Failure Recovery Methods in Critical Communication Networks

Ferdinand von Tüllenburg and Thomas Pfeiffenberger

Salzburg Research Forschungsgesellschaft mbH
Advanced Networking Center
email: ferdinand.tuellenburg@salzburgresearch.at
email: thomas.pfeiffenberger@salzburgresearch.at

***Abstract*—Service interruptions in critical infrastructures, like the power grid, can lead to serious consequences for safety and security of people. To avoid such interruptions of distributed applications or process control systems belonging to a critical infrastructure, reliable recovery mechanisms for the associated communication systems are essential. OpenFlow, a standard for software defined networking (SDN), provides the fast failover group mechanism to forward packets via alternative paths in case of link failures. In contrast to the conceptual and theoretical discussions of this concept, in this work, the performance of path restoration using SDN fast-failover groups is compared to the performance of path computation when using the Rapid Spanning Tree Protocol (RSTP). Our results show, that current implementations of OpenFlow can significantly improve the failover performance compared to RSTP, which makes it possible to use SDN in ultra high reliability communication networks. But it is also shown that there is a potential to further improve the SDN recovery mechanisms by deeply inspecting the correlations between OpenFlow/SDN implementations, the used hardware and the operating system.**

***Index Terms*—Critical infrastructure; Fast failover evaluation; Software defined networking; Reliability; Network recovery**

I. Introduction

Some technical systems like the electrical grid or other utility systems are of special importance for our modern society as they are providing the basis on which our communities, economies and everyday lives are founded. Such technical systems are referred to as critical infrastructures. In the last years, there has been a recognizable trend of a proceeding augmentation with Information and Communication Technology (ICT) to increase advantages and efficiency of such systems. With this progress, critical infrastructures are getting highly dependent on a working communication infrastructure, making this ICT itself to a critical infrastructure [1]. One example for this development can be seen in case of power grids, which are evolving towards Smart Grids. Here, various entities of the power systems like generators, sensors, and intelligent devices are getting interconnected using ICT in order to enrich the power grid with more sophisticated functions for monitoring and control, trading, and Demand Side Management [2].

Nowadays, communication networks for critical infrastructures are often operated as dedicated networks where connections to other networks (especially the Internet) are avoided. Mainly due to the risk of introducing security and performance issues as certain ICT functions in critical infrastructures have special requirements for reliability, data security and quality of service (QoS). This however, has several disadvantages such as high operating and installation costs for dedicated networks and the impossibility to share information between systems belonging to different critical infrastructures. But, when already existing communication infrastructures are extended to be used for critical infrastructures beside its originary operation purpose, methods are needed that guarantee the reliability of critical traffic. To achieve this, (1) critical traffic should be separated from non-critical traffic and (2) for critical traffic special treatment is needed in order to guarantee communication reliability. One approach often discussed in current and recent research project is the use of Multiprotocol Label Switching (MPLS) networks. With MPLS and its traffic engineering extension Ressource Reservation Protocol - Traffic Engineering (RSVP-TE), traffic of distinct applications can be forwarded differently within the network, which leads to traffic separation. Furthermore, with RSVP fast reroute a fast method is given to reroute packets as soon as link failures occur. This can be used to increase the communication reliability of critical traffic. The disadvantage of MPLS, however, are high efforts for maintenance and often high costs for provisioning of MPLS services (e.g., renting MPLS lines from service providers).

Software-defined networking (SDN) provides other approaches to tackle the aforementioned topic. This can be shown in the SDN testbed for critical and non-critical applications. Here, SDN is considered as a promising candidate to separate traffic of critical and non-critical applications. This also goes in conjunction with better mitigation of potential security risks, increased reliability through isolation from configuration errors of other applications and networks, and a simplified configuration and management for both, infrastructure users and providers.

The SDN testbed implements solutions as a proof of concept in a real-end user, OpenFlow enabled [3] fibre to the home infrastructure operated by a district heat provider. The district

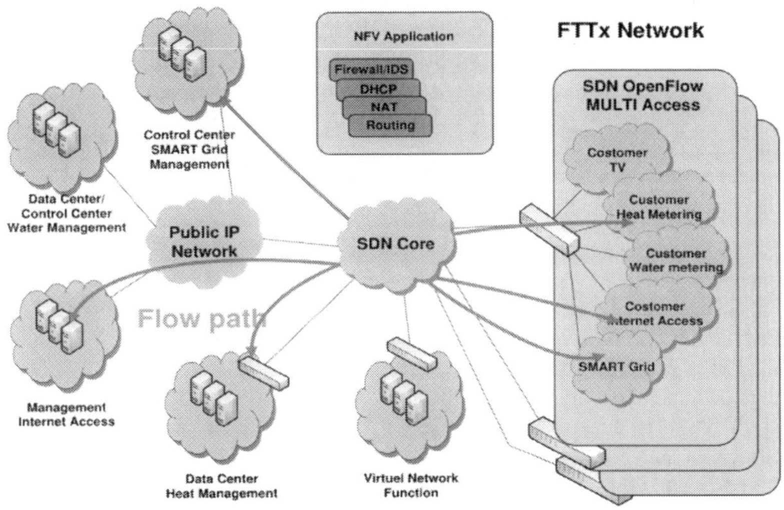

Figure 1. SDN testbed for co-existence of critical and non-critical network applications.

heat provider uses this infrastructure on the one hand for controlling purposes of the heating system, and on the other hand to offer his communication infrastructure to service operators, which in turn offer additional services (such as high speed Internet) to customers. Also the integration of metering solution for smart grids or water systems for utility service providers or the local government is possible. Figure 1 gives an overview of the SDN based testbed.

The topic addressed in the current study is reliability of critical infrastructure communication. Certain applications of critical infrastructures require a high degree of reliability regarding communication interruptions. Here, OpenFlow provides a special fast failure recovery method allowing for configuring switches at the SDN forwarding plane with fast-failover groups. Such a group defines a list of alternative ports on which packets can be sent out belonging to a certain traffic trunk. This means, that for all computed paths between a source and a destination, all switches on these paths can have multiple opportunities to forward packets to follow one of the precomputed paths. As soon as one forwarding port is not usable in case of a link failure the alternative port can be used. The decision, which one of the possible output ports is used, is taken at each switch based on the locally available link state information.

In the present performance comparison study, OpenFlow fast-failover is compared to the commonly used rapid spanning tree protocol (RSTP) that also provides the reroute capabilities when link failures occur. In difference to OpenFlow's failover groups, alternative paths are computed by a distributed algorithm right after a link failure occurs [4]. In this paper, we focus on the comparison of the OpenFlow fast failover groups with RSTP as we had a focus on layer 2 of the OSI model. Further more the study is done to examine the applicability of SDN/OpenFlow for reliable communication in the SDN Testbed. The aim of this work is also to encourage further discussions on augmenting communication networks of critical infrastructures with SDN technology.

The paper is organized as follows: Section II contains a brief overview of other work related to this paper. In Section III a short introduction to MPLS fast reroute method is depicted. Section IV describes the network infrastructure used for the tests as well as the methodology of the tests. Section V describes the validation results in detail before we give an outlook on future work in Section VI.

II. Related Work

Several studies have investigated the application of SDN in Smart Grid communication systems. Dong et al. focus on possibilities of SDN to improve the resilience of a Smart Grid. They also discuss critical issues of SDN, which need to be taken into account before deploying SDN to Smart Grids [5]. The use of SDN in the area of substation automation based on IEC-61850 is discussed in [6]. Here, Cahn et al. describe a system that automatically configures the network infrastructure of a substation with respect to the communication requirements of present IEDs and monitoring devices. This work is brought to a more practical level in [7], where the current development state of SDN/OpenFlow implementations was investigated in detail and, in addition, the ability of SDN to fulfill communication requirements of Smart Grid communication networks was evaluated. [8], [9] and [10] evaluates different methodologies to implement failure recovery in SDN based networks. Dorsch et al proposed approaches for fast-recovery and guaranteed quality of service [2]. In contrast to the fast-recovery approach proposed in our work, the logic for re-routing of packets is centralized at the SDN Controller - i. e., if a link failure occurs, the corresponding switches send a message to the SDN controller, asking for an alternative forwarding rule. The approach of our work utilizes OpenFlow fast-failover groups to provide multiple alternative paths to the switches at the same time. Switching to alternative paths can be done based on local decisions of switches, which is expected to reduce link down time and packet loss. Our approach could be extended by the work of [11] where a SDN Controller precalculates multiple forwarding paths from a sender to a destination at the same time, and download the corresponding forwarding rules to the switches. In such an approach OpenFlow enabled switches have to deal with a significant higher number of flow entries and this harbours the risk of flow table explosion.

III. RSVP-TE Fast Reroute

For critical infrastructure communication, MPLS (and especially its extension RSVP-TE) is frequently proposed in order to guarantee reliability, traffic separation, reliable bandwidth separation and the like. RSVP-TE enables to establish label switched paths (LSP) throughout an MPLS network including resource reservation on end-to-end links such as minimum bandwidth or delay requirements. One extension of RSVP-TE to LSPs is fast reroute functionality. Fast reroute allows the establishment of additional backup LSPs which can be switched to as soon a link failure or network failure occurs. RSVP-TE fast reroute is specified in RFC 4090 [12].

In general, fast reroute works according to the following simplified model: When a new LSP is requested (usually by the network administrator), several detours are precomputed and preestablished along the LSP. These detours are paths between MPLS routers, which provide local repair capabilities. After a link failure has been detected by a directly connected Label Switching Router (LSR) it becomes to the point of local repair and uses one of the preestablished detours to quickly reroute traffic around the failure point. In a second step, after rerouting the traffic via the detour, the router sends a notification to the MPLS ingress router, which then, establishes a complete new LSP avoiding the network failure point. While the computation of a new LSP takes several seconds, the local repair can be established within several milliseconds after a failure has been detected.

For the detection of link and node failures, the fast reroute makes use of MPLS hello messages for the detection of unreachable neighbour MPLS nodes and additionally can make use of local physical layer information to detect link failures to next-hop neighbours. While rerouting based on the local link information can be done within some milliseconds, using hello messages to detect failed neighbor nodes takes times in the scale of some seconds. In the latter case, hello messages are periodically (every two to five seconds) sent out by LSRs to their neighbours and if no reply is received from a neighbour LSR, this LSR is considered as broken. Due to this, a link failure can remain undetected several seconds before the local repair mechanism starts to work. In several practical implementations and evaluations, it has been shown that fast reroute can reach failure recovery times in the range of up to 50 milliseconds for the local repair mechanisms when physical layer information is used [13].

While a direct comparison between MPLS fast reroute networks and SDN approaches would be highly interesting, in this paper we are focusing on pure layer 2 link failure recovery techniques. For a comparison of MPLS fast reroute and SDN approaches, a more comprehensive evaluation should be done including also features like bandwidth protection, which are provided by RSVP-TE fast reroute.

IV. Validation Architecture and Methodology

Content of this section is a description of testbed architectures and testing methodologies for the failover performance evaluation of SDN/OpenFlow and RSTP.

A. *RSTP fast-failover evaluation*

The network infrastructure used for RSTP evaluation consists of two hosts A and B, connected with a network of four switching devices S1, S2, S3, and S4 (see Figure 2).

Both end devices are standard desktop computers using 1 Gbit/s standard Ethernet interface cards. On host A a sending application is able to send UDP flows with a configurable packet size and sending interval. During the evaluation measurements, the packets are forwarded through the network and finally delivered to the destination host B. At host B a receiving application is running, which captures the packets sent by host A and keeps track of receiving timestamps of each packet. The UDP packets' payload containing their sending timestamps and a packet number increased by 1 for each packet sent out (the first packet has number 0). Both contents are written by the sending application. By utilizing the packet numbers stored in the packet's payload, it is possible to compute lost, reordered, and duplicated packets. The receiving application keeps track about the packet numbers of incoming packets. If gaps are detected the according packets are considered as lost. In the case of out-of-order packet numbers of incoming packets, packet reordering is considered. If one packet with the same packet number is received twice, packet duplication can be assumed.

In the RSTP test network, standard desktop computers are used as switching devices running Open vSwitch 2.3.90 supporting RSTP IEEE 802.1D-2004 [4]. All PC based switches

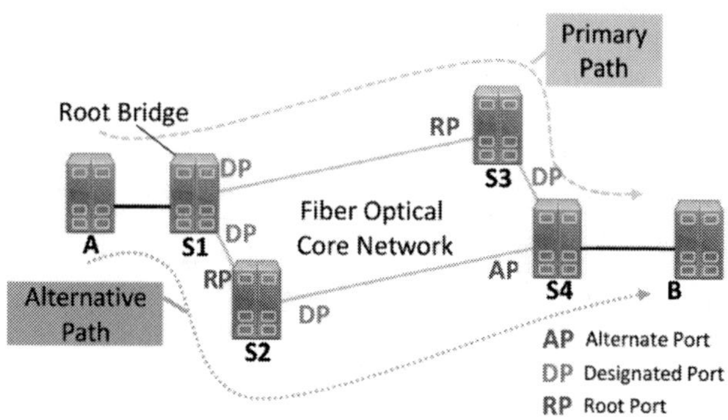

Figure 2. Overview of RSTP evaluation network infrastructure.

TABLE I. OPTIMIZED RSTP PARAMETERS

Parameter	standard value	optimized value
Forwarding Delay	15	4
BPDU max. age	20	6
Transmit Hold Count	6	1
BPDU timeout	1200	1

(S1, S2, S3 and S4) are equipped with identical fiber optical network interface cards in order to make sure that impacts of different network hardware on the recalculation performance can be excluded.

At the beginning of the test, a primary path is computed by RSTP leading via the switches S1, S3, and S4 to the destination host B. When a link failure occurs between S3 and S4, RSTP establishes the alternate path via S2 and S4 to host B (see Figure 2). As soon as the connection between S3 and S4 is available again, the primary path gets restored by the RSTP path computing algorithm.

During the test, the fiber optical connection of the primary path were automatically (by a test program) disconnected and reconnected in time-intervals of 10 seconds. In total 40 disconnect and reconnect actions has been executed during the tests. Each action led to path recalculations of the RSTP protocol in order to find most cost-efficient path towards its neighboring switches and establish a new forwarding path. When the link failure occured (after disconnection of the primary path) RSTP re-established a path via the alternate path and the computation time for the alternate path was recorded. When the broken link has been reactivated, the time needed to return to the default route has been measured.

To maximize the speed of RSTP link failure detection and path calculation, the algorithm parameters forwarding delay, BPDU sending interval, and maximum age of BPDUs are reduced compared to standard values. Table I contains a comparison between RSTP standard values and optimized values.

B. OpenFlow fast-failover evaluation

The network infrastructure for the evaluation of OpenFlow fast-failover performance has the setup shown in Figure 3. The hosts A and B are standard desktop computers, equipped with 1 Gbit/s standard Ethernet network interface cards. These interfaces are faced to the network used for OpenFlow performance evaluation. The switch S1 is a standard desktop PC configured as switch and is running Open vSwitch Version 2.3.90 as Linux Kernel module supporting OpenFlow until Version 1.3. S1 is equipped with a dual port fiber-optical network interface card. One of the ports is connected to switch S2, the other to switch S3. Finally, the switches S2 and S3 are connected to switch S4, which in turn is connected to host B. The switches S2, S3, and S4 are identically built switching devices providing a 1 Gbit/s fiber-optical network. The hardware is natively running Open vSwitch Version 1.9.90, also supporting OpenFlow up to Version 1.3. The switching hardware S2, S3, and S4 are generally i386 Linux boxes with designated TCAM based switching hardware bringing mainly a performance boost for their forwarding actions (TCAM based rule selection).

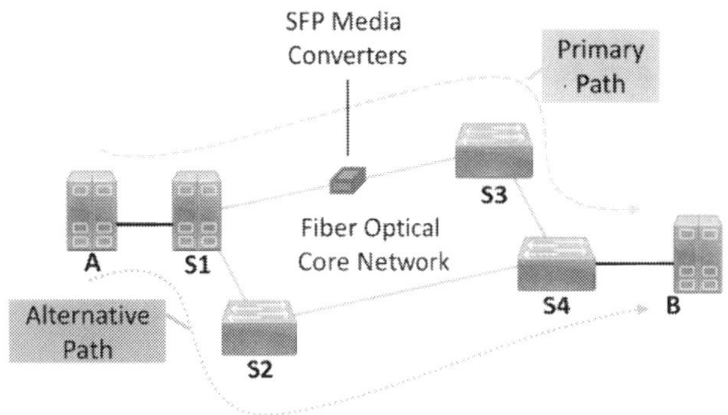

Figure 3. Overview of the OpenFlow/SDN evaluation network infrastructure.

Like in the RSTP tests, on host A, UDP traffic is generated and sent to host B, using the same applications and configurations as in the RSTP evaluation.

To evaluate the OpenFlow fast failover behavior, the network is configured with a fast-failover group at S1, which forwards packets to switch S3 during default operation (primary path). When S1 looses its connection to S3 the alternate path via S2 is used. Furthermore, switch S2 and switch S3 are configured with static flow entries in order to forward packets to switch S4. Switch S4 also has a static flow entry to forward all incoming packets to destination host B.

The sending application is configured to generate Ethernet traffic of about 4.6 MBit/s with following properties:

- 242 Bytes payload of each UDP packet
- 8 Bytes for the UDP header
- 20 Bytes IP header
- 18 Bytes Ethernet header
- 500 microseconds mean packet sending interval

The performance tests were carried out in one automated test scenario to emulate software failures, and one manual test scenario to emulate hardware link failures. This is also done to unveil impacts on the link failure detection mechanism, depending on whether the link failure is produced by turning off the network interface via a user space command or when a physical network connection breaks.

In the automated test scenario, the link between S1 and S2 is interrupted by a disconnection command, which instructs the operating system to deactivate the network interface on switch S1, which is connected to S2. After a waiting time of 10 seconds, the network interface is reactivated again. This procedure is repeated every 10 seconds until the UDP traffic flow from host A to host B has stopped. The automated test is done during a test period of 40 switching actions. The manual test scenario, the link interruption is done manually by interrupting the physical optical fiber connections. Like in the automated scenario, the 10 seconds interval when connecting and disconnecting the link is kept and also 40 switching actions are performed.

In the manual test scenario a SFP-based fiber optical media converter is placed between the switches S1 and S3 (see Figure 3). These devices are normally used, e.g., to convert a single mode fiber optical connection into a multi-mode connection. In the manual test, however, the media converters are used to manually interrupt the connection between S1 and S3. For this purpose the external power connection of the media converter is used. This has the benefit, that contact chatter can be avoided, which was observed when manually plug and unplug optical fibers into the NIC ports. When the media converter is turned off, a link failure appears at both sides of the connections, i. e., both switches S1 and S3 will detect the link failure.

V. RESULTS

In the following section we present and discuss our fast-failover evaluation results with RSTP and OpenFlow.

A. RSTP fast-failover evaluation

When looking at RSTP, the protocol need to recompute the path in two cases: As soon as the primary path fails, which results in a fast transition of the forwarding behavior of switch S4 from its preferred designated port (connected to S3) to its alternate port (connected to S2), and as soon as the primary path has been restored. Then, switch S3 changes to use the more cost efficient (originary) designated port.

For changing the forwarding behavior at switch S4 from the designated port to the alternate port in case of primary link failures, it took 3 ms in minimum and 65 ms in maximum. The average time to establish the backup connection between both hosts were 26 ms. For link reactivations after the primary path has been re-established, RSTP need in minimum of about 500 microseconds and in maximum 809 milliseconds. The mean time for re-establishing the primary path after a reconnect (path restore) is about 401 ms. The differences between first and second case as well as the large interval between minimum and maximum values (in the second case) cannot be conclusively explained but one reason is surely introduced by operating system scheduling and hardware control at the computer hosting switch S4. For the evaluation of these path computation times all 40 connection and disconnection actions has been considered.

One hint in this direction is also given, when comparing our results to those published in a Siemens Whitepaper covering a RSTP performance evaluation [14]. In this work failover times between 50 ms and 100 ms has been measured depending on the networks' size and using specialized RUGGEDCOM switches supporting RSTP standard 802.1D-2004.

B. OpenFlow fast-failover evaluation

The results of the OpenFlow fast-failover evaluation are given by packet losses occurred following a switching action. From the amount of lost packets a worst-case estimation for the interruption time can be made.

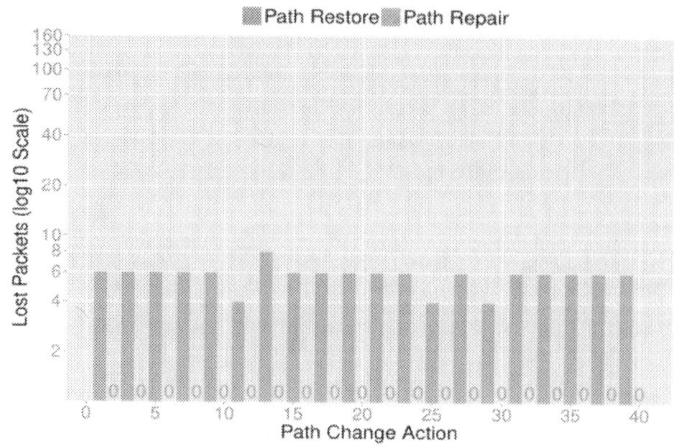

Figure 4. Losses appeared in the automated test scenario.

The bar plots 4 and 5 showing the packet losses resulting from switching actions. On the horizontal axis, the switching actions (Path Change Action) are depicted, on the logarithmic scaled vertical axis, the amount of lost packets per switching action is outlined. All three figures using the same scale for x and y axis. The bars denoted with 'Path Repair' representing packet losses occurred when the primary path in the evaluation architecture is deactivated in a automatic or manual manner. The bars denoted with 'Path Restore' representing packet losses occurred after the primary path was restored and the packet flow was switched back to use the primary path. When no packet losses occurred after a switching action the symbol '0' is written to the plot.

Figure 4 shows the packet losses in case of the automated test scenario when link interruptions were initiated by software. As can be seen from the plots, no packet losses occurred when packet forwarding was switched from alternate to primary path ('Path Restore'). When looking at packet losses occurred after the primary path was interrupted, the mean amount of packet losses was 5.8 packets (minimum 4 packets, maximum 8 packets). As it can be seen from the figure, mostly, the amount of lost packets were 6. This results in a estimated worst-case interruption time between 3 ms and 5 ms (considering a mean packet sending interval of 500 microseconds).

Figure 5 shows the packet losses in case of the manual test scenario with 1 converter, and the link between switch S1 and switch S3 is physically disconnected. Looking at the 'Path Restore' bars, packet loss after switching from the alternate path to the primary path occurred only once. Here, 18 packets got lost meaning a worst-case interruption time of 10 ms. When looking at packet losses occurred after the primary path was interrupted, the mean amount of packet losses was 32.45 packets. The minimum of lost packets was 2, and the maximum 160. As the median of the amount of lost packets were 4, it can be seen that high loss values are not frequent. This also is shown by the 3rd quantile of the measured values lying at 28.00 packets. Considering the

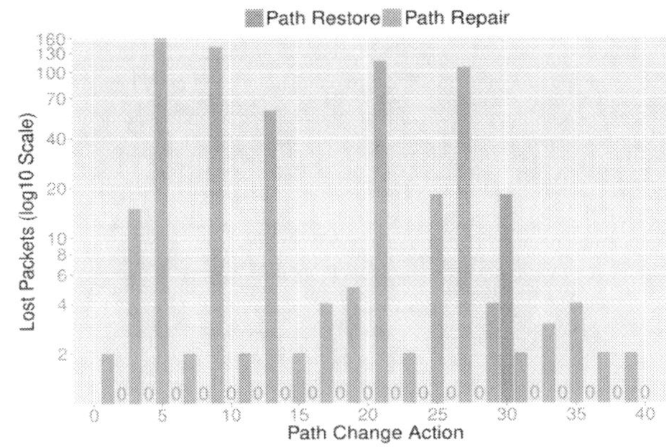

Figure 5. Losses appeared in manual test scenario 1.

mean amount of lost packets, the worst-case interruption time was around 17 ms. Taking the maximum packet loss as a basis, the worst-case interruption time is around 81 ms. For the worst-case estimation, again, a packet sending interval of 500 microseconds is considered.

Comparing the OpenFlow fast-failover scenarios, a very important result is that in most of the cases, no packet losses occurred when switching back from the alternate path to the primary path. Furthermore, the amount of packet losses and interruption has a larger spread and variability in case of the manual test scenario. Comparing the results of RSTP and OpenFlow/SDN, the fast-failover performance using SDN/OpenFlow is significantly improved. While the maximum time for switching a path with RSTP was measured with about 800 ms (mean: 200 ms) in our measurements (Siemens measured with specialized Hardware up to 100 ms) with OpenFlow we measured a maximum interruption time around 81 ms (mean: 17 ms).

VI. Conclusion and Future Work

Our results show that using OpenFlow fast-failover recovery clearly outperforms path recovery mechanisms of RSTP. This makes SDN/OpenFlow a promising approach for establishing an ultra-high reliable communication network for critical infrastructures. A further aspect is that OpenFlow based fast-failover mechanism is able to manage a symmetric loss and timing behaviour. RSTP uses different port roles and port states and this result in an asymmetric behaviour.

On the other hand, our results showed, that the performance of SDN fast-failover highly correlates with used Open vSwitch implementations, networking hardware and operating system support. To fully understand these correlations, it is necessary to extend our validation methodology, e.g., to be able to measure the packet one way delay accurately in the range of small fragments of microseconds. Possibly, clock synchronization using PTP or Sync-E could be used. A further question we want to answer is, how hardware based and high performance network stacks and package processing approaches like DPDK [15] or OpenOnload [16] can improve the quality of failure resistance of SDN/OpenFlow networks.

Answering these questions can lead to high quality productive networks usable for critical infrastructures and other domains like industrial automation systems where latency in the range of micro- and nanoseconds is requested.

VII. Acknowledgment

The work described in this paper was funded by the Austrian Federal Ministry for Transport, Innovation and Technology (BMVIT).

References

[1] Council of the European Union, "Council Directive 2008/114/EC of 8 December 2008 on the identification and designation of European critical infrastructures and the assessment of the need to improve their protection," *Official Journal of the European Union*, vol. L 345, pp. p. 75 – 82, 2008.

[2] N. Dorsch, F. Kurtz, H. Georg, C. Hagerling, and C. Wietfeld, "Software-defined networking for Smart Grid communications: Applications, challenges and advantages," in *Smart Grid Communications (SmartGridComm), 2014 IEEE International Conference on*. IEEE, Nov. 2014, pp. 422–427.

[3] Open Networking Foundation, "OpenFlow Switch Specification 1.4.0," Oct. 2013, technical Specification TS-012.

[4] IEEE, "IEEE Standard for Local and metropolitan area networks: Media Access Control (MAC) Bridges," 2004.

[5] X. Dong, H. Lin, R. Tan, R. K. Iyer, and Z. Kalbarczyk, "Software-Defined Networking for Smart Grid Resilience: Opportunities and Challenges," in *Proceedings of the 1st ACM Workshop on Cyber-Physical System Security (CPSS '15)*. ACM Press, 2015, pp. 61–68.

[6] A. Cahn, J. Hoyos, M. Hulse, and E. Keller, "Software-defined energy communication networks: From substation automation to future smart grids," in *Smart Grid Communications (SmartGridComm), 2013 IEEE International Conference on*. IEEE, 2013, pp. 558–563.

[7] T. Pfeiffenberger and J. L. Du, "Evaluation of software-defined networking for power systems," in *Intelligent Energy and Power Systems (IEPS), 2014 IEEE International Conference on*, June 2014, pp. 181–185.

[8] M. Reitblatt, M. Canini, A. Guha, and N. Foster, "Fattire: declarative fault tolerance for software-defined networks," in *Proceedings of the second ACM SIGCOMM workshop on Hot topics in software defined networking*. ACM, 2013, pp. 109–114.

[9] S. Sharma, D. Staessens, D. Colle, M. Pickavet, and P. Demeester, "Fast failure recovery for in-band openflow networks," in *9th International Conference on Design of Reliable Communication Networks, Proceedings*. IEEE, 2013, pp. 52–59.

[10] O. Tilmans and S. Vissicchio, "Igp-as-a-backup for robust sdn networks," in *10th International Conference on Network and Service Management (CNSM)*. IEEE, 2014, pp. 127–135.

[11] T. Pfeiffenberger, J. L. Du, and P. Bittercourt, "Reliable and flexible communications for power systems: Fault-tolerant multicast with sdn/openflow," in *7th IFIP Soft Computing Methods for the Design, Deployment, and Reliability of Networks and Network Applications*, July 2015, pp. 1–6.

[12] P. Pan, G. Swallow, and A. Atlas, "Fast Reroute Extensions to RSVP-TE for LSP Tunnels," RFC Editor, RFC 4090, May 2005.

[13] "MPLS Traffic Engineering Fast Reroute – Link Protection - Cisco Systems," URL: http://www.cisco.com/en/US/docs/ios/12_0st/12_0st10/feature/guide/fastrout.html [accessed: 2016-05-17].

[14] M. Pustylnik, M. Zafirovic-Vukotic, and R. Moore, "Performance of the Rapid Spanning Tree Protocol in Ring Network Topology," Siemens AG, Whitepaper, 2007.

[15] "DPDK," URL: http://dpdk.org/ [accessed: 2016-05-17].

[16] "OpenOnload," URL: http://www.openonload.org/ [accessed: 2016-05-17].